With
HIROSHIMA
Eyes

**Atomic War, Nuclear Extortion,
and Moral Imagination**

Joseph Gerson

New Society Publishers
Philadelphia, PA   Gabriola Island, BC

Published in cooperation with
American Friends Service Committee
New England Regional Office

Library of Congress Cataloging-in-Publication Data
Gerson, Joseph.
  With Hiroshima eyes : atomic war, nuclear extortion, and moral imagination / Joseph Gerson.
    p.   cm.
  Includes bibliographic references and index.
  ISBN 0-86571-329-4. ISBN 0-86571-330-8 (pbk.)
  1. United States—Foreign relations—1945-1989—Moral and ethical aspects. 2. United States—Foreign relations—1989- —Moral and ethical aspects. 3. Nuclear weapons—United States—Moral and ethical aspects. 4. United States—Military policy—Moral and ethical aspects. I. Title.
E840.G47 1995   327.73—dc20   95-1999

Inquiries regarding requests to reprint all or part of *With Hiroshima Eyes: Atomic War, Nuclear Extortion and Moral Imagination* should be addressed to New Society Publishers, 4527 Springfield Avenue, Philadelphia, PA, 19143.

| ISBN Hardcover | USA 0-86571-329-4 | CAN 1-55092-280-7 |
| ISBN Paperback | USA 0-86571-330-8 | CAN 1-55092-281-5 |

Cover photograph by Roberta Foss. Cover design by Parallel Design of Philadelphia, Pennsylvania. Book design by Martin Kelley. Index by IRIS of Kingston, Washington. Printed on partially-recycled paper using soy-based ink by Capital City Press of Montpelier, Vermont.

Page iv: Matsuyama-Cho in Nagasaki near the hypocenter, around noon August 10, 1945; photograph by Yosuke Yamahata. Page xx: "Rescue" from the Hiroshima Panels of Iri Maruki and Toshi Maruki. Page 24: west of Miyukibashi Bridge, Hiroshima, 11 AM, August 6, 1945, 2.2 kilometers from the hypocenter; photograph by Yosuke Yamahata. Page 92: religious activists conduct a sit-in to oppose the U.S. war against Vietnam; photograph by Ihe'e Kimura. Page 126: protest greets U.S. nuclear-powered submarine *Sea Dragon* in Sasebo; photograph from Japan Press.

To order directly from the publisher, add $3.00 to the price for the first copy, and add 75¢ for each additional copy. Send check or money order to:

In the United States:	*In Canada:*
New Society Publishers	New Society Publishers
4527 Springfield Avenue	PO Box 189
Philadelphia, PA 19143	Gabriola Island, BC VOR 1XO

NEW SOCIETY PUBLISHERS is a project of the New Society Educational Foundation, a nonprofit, tax-exempt, public foundation in the United States, and of the Catalyst Education Society, a nonprofit society in Canada. Opinions expressed in this book do not necessarily represent positions of the New Society Educational Foundation, or the Catalyst Education Society.

The AMERICAN FRIENDS SERVICE COMMITTEE is a Quaker organization which includes people of various faiths who are committed to social justice, peace, and humanitarian service. Its work is based on the Quaker belief in the worth of every person, and faith in the power of love to overcome violence and injustice.

Never Again the A-Bomb

In the place where our city was destroyed
Where we buried the ashes of the ones that we loved
There the green grass grows and the white waving weeds
Deadly harvest of two atom bombs
Then brothers and sisters you must watch and take care
That the third atom bomb never comes.

Gentle rain gathers poison from the sky
And the fish carry death in the depth of the sea
Fishing boats are idle
Their owners are blind
Deadly harvest of two atom bombs
Then landsmen and seamen watch and take care
That the third atom bomb never comes

The sky hangs like a shroud overhead
And the sun's in the cage of the black lowering cloud
No birds fly in the leaden sky
Deadly harvest of two atom bombs.
The brothers and sisters watch and take care
That the third atom bomb never comes

All that people have created with their hands
And their minds for the glory of the world in which we live
Now it can be smashed in a moment destroyed
Deadly harvest of two atom bombs
People of the world watch and take care
That the Third Atom Bomb never comes.

— Ishiji Asada
Translated by Ewan MacColl

Table of Contents

Publisher's Note

WE HAVE LIVED half a century now under the shadow of nuclear war. This book speaks to that history, tells us how our leaders have justified this, our twentieth-century nightmare. But the book does more than explain, because we must do more than understand. We must confront the people who have already experienced our nightmare—the *hibakusha*, the survivors of Hiroshima and Nagasaki's bombings. We must do this because atomic war is real: it has happened in these cities and it could happen again.

Imagine bringing the *hibakusha* into our lives. Imagine trying to explain to a survivor the need for more testing, the calculation of "acceptable losses," or the inpracticality of reducing the stockpiles. The cynical logic we use to defend our nuclear gambling falls apart once we realize the true stakes which the *hibakusha* know.

It is easy to lose ourselves in the details of this nuclear age: to tabulate megatonnage, to debate delivery systems. But to end the nuclear threat in our lives, we must remember the very real people that are threatened. We must remember that there have been *hibakusha*, and that there could be more in our future. We must all look through the eyes of the *hibakusha* and say "No More Hiroshimas."

In these pages, Joseph Gerson shows us our nuclear history. But he also remembers our collective human history, and for that reason we here at New Society Publishers are proud to publish *With Hiroshima Eyes*.

— Martin Kelley
for the New Society Publishers Collective

Acknowledgements

THIS BOOK IS dedicated to the *hibakusha* of Hiroshima and Nagasaki, and particularly to Junko Kayashige, Mitsuo Kojima, Shoji Sawada, Sumiteru Taniguchi, Senji Yamaguchi, and to the memory of Chieko Watanabe—friends, models of courage and vision.

I want to recall here the gifts of Leon Gerson, a child of immigrants, who helped me understand my connection to the world and to history; of Evelyn Gerson (Burrell), who taught me to see the sea and sky, and who shared lessons of "The Holocaust"; and of L. Mayland Parker, a second father whose vision of justice and whose support were invaluable to me.

This book could not have been written without the help, patience, translation, and endurance of my friend Rieko Asato. Rieko, Hiroshi Taka, Kiyotami Nabeshima, Ai Ta Kada, Yayoi Tsuchida, and Kazuya Yasuda of the Japan Council Against Atomic and Hydrogen Bombs, Gensuikyo, and Miwa Yamasaki of Nihon Hidankyo, made it possible for the suffering, vision, and courage of *hibakusha* to be shared and to continue to affect the thinking and political actions of others through this book.

Other friends and colleagues in Japan have touched my life, been my teachers, and deepened my understandings of love, generosity, commitment, courage, community, and political history. Among them are: Ikuro Anzai, Nobuyuke Kayashige, Fumiko Kataoka, Shoji Niihara, Susumu Ozaki, Hiroaki Yoshizawa, and many others.

I have enjoyed the rare gift of the support of colleagues and committee members of the American Friends Service Committee. They have understood the importance of supporting the *hibakusha*, building links with the Japanese peace movement, and the potential value of this book. David Gracie's encouragement and critical suggestions were particularly helpful. I want to thank colleagues, friends and family whose critical reading of one or more chapters contributed to the quality of this book; they certainly bear no responsibility for any flaws herein: Andrew Hughes, Phyllis Cohen, Debka Colson, Karen Cromley, Howard Fredrick, Lawrence J. Friedman, Lani Gerson, David Gracie, Keith Harvey, Bill Pierre, and Hilda Silverman.

William Arkin, Barton J. Bernstein, Dan Ellsberg, Kazuaki Kita, Michael T. Klare, Iri and Toshi Maruki, Mioko Suzuki, and Hiromi Turnage made important contributions to this work. Skip Atkins, Alberto Barreto, Judith Campbell, Maureen Colton, Paul Cravedi, Rick Davis, Pat Farren, Louis Kampp, Tony Palomba, May and Tetsuo Takayanagi, Lawrence S. Wittner, and my students at Regis College were all more helpful than they knew. Martin Kelley of New Society Publishers has been a friend, and a supportive and patient editor, since we first began discussing the possibility of this book...and its title. Kenneth Sutton's copyediting made the text more reader-friendly.

Several teachers must be gratefully acknowledged. Wilfred Desan's metaphysics and ethics helped name the universe I had begun to experience and intuit. I remain indebted to him for his support and the encouragement he gave me to write. Robert Jackall gave an undergraduate student the liberating freedom to explore causes and consequences of racism and the U.S. war in Vietnam, and the means to challenge them. Elizabeth Minnich's troubling and challenging questions led me deeper into the world, gave me a deeper appreciation of my knowledge and voice, and helped illuminate the fundamental importance of exploring marginalized knowledge. Colin Greer was there when I needed him. He read this work thoughtfully and sympathetically, making critically supportive suggestions, which deepened it. Paul Walker and Irene Gendzier have been my teachers and friends longer than they know. Their insights, suggestions, and contributions have been essential.

I am especially thankful for my wife, Lani Gerson's, support which helped to make both my path and this book possible.

— Joseph Gerson

Preface

All I ask is that, in the midst of a murderous world, we agree to reflect on murder and to make a choice.
— Albert Camus, *Neither Victims Nor Executioners*

I am of the opinion that there is such a thing as a collective memory and a collective responsibility.
— Adam Michnik

One critical reason not to lie to ourselves…is that you cannot think well when there are things you cannot allow yourself to think about, and you cannot communicate with others when you have stopped being able to communicate with yourself.
— Elizabeth Minnich

The *hibakusha* feel that they must not die until the abolition of nuclear weapons is realized.
— Masanori Ichioka

On August 8, 1992, at about six o'clock in the morning, I was walking beside a canal in Nagasaki. I had returned to Hiroshima and Nagasaki ostensibly to serve as a speaker at the annual World Conference Against Atomic and Hydrogen Bombs. In fact, I had come to remind myself what it means to be human, to reengage with the cinders and courage that remain at the epicenter of this murderous century, to be revitalized by the steadfast spirit of the Japanese peace movement and Japanese friends, and to continue learning about the contours and implications of the post-Cold War global "order."

That morning the sky was a perfect, cloudless blue, a brief interval in a week of cool rain, which was to be punctuated the following day by a typhoon. The heat was not yet insufferable, but the sun's intensity intimated what was to follow.

That morning walk was the first extended, quiet repose and reflection I had had in two months. Shops were not yet open. If others were awake, they were not yet making their way to work. I enjoyed the quiet beauty of obscure corners of the city near my hotel: white and orange speckled carp in the canal, small houses built on the canal's banks, and weeping willow trees that seemed to flow into the water. Elsewhere, trimmed and potted plants graced otherwise unadorned doorways and windows.

After months of emotional and intellectual stress, I relaxed. I wasn't thinking about my mother's recent death or the related tears that had crept from the corners of my eyes the day before when a choral suite honored Chieko Watanabe, who also had died within the past year. I thought I was watching nature and life, in and around the canal, not subconsciously struggling with conflicting ideas from a recent seminar on postmodern philosophy, racism, and feminism. I wasn't aware that beneath the surface I was still wrestling with discussions in Hiroshima about the meanings of the Cold War, or debating how to recast a book about the relationship of nuclear weapons to U.S. foreign military intervention.

Without warning, thoughts, connections, and possibilities ignited within me. I began to see how I could integrate testimonies and friendships of *hibakusha* (a Japanese word literally translated as explosion-affected person, popularly translated as A-Bomb witness/survivor), debates about the meaning of the Cold War, and insights of Foucault into a single work, possibly in time to influence the debates that would attend the fiftieth anniversaries of the atomic bombings of Hiroshima and Nagasaki.

As I continued to walk, I began to envision a book that had similarities to a Picasso cubist painting. Much of the analytical structure I had previously envisoned—the history of the use of nuclear weapons for the maintenance of empire—could remain. But I could shatter, base, and infuse my initial conception of the book with the memories, meanings, and histories of the atomic bombings. Instead of writing one more abstract, analytical political history, like Patricia J. William's *The Alchemy of Race and Rights,* I envisioned a book filled with life, pain, personal observations, and experiences. It could be a natural reflection on the history and meaning of nearly five decades of nuclear war, nuclear threats, atomic diplomacy, and the resistance of hibakusha.

Over breakfast at the hotel I began talking about these ideas with the young people who served as interpreters and attended to the details that made the conference possible. These largely one-sided conversations led to more thoughts, ideas and notes. A panel discussion with Philippine and Japanese movement leaders later that day became an opportunity to listen more intently and acquisitively, and to sharpen, more than share, my thinking. At lunch, when I discovered that what I thought was a green

Japanese pickle was in fact an apple, I lost myself and tormented my friends with abstract philosophical flights about "constructs" of "atomic weapons," "apple," "Hiroshima," "Nagasaki," "Cold War," and Foucault's concept of localized truths.

We all know what nuclear weapons are, but they have specific meanings for hibakusha, different meanings for other Japanese, and yet different meanings for the governments and people of the United States. These differences result from differing relationships to power, unique histories, and geographical distance. These differences are reflected in the very different exhibitions and commemorations being planned in Hiroshima and Washington on the fiftieth anniversaries of the atomic bombings of Hiroshima and Nagasaki, the first focusing on the civilian victims of the bomb, the latter (after being modified under the pressure of veterans groups and conservative politicians) on the legitimate use of nuclear weapons to achieve military victory in a "just war."

That morning in Nagasaki was the most immediate origin of this work. There are, of course, other origins, rivulets of experience that led to that moment.

Over time I began to see connections between the thoughts of that day and articles I had been reading about the memories and meanings of the European Judeocide.

Rod Stewart sings that "the first cut is the deepest." For me that cut was the European Holocaust, more precisely the Judeocide. I was born in 1946, the year following the liberation of the extermination camps and the end of what is commonly termed the Second World War. My childhood was lived under the shadow of the Holocaust and its legacies of loss, fear, and insecurity. As a child I only vaguely grasped its meaning; "my people," including distant relatives, had been exterminated in numbers that I could name but not imagine. They were killed because, like me, they had been born into Jewish families. I knew, but did not understand, that my life was, and in some ways would remain, uniquely vulnerable.

Within my family and my circle of friends, there were frequent references to the remembered dead and to those who had somehow survived, some with concentration camp numbers tattooed on their arms. Hitler and Mussolini were the objects of our preadolescent semipornographic rhymes. To this day I associate Adolph Eichmann's arrest and trial with the flood of paperback histories that stared at me from drug store bookshelves and made their ways into my hands and mind. Their descriptions of the terror and re-ghettoization of Jews, of Jewish complicity, of extermination camps, and of lampshades, soap, and cinder paths made from the remains of Jewish people horrified me and marked my identity.

In countless, and now only dimly remembered, conversations with my parents, two fundamental lessons from the Holocaust were communicated to me. They became essential to my identity: Never again to anyone. Never participate in the crime of silence. Two corollaries that I learned over time are first, that we are all agents of history, regardless of our consciousness or intentions. We bear responsibility to the past and for creation of the future. Second, that justice and human survival are closely related to honesty and intellectual integrity.

These defining events and values, reinforced by the peculiarities of my family life, experiences of discrimination, and class marginalization in wealthy schools, led me to the fringes of the Civil Rights movement, to active nonviolence, to resistance to the U.S. war in Indochina, and ultimately to the American Friends Service Committee (AFSC), and Japan.

For me, opposition to the Vietnam War first meant studying U.S. and Vietnamese history. This led to an understanding that the war was not an aberration. It was the logical extension of centuries of U.S. foreign military intervention. I gradually learned that Manifest Destiny, U.S. wars of foreign intervention, and the building of the American Empire were also, in large measure, expressions of racism and had origins in the Pilgrims' identity as God's "chosen people." That resonated with my experience as a Jew.

I learned that after defeating the Spanish in 1898, the United States dehumanized and fought the people of the Philippines, killing and torturing hundreds of thousands in order to gain control over Subic Bay and thus secure a base from which to exploit China. My later work with the AFSC brought me in contact with women like Charito Planas. Charito ran against Imelda Marcos, the dictator's wife, in the 1978 election for mayor of Metro Manila. After Charito's electoral victory was stolen by fraud, she was forced to go underground and ultimately into exile. Responding once to a student's question, Charito assured her that the United States was unlikely to repeat Vietnam in the Philippines. The Philippines had been repeated in Vietnam.

The application of the fundamental lessons of my childhood also meant confronting the Israeli-Palestinian-Arab conflict. While living in Europe after the war in Indochina, I had access to a body of literature about the Middle East that was then unavailable in the United States. I had the opportunity to work with expatriate Israeli dissidents and Palestinians and to travel to the region. Once again, I was confronted by the legacies of European and U.S. racism, and the subversion, military intervention, and threats of nuclear war that had been used to gain and retain control over the oil of the Middle East. I recall standing with a Palestinian man beside the remnants of his recently demolished home on the outskirts of Hebron as his wife and neighbors served us coffee. The Palestinians, he reflected, had survived the Ottoman and British conquests. They would, he assured me, survive the worst of them all—the Israeli-U.S. conquest and occupation, which sought to steal their land and to destroy their identity. The long-term inability of the U.S. peace movement to confront issues of intervention, justice, and peace in what Eqbal Ahmad termed "the geo-political center of the struggle for world power" has never ceased to disappoint me. I believe this inability has less to do with the "complicated" politics of the region and more to do with "Orientalism", a centuries-old manifestation of racism.

The realities of U.S. intervention in the Americas are unavoidable in the United States. As I graduated from college, I came into contact with liberation theologians fleeing Guatemala and Brazilian literacy workers escaping that U.S.-supported dictatorship. I first learned about the consequences of the U.S.-sponsored coup in Chile on Swedish television from Sweden's briefly imprisoned ambassador to Chile. He had been taken from the stadium prison to the Santiago airport, and directly from the Stockholm airport to the television studio. Later, a Chilean minister, tortured during the first three months of his imprisonment, became my teacher and friend. And in the 1980s the U.S. peace movement became almost as deeply engaged in solidarity with the people of Central America as it was in resistance to Reagan's nuclear madness.

My studies and work taught me that nuclear weapons have been used to expand and maintain the U.S. "sphere of influence" since the bombings of Hiroshima and Nagasaki, notwithstanding the use of the Cold War with the Soviet Union as the sole rationale for the nuclear arms race. This was true of the Eisenhower administration's offer to use tactical nuclear weapons to break the Vietnamese siege at Dien Bien Phu, John Kennedy's willingness to use nuclear weapons during the Cuban missile crisis, and the nuclear alert of U.S. forces in the last hours of the 1973 October War in the Middle East. Nuclear weapons are part of the "seamless web" of the U.S. military arsenal, the biggest stick, about which our government speaks softly but which it carries incessantly.

This work also grows from my contact and friendship with hibakusha and other Japanese peace activists during the past decade. For most Americans, even those engaged in the peace and nuclear disarmament movements, the victims of the atomic bombings of Hiroshima and Nagasaki are abstractions, marginalized *others*. Some of us have been privileged to meet survivors of Hiroshima or Nagasaki and to listen to their harrowing testimony, but their lives, experiences, spirit, and political will, which make them fully and uniquely human, lie beyond our understanding. They are not central to the consciousness of the peace movement, or the culture of nonviolent resistance in the United States.

My understandings of Hiroshima, Nagasaki, and the hibakusha have grown gradually, often painfully and sometimes through missteps and embarrassment, during my initial pilgrimage and subsequent working visits to these epicenters of this murderous century. I was overwhelmed in 1984 when I first participated in the World Conference Against Atomic and Hydrogen Bombs in Tokyo, Hiroshima, and Nagasaki. First were the anticipated layers of disorientation: culture shock, jet lag, and the attempt to discern new structures of political organization, dialogue, and analysis. Then came the more profound personal encounters and experiences, among them that a person cannot visit Hiroshima in innocence.

I still react viscerally when I remember my first visit to the A-bomb dome, the symbol of the incineration and suffering of hundreds of thousands, illuminated at midnight—silent, haunting, transcendent, and graceful. During that first trip, and subsequently, I was humbled by people's kindness and inspired by the spirit of the Japanese nuclear disarmament movement, communicated in music and art as well as in political rallies and demonstrations. Despite excruciating encounters with the death, suffering, and symbolism of Hiroshima and Nagasaki and the challenges of Japanese peace movement politics, on returning to the United States I did not want to return. I awoke from dreams of death and cinders, buoyed by lingering images of the brilliant colors of origami peace cranes, subconscious and material affirmations of life.

Between the subtleties of Japanese society, my limited time in Japan, and my blindness as a *gaijin* (hairy, bearded foreigner) there is, of course, much that I have missed. I have depended on hosts and friends for much of what I have learned. When self-effacing physics professor Shoji Sawada invited me to speak in Nagoya to reinforce the local movement's struggle to prevent port calls by nuclear armed U.S. ships, I did not know that he was a hibakusha, or what those nuclear weapons meant to him. An Okinawan attorney, who later introduced me to the second-class status of Okinawans, told me more about Professor Sawada's life, and thus helped to prepare my way. Similarly, when I first saw Chieko Watanabe speaking from her wheelchair, and Senji Yamaguchi standing at the podium, I could not understand the acts of will and courage that brought them there; nor did I know what they meant to the Japanese peace movement, or what they would come to mean to me. This required understated words and assistance from Japanese friends.

This book is, in part, an effort to translate some of what I have learned in Hiroshima and Nagasaki and from politically engaged hibakusha, and to relate it to a larger sweep of history. By definition, translation is imperfect. Michel Foucault observed that particular histories and structures of power create unique local truths or knowledge. There are things I have observed and know in Japan that I know less well in the United States. They can be intimated, but not fully translated into the American language and power/knowledge dynamic.

There are also limitations of medium and distance. Listening to the deep and haunting strains of the orchestral anthem "Never Again the Atom Bomb" or to the soaring choral harmonies of "Blue Sky," a person is exposed to memory, vision, and commitment in ways that printed words cannot communicate. Seeing and listening to a chorus of unionized industrial workers sing anthems for nuclear disarmament, or swaying hand-in-hand with ten thousand Japanese peace activists singing "We Shall Overcome," are best understood by experience.

The problem of communication and representation is not limited to trans-Pacific translation. For years, hibakusha have complained that the media's descriptions of the holocausts of Hiroshima and Nagasaki do not begin to communicate what they endured and saw. They were transformed, and remained marked, by a unique dynamic of power and knowledge—atomic bombs and the U.S. military occupation which followed. When the NHK television network invited hibakusha to paint what they remembered for a broadcast titled "Unforgettable Fire," they felt that even their own terrifying images of Hell revealed only a fraction of what they had suffered and seen.

For this reason Claude Lanzmann scrupulously avoided representing the suffering of the Judeocide in his film *Shoah* with anything but absence. He used absence to communicate presence and loss. I acknowledge the impossibility of fully understanding or describing what was experienced in Hiroshima and Nagasaki. In *With Hiroshima Eyes*, I have used memories and remnants of the cataclysm to intimate the larger, unknowable experience, and to communicate the very real experiences of people with whom we can, and should, identify.

An Orwellian understanding that integrity of language and memory are essential to our ability to think, to be, and to become more free also flows in this work. My understanding and appreciation of the dissertations of George Orwell, Kurt Vonnegut, and Milan Kundera on the importance of memory and history (particularly in *1984*, *Sirens of Titan*, and *The Unbearable Lightness of Being*) have deepened and grown as the years have passed. If we do not know where we have been, we cannot know where we are, let alone where we are going. We are manipulated and placed in jeopardy when distorted memories and "lessons" of history are used to legitimize political and military decisions. We can not be free if we are ignorant of our past. Howard Zinn put it this way:

When Orwell talked about controlling the past in order to control the present and, therefore, the future, I think he meant that if you can control people's sense of history, you can make them believe anything. So that if the American people are not told,... are not given the information about the history of American intervention in the world, it is as if we were all born yesterday... The President's speech on T.V. becomes the only fresh bit of information we have, and ...if he says, 'Ah, we're in danger in the Caribbean, the Russians are threatening us here and there,' without a sense of history you believe that.[1]

Santayana's dictum that those who do not learn from history are doomed to repeat it assumes a different existential edge in a world in which eleven countries have the weapons to threaten nuclear cataclysms, and in which the fifty-year-old weapons-related technology is accessible across the planet.

There is also the challenge of history returning in disguise. The bombings of Hiroshima and Nagasaki, the Cuban missile crisis, the U.S. war in Indochina, and the repeated U.S. military interventions in the Middle East explored in this book were masked reincarnations as well as critical moments of history.

As Vaclav Havel observed in 1994, we are "going through a transitional period, when it seems that something is on the way out and something else is painfully being born."[2] The post-Cold War era, the fiftieth anniversaries of the liberation of Auschwitz and the atomic bombings of Hiroshima and Nagasaki, and the approaching twenty-first century are all elements of this fundamental transition in human history. This year, and in the coming years, the people and government of the United States will face questions about our identity, our commitments, and our future. Can we still envision a world like that described in Article 6 of the Nuclear Non-Proliferation Treaty signed in 1970, one without genocidal nuclear weapons and in which there is "general and complete disarmament under strict and effective international control?" Can we envision a secure United States, finally independent of the subversive military-industrial complex about which Dwight Eisenhower warned in 1960? Can we embrace a politics of imagination and real national security, rather than legacies of militarism and deadly foreign intervention? Are we doomed to repeat the holocausts of modern history, or is some liberation, some greater security, possible?

How we answer these questions depends in significant measure on how the United States defines itself and its values, how the people of this country respond to our historic responsibility for the atomic bombings of Hiroshima and Nagasaki, how we regard our declared commitments to democracy and self-determination, and how we face our repressed legacies of foreign military intervention and related nuclear blackmail. Fundamentally, we face the questions posed by Albert Camus and Adam

Michnik: How do we value life and murder? Do we have a sense of collective responsibility, and if so, what does it mean for the future?

This book is written to contribute to the debates during this transitional time. My hope is that by remembering and reflecting upon our murderous recent past (particularly those times when nuclear weapons have been used) and by placing victims, as well as executioners, closer to the center of our history, thinking, and policy making, a more life-affirming and secure vision can be constructed.

One other origin of this work remains to be identified: the racism of society, which has infected the traditional, white, U.S. peace movement and many other political initiatives designed to improve society and the quality of life. With the exception of the U.S. war in Vietnam, when popular protest surged and correlated with the death toll of U.S. forces half a world away, this usually unconscious racism has made it possible for many well-meaning people to ignore the suffering inflicted by U.S. military intervention on Third World peoples, and the roles nuclear weapons have played in these interventions and in the maintenance of less visible structures of oppression. As my then seven-year-old adopted daughter once asked, why is it that the bombs are always dropped on darker-skinned people like me?

White racism is at least as old as the Crusades. Its dehumanizing influence helped fuel the Pacific War of 1941 to 1945 and contributed to the legitimization of the atomic bombings of Hiroshima and Nagasaki. The same racism leads people to work for non-proliferation of nuclear weapons while remaining silent about the violence in their communities. It has been a barrier to joining with others, committed to justice and peace, to build the social and political power needed for fundamental change. I have written about this in *The Deadly Connection: Nuclear War and U.S. Intervention* and will not belabor the point here.

It is natural to want not to die in a global repetition of Hiroshima and Nagasaki. Not to worry about, and struggle for, our security and survival and that of our children and loved ones is unthinkable. But a central question, once asked by Bob Moses, remains: "Who is 'we'?"

It is my hope that by understanding the hibakusha as "we," as I have had the privilege to do, people in the United States will finally face the enormity of what our society has done and continues to threaten to do. If there can be no peace without justice, total nuclear disarmament is unlikely without greater strides toward ending racism.

Each of the case studies in these chapters, are related to the racism of U.S. culture. I came into the peace movement from the Civil Rights movement. The analysis growing from the Black Power movement in the mid-1960s was that Whites should address the racism in their own communities. David Donald Duncan's photographs of civilian victims of the U.S. war in Indochina shattered what illusions I still held about U.S. foreign policy and U.S. history. What greater manifestation of U.S. racism was there at the time? This awareness, and the very real pressures of the military draft, led to my deepening engagement with what has been described as the anti-intervention wing of the U.S. peace movement.

In seeking to understand, analyze, and describe the decision to bomb the people of Hiroshima and Nagasaki, the consequences of that decision, the subsequent practice of nuclear extortion, and the patterns of U.S. foreign policy that make up the whole cloth, I have attempted to be both truthful and compassionate in exploring what can be learned from long repressed truths. As Akira Kurowaswa illustrated so clearly in *Rashomon*, our limited angles of vision make even discrete events subject to wildly different interpretations. On a grander scale, if one is to speak of *a* or *the* Truth, the Universe or *Totum*, it is by definition unknowable, as it extends in time and space far beyond our limited angles of vision.[3] This book does not attempt to name or describe "the whole Truth." Nor does it attempt to describe the entire history of atomic diplomacy and nuclear extortion. It concentrates, instead, on the the bombings of Hiroshima and Nagasaki, which served as the models for their repeated use by the United States and, to a lesser extent, by other nuclear powers. This work does not underestimate the possible consequences of nuclear extortion and nuclear war initiated by the other nuclear powers. It does, however, confine its scope to the U.S. practice of nuclear extortion which has encouraged and, within the game of nations, legitimized its imitation by other nations unwilling to accept the discriminatory nuclear order codified in the non-proliferation regime. Those seeking a more universal understanding of the practice of nuclear extortion may wish to make use of the bibliography.

Three other points should be briefly touched upon. The title, *With Hiroshima Eyes*, is not without problems. The double entendre of *with* captures both the spirit and content of this work. The book shares some of what hibakusha have seen, and it is written as an homage to, and act of solidarity with, politically engaged hibakusha. *Eyes* is somewhat more problematic. The book draws on what the hibakusha endured, thought, willed, and dared as well as what they have seen. More difficult was the choice of the word *Hiroshima*. As readers will discover, I have drawn at least as heavily on the testimonies and actions of the Nagasaki hibakusha as I have on those who survived Hiroshima. Like many before me, I have hesitantly used Hiroshima as emblematic of the two nuclear holocausts inflicted on Japan in August 1945, in much the same way that Auschwitz has come to be used as a symbol for the entire European Judeocide and Holocaust.

This book is a work of condensation. Each chapter could be, and has been, the subject of many scholarly works. The need to condense volumes into paragraphs and pages has been a source of constant frustration. Vast histories have been summarized and thus somewhat distorted. They are included here to provide context, to make the thoughts, decisions, and patterns of policy makers and governments comprehensible. My hope is that this background will contribute to, and not detract from, the three essential points of this book: that nuclear weapons have always been targeted against human beings; that the U.S. practice of nuclear extortion has been an essential element of the maintenance and expansion of its global sphere of influence; and that politically engaged hibakusha are undervalued moral and political exemplars for all people.

Finally, a note about my use of Japanese names and honorifics. In Japanese, the family name is used first and the given name last. This has been a source of confusion to many in the West. To facilitate understanding of readers in the United States I have reversed Japanese names. Throughout the text, given names appear first and family names last. It is a courtesy to refer to respected adults as -*san*, and teachers as -*sensei*. In fact, all the politically engaged hibakusha are my *sensei*, but here I have appended these honorifics where it seemed most appropriate.

Notes

1. *The Last Empire*, Cambridge, Mass: Cambridge Documentary Films, 1985.
2. *New York Times*, July 8, 1994.
3. I am referring to Akira Kurosawa's 1950 film, *Rashomon*, and to Wilfred Desan's *The Planetary Man*, New York: Macmillan Co., 1972.

CHAPTER ONE

Memories and Meanings

The painful page in our history cannot be turned before it is written.
— Alain Jacubowicz, Prosecutor at Paul Touvier War Crimes Trial[1]

There is a crack in everything / That's how the light gets in
— Leonard Cohen[2]

Silent holes say so much.
— Yamane Masako[3]

IN MAY 1994, five years into the post-Cold War era, Nihon Hidankyo, the Japanese Confederation of Organizations of Atomic and Hydrogen Bombs Sufferers, published a statement in anticipation of the fiftieth anniversaries of the atomic bombings which its members endured and survived. With characteristic directness, understatement, and formality, these scarred survivors of Hiroshima and Nagasaki decried the danger and hypocrisy of the Clinton administration's nuclear threats against North Korea. Calling for the abolition of nuclear weapons, these hibakusha declared:

> We have recently felt disturbed about the nature of American efforts to stop North Korea from developing nuclear weapons. America has renewed its nuclear weapons stockpiling and is considering sanctions which include the possible use of nuclear weapons. Of course we oppose the proliferation of nuclear weapons. However, the position that says that only "we" can have nuclear weapons, and that "we" might actually be forced to use them if others do not listen to us, is the same argument which justified the atomic bombings of Hiroshima and Nagasaki. We, utterly, cannot accept this.[4]

Creating and returning to history in the first months of his presidency, Bill Clinton journeyed to one of the last boundaries of the Cold War, the thirty-eighth parallel in Korea. His purpose was to reinforce pressures initiated by George Bush to prevent North Korea from becoming a nuclear weapons power. Calling the North Korean domain the "scariest place on earth," the new president threatened the government in Pyongyang with nuclear annhiliation. It "would be pointless for them to try to develop a nuclear weapon because if they use it," Clinton said, "it would be the end of their country."[5] This threat was followed by leaked reports of U.S. and South Korean preparations for "a pre-emptive strike against Pyongyang in the event of any sign of mobilisation in the North."[6]

The Post-Cold War Context

The end of the Cold War marked a return to historical patterns repressed or obscured by the U.S.-Soviet confrontation. From Chile to China, U.S. presidents again explained U.S. foreign and military policy in terms of access to markets and human rights, as their predecessors had done a century earlier. There was again, as the poet Edna St. Vincent Millay wrote on the eve of the First World War, "fighting in the Balkans." U.S. Marines once again occupied Haiti in the name of "democracy." Half-hearted "humanitarian" military interventions in Rwanda and Somalia served to legitimize militaries and their budgets in the United States, Europe, and Japan. In Asia, the fate of the Korean people was again the subject of the ambitions of powers that long dominated the peninusla: the United States, Japan, China, and Russia.

History, as always, returned in disguise. Although the nuclear sword of Damocles was popularly thought to have been returned to its scabbard, in the early years of the Clinton administration the U.S. nuclear arsenal continued to include an estimated 8,300 strategic nuclear weapons, 950 tactical nuclear warheads, and more nuclear weapons in inactive reserve.[7] Daily alarms of the dangers of nuclear weapons and nuclear war screamed silently from the headlines: North Korea might have nuclear weapons. A Korean bomb could "force" Japan to recant its peace constitution and to become a nuclear weapons power. The Ukrainian arsenal was the third largest in the world, complicating U.S. and Russian negotiations and threatening to "force" Germany to become a nuclear power. Ukraine and Kazakstan each had more nuclear weapons than France, Britain, China, Pakistan, India, and Israel combined. Weapons grade plutonium was being smuggled from Russia through Germany. India refused to surrender its nuclear weapons and, with other Third World nations, it challenged U.S. proposals for the indefinite extension of the 1968 Nuclear Non-Proliferation Treaty. Pakistan would not cap its nuclear weapons program in exchange for U.S. jet fighters. Iran, Algeria, Libya, Egypt, and even Saudi Arabia had nuclear weapons programs that threatened to undermine the U.S.-Israeli regional nuclear monopoly.

U.S. foreign policy for the post-Cold War era was framed by *Discriminate Deterrence*, the bipartisan report of the Pentagon's Commission on Integrated Long-Term Strategy. The report, which was promulgated in the closing years of the Reagan administration, proposed a U.S. global strategy to ensure that the United States remained the dominant global power in the first decades of the post-Cold War era.

The commission's diagnosis was clear: Japan and Western Europe were beginning to challenge U.S. global hegemony. The power of U.S. conventional weapons was declining in relation to several increasingly well-armed Third World nations. As many as forty countries could become nuclear weapons powers by the year 2010. To remain the dominant global power, the commission recommended the United States should not attempt to control every development in the world. Instead, it must retain control over three regions: the Persian Gulf, the Mediterranean Sea, and the Pacific Ocean. As it faced difficult budget choices, the commission advised the Pentagon to continue modernization of its nuclear arsenal, increase air- and sea-lift capabilities for rapid military intervention, and invest in high-tech weaponry.[8]

Discriminate Deterrence provided the "vision" for George Bush's 1990–91 "Desert Storm" against Iraq. It was a war fought to reassert U.S. control over the Persian Gulf region, and it was fought with high-tech cruise missiles, rapidly deployed ground forces, threats of nuclear attack made by President Bush and others, and the encirclement of Iraq with and estimated 1,000 nuclear weapons.

Before leaving the White House the Bush administration had refined *Discriminate Deterrence* for its successors. The initial draft of its strategic policy document, leaked to the press in March 1992, bluntly described the unrefined commitments of "national security" planners in Washington. "Our first objective," it read, "is to prevent the reemergence of a new rival." In the Asia/Pacific region that meant "Defense of Korea will likely remain one of the most demanding major regional contingencies…we must maintain our status as a military power of the first magnitude in the area."[9]

It was in this context that Bill Clinton journeyed to the thirty-eighth parallel, approached the brink of a second Korean war, and negotiated an ambiguous resolution of the U.S.-North Korean confrontation. Threatened by the Clinton administration's atomic and economic diplomacy, North Korea reaffirmed its commitment to the Nuclear Non-Proliferation Treaty. It also agreed not to reprocess its spent nuclear fuel rods, halted construction of two nuclear reactors, and reaffirmed its willingness to comply with the inspections demanded by the United States, some of them to occur after a "decent interval." In exchange the Clinton administration promised North Korea economic and technological aid, diplomatic recognition, and security guarantees.[10]

The confrontation between Washington and Pyongyang and Nihon Hidankyo's statement were about North Korea, and more. Nuclear weapons technology was fifty years old. As one engineer put it, "If a country has the technology to grind lenses, it can build a nuclear bomb." The global structure of power based on U.S. nuclear dominance and the implicit threat of U.S. first-strike nuclear warfighting was being challenged. Half a century of U.S.-initiated atomic diplomacy and nuclear extortion, begun by Franklin Roosevelt before unforgettable fires were inflicted on Hiroshima and Nagasaki, had created imitators, competitors, and steadfast opponents.

The post-Cold War threats of nuclear war were direct descendents of the 1945 atomic bombings. Like the repeated use of nuclear extortion throughout the Cold War, they resulted from what many practitioners of realpolitik viewed as the successful "diplomatic" use of nuclear weapons.

President Clinton's nuclear threat against North Korea and the Bush administration's multiple nuclear threats against Iraq, like those of other U.S. presidents, were what former Secretary of War Henry L. Stimson described as playing the master card in the game of nations.[11] Daniel Ellsberg, who helped design nuclear warfighting doctrines for Presidents Johnson and Nixon, has explained that "the United States has used nuclear weapons at least a dozen times or more since Hiroshima and Nagasaki." Included in Ellsberg's list are U.S. nuclear threats made during the Korean and Vietnam Wars and numerous wars in the Middle East. Building on another of Stimson's analogies, that having an atomic bomb is like having a "gun on your hip," Ellsberg has also described how successive U.S. presidents used nuclear weapons "in the way that you use a gun when you point it at someone's head in a confrontation…whether or not you pull the trigger…You're also using it when you have it on your hip, ostentatiously."[12] Like the bombings of Hiroshima and Nagasaki, when U.S. presidents have played gunslinger with nuclear master cards, they have usually done so in ways that were secret to the U.S. public, but quite visible to those attempting to resist the will of the U.S. government.[13]

Challenging the Myths

What can another writer add to the literature of the atomic bombings of Hiroshima and Nagasaki that has not already been said? What does another book about the history and possible uses of nuclear weapons contribute to our understanding? My answers are simple and complex, personal and philosophical.

This book was conceived with three goals in mind. First, it seeks to challenge the popular conceptions of Hiroshima and Nagasaki. It asks, and in part describes, what the bombings meant for the *people* of those two cities, and why the Truman administration imposed two nuclear holocausts. Second, this book continues to revise popular understanding of the nuclear arms race and the use of nuclear weapons as deterrents against the Soviet Union. It emphasizes that U.S. nuclear weapons have been used to maintain and expand U.S. global power, particularly in the Third World. The Middle East, East Asia, and Latin America were more frequently the focal points of nuclear threats and atomic diplomacy than were Berlin and the Fulda Gap (the anticipated invasion route of a Soviet invasion of Western Europe). Finally, this book seeks to present the politically engaged hibakusha to a wider audience. These damned, scarred, and courageous survivors, who have confronted and transformed their painful identities in ways similar to the morally engaged survivors of the European Judeocide, should serve as role models. For their own survival, and ours, they have established the fundamental frame of reference for understanding the continuing urgent danger of nuclear weapons, and they are models for understanding the resiliency and potential of human life.

The Moral Imperative of the Hibakusha

Beginning with the atomic bombing of Hiroshima, nuclear weapons have been targeted and used against human beings. Throughout this book, with special attention to the atomic bombings of the people of Hiroshima and Nagasaki, I have explored some of the meanings of this continuing crime against humanity.[14] By remembering that the hibakusha were literally at the vortex of events and human history in August 1945, and by placing them, along with U.S. policy makers, at the center of this book and our thinking, I have sought to illuminate our understanding of the meaning of nuclear weapons. Democratizing the discourse by listening to and considering people immersed in death by the Truman administration challenges the idealistic, chauvinistic, racialized, and imperial structures of knowledge created by the mandarins of American academia.[15]

Since 1945 there has been broad understanding that the atomic bombings of Hiroshima and Nagasaki, like Auschwitz, demonstrated "the existence of a will to genocidal, absolute destruction."[16] The existential and moral imperatives of preventing nuclear war have been manifestly clear, even as the "will to power" by states, military-industrial complexes, and individuals has, since 1945, increased the possibilities of "limited" nuclear wars and global nuclear omnicide. Few in the United States, however, and certainly not the Hawks and Owls from academia who advise policy-makers,[17] have attempted to learn from the hibakusha, or to challenge the barriers of distance, language, and culture, the politics of history, and the history of politics that have reinforced the dehumanization of the people of Hiroshima and Nagasaki and transformed them into disembodied numbers: phantoms.

The issue at stake is whose memories, whose words, and whose understandings will define *Hiroshima* and *Nagasaki* in the present and for the future. Will it be those who made and implemented the decision to bomb the people of these two cities, those who made subsequent nuclear threats, concerned scholars, or the hibakusha who survived? In the United States, the testimonies of hibakusha have rarely led political scientists or community activists to reflect about the unique political and moral dilemmas they present to Americans. For example, Michiko Yamaoka was fifteen years old and eight hundred meters from the epicenter of the atomic bombing of Hiroshima. She remembers that:

> There was no sound. I felt something strong. It was terribly intense. I felt colors. It wasn't heat. You can't really say it was yellow, and it wasn't blue. At that moment I thought I would be the only one who would die. I said to myself, "Goodbye, Mom." I remember my body floating in the air...I don't know how far I was blown. When I came to my senses my surroundings were silent...Nobody there looked like human beings...Everyone was stupefied. Humans had lost the ability to speak. People couldn't scream...even when they were on fire... They just sat catching fire...
>
> I made my way towards the mountain, where there was no fire. On this flight I saw a friend of mine ...I called her name, but she didn't respond. My face was so swollen she couldn't tell who I was. Finally she recognized my voice. She said, "Miss Yamaoka, you look like a monster!" That's the first time I heard that word. I looked at my hands and saw my own skin hanging down and the red flesh exposed.[18]

Michiko Yamaoka's memories have not been at the center of U.S. political and moral discourse. What responsibilities follow from confronting her memories?

I have sought to help make "silent holes" audible. I have sought to let their voices penetrate the repressed silence of trauma and to amplify the voices of the growing body of hibakusha testimony. I seek to place the hibakusha in their proper place, at the center of our thinking about Hiroshima and Nagasaki. We can learn from victims, at least as well as from executioners.

Accidents of life and history, as well as my personal commitments, have led me to be among those privileged to have had extended contact with leading political activists among the hibakusha. Within Japan, many hibakusha have suffered discrimination because of their victimization, their physical scars, and popular fears of the potential consequences of radiation-induced genetic damage. Among many people in Japan and the United States there is, I fear, also a dehumanizing belief that the hibakusha have nothing to share but their pain. This discrimination and denial grow from fears of confronting and sharing the pain of the hibakusha and from the preoccupations of the consumer culture, dominated by market relations and the requirement that people must come together to buy and sell things.[19] In the United States, national chauvinism is also a factor.

These fears and preoccupations have diminished not only countless lives on both edges of the Pacific Rim, but also the moral and political awareness necessary to confront the dangers of nuclear weapons and to struggle for their abolition. For these reasons I have drawn on my experiences with politically engaged hibakusha, their public testimonies, and less accessible archives to make the courage, vision, and commitments of these survivors available to a wider public.

In her book *In the Realm of a Dying Emperor*, Norma Field describes the "especially precious" role of courageous and abused minorities who "do battle for themselves and for majorities."[20] This applies universally, and precisely describes my understanding of the contribution and role of the politically engaged hibakusha. Their courage, memories, testimonies, and witnesses are moral frames of reference for all who live under the shadows of Hiroshima and Nagasaki and their nuclear progeny.

I have sought to avoid romanticizing hibakusha, who are, simply, people. Like all of us, they suffer from limits to their courage and wisdom, and not a few struggle with self-doubt. Many hibakusha committed suicide to escape their agony. More died from radiation poisoning and other bomb-inflicted wounds. Some repressed their traumatic memories in order to continue with their lives. Others sought to hide their identities and thus avoid discrimination. Some have been heroic, transforming their suffering into moral and political forces to create a world in which there will be no more Hiroshimas, no more Nagasakis, and no more hibakusha.

A story may serve as an illustration of these different lives of hibakusha.

In 1987, when I returned to Japan to participate in the annual World Conference Against Atomic and Hydrogen Bombs, I asked to stay in private homes rather than in hotels. My intent was to learn more about Japanese life and culture. In Hiroshima, Morteza Abdolalian, a refugee from Khomeini's Iran, and I stayed in the suburban home of Junko Kayashige, a hibakusha, and her husband. We depended on the Kayashiges' heroic efforts to speak English for communication. That night Morteza and I slept on futons in a tatami room with the Kayashige's books, armoire, and many of their prized possessions.

On the morning of August 6 we rose early, well before the sun was strong and the cicadas grated the air with their searing buzz. Neither Morteza nor I were fully awake when we climbed into our clothes, forced food into our mouths, and struggled to keep up with Kayashige-*san* as she led us along the road beside the irrigation canal, past modern homes, rice paddies, the Buddhist temple, and food shops to the Midorii railroad station. We were, finally, almost awake when our train pulled into Hiroshima station and Kayashige-*san* hailed a cab to take us across town for the official memorial ceremony.

Sitting with Kayashige-*san* in the front seat was a middle aged, crew cut, white gloved taxi driver. As Morteza and I talked about political developments in the Middle East, I gradually became aware that Kayashige-*san* had disengaged from us and was engrossed in a politely intense exchange with the taxi driver. When we arrived at the Peace Park their conversation subsided, and I risked asking her what they had been talking about.

The taxi driver was upset by our presence and by the thousands of other pilgrims, political activists and politicians who had converged on the city. He had challenged Kayashige-*san*'s participation in the meetings and demonstrations that brought people to Hiroshima from across Japan and abroad. He felt that we could have little regard for the suffering he and others endured. Our activities, he felt, exploited the anguish of those who had died and those who had survived. Junko had countered that even if we could not fully understand what had happened when the city was bombed, our presence in Hiroshima was important. We could learn. Our demonstrations, political discussions, and organizing were, she said, the only way to stop the nuclear arms race and to ensure that nuclear weapons were never used again.

The tense discussion between Kayashige-*san* and the taxi driver was an undeniable lesson that the hibakusha have many voices. They share their survival of Hell, but they have different memories, and they have made different meanings of those memories, their survival, and their lives.

Years later, after meeting, working with, and becoming friends with politically engaged hibakusha , I discovered the opening words of Robert Lifton's 1967 essay "Atomic Bomb Leaders" were particularly helpful in understanding what I had observed and experienced. "A few in Hiroshima," Lifton wrote, confronted "their hibakusha identity and put it to public use." Like the survivors of the European Judeocide and other cataclysmic crimes and events, through speaking about what they endured, the hibakusha have moved to release themselves from "death anxiety and death guilt…The unifying theme of hibakusha leaders…has been… 'conquering death'—of demonstrating ways of comprehending a profound upheaval in patterns of life and death, and ultimately of comprehending the fact of human mortality itself." This, Lifton reminds his readers, "is the primary function of all leaders."[21]

The censorship of the U.S. military occupation severely limited the ability of the Japanese to learn about or publicly discuss what the hibakusha had suffered or about the causes and meanings of the atomic bombings. Despite the occupation's restrictions, the first stirrings of a peace movement grew from the suffering and grieving of the hibakusha. In Hiroshima they met for poetry readings, and in March 1946, Hiroshima intellectuals began the publication of *Chungku Culture*, a magazine whose first issue focused on the atomic bombings. A 1946 Memorial Day organized by religious leaders, brought together three hundred fifty groups and contributed to the founding of the Hiroshima Peace Association. Not until the U.S. military occupation ended in 1952 were Japanese free to publish and broadcast descriptions of the catastrophic attacks they had suffered or to explore the meanings of the nuclear holocausts in relative freedom. Yet as late as 1960, the U.S. government worked to withhold the release of photographic documentation of the damage caused by the bombings. As Secretary of State Christian A. Herter wrote to John A. McCone, the Director of the Atomic Energy Commission, "the Department of State has serious reservations about the release of these photographs because we have been concerned over the political impact in Japan particularly, and because of our reluctance to present the Communists with a propaganda weapon they would use against us in all parts of the world."[22]

Japanese organizing against the possible use of nuclear weapons, and for the abolition of nuclear weapons, which began when Presidents Truman and Eisenhower threatened nuclear attacks during the Korean War, intensified in 1954 when the crew of the *Lucky Dragon Number Five*, a Japanese fishing vessel, was showered with radioactive fallout from a U.S. hydrogen bomb test at Bikini atoll. The end of U.S. military occupation, continuing U.S. preparations for nuclear war, and the third atomic bombing of Japanese gave birth to the modern Japanese peace and nuclear disarmament movement. It, in turn, provided encouragement and forums to the hibakusha to confront and to share their agonizing memories.

Hibakusha, including Misako Yamaguchi, Chieko Watanabe, Senji Yamaguchi, and Sumiteru Taniguchi, overcame fears of exposing their "ugly features" to the world. Standing on their own, or in Chieko Watanabe's case, carried by her mother, they began to address Japanese audiences and the World Conferences Against Atomic and Hydrogen Bombs, the first of which was organized in 1955. They formed local organizations of hibakusha and the Confederation of Organizations of Atomic and Hydrogen Bombs Sufferers, Nihon Hidankyo.

Sumiteru Taniguchi, who was hideously maimed and to this day endures open wounds from the Nagasaki bombing, once explained in an interview that, "In August 1955 the First World Conference Against Atomic and Hydrogen Bombs was held and one atomic victim stood on the stage and rendered his plea. When I realized how other victims were opposing the Bomb, I decided that I too should throw away my hesitation and become a witness for peace."23 Taniguchi-san feared the consequences of forgetfulness, that "those who have forgotten the past are going ahead in support of nuclear weapons."

For many hibakusha, becoming a public witness was not a simple matter. Taniguchi "hated showing [his] deformed body," and understandably did not want to "become an object of display." But he "put his hibakusha identity to use" and spoke for many of the politically active hibakusha when he said,

> that does not mean that we victims should hide in the shadow. We must not give in to just struggling with our own personal despair and not working for peace. Living and struggling for peace is my joy and consolation, but those of us who have walked forward out of Hell know that there has been enough suffering. We want our sons and our daughters to live rich, happy lives in peace. And for this we depend on everyone to struggle with all their might for peace.[24]

Junko Kayashige, who is steadfastly active, if not a hero in the Western sense of the word, put it differently in a speech:

> I always feel reluctant to speak about what happened in the summer forty-nine years ago, because it means to touch my unhealed wounds which still hurt me. The scars don't heal even if I avoid talking about it...not talking about my scars means escaping from myself and society. Therefore I must take courage to open my mouth to tell people about my scars...It was in the ninth year of my teaching career that I spoke to my students about the A-bombing for the first time. Even junior high school students of Hiroshima don't know about the A-bombing. How can those of other prefectures come to know it?
>
> ...Memories usually become sweet as time goes by, unless they are grossly disgusting. Now I even remember with nostalgic feeling the life in the shack and a welcomed meal made from stripped bullfrogs. But keloids* on my body would not turn into good memories.

---

*Like many other hibakusha, Junko Kayashige and her family were initially evacuated to a suburban village where they were made to feel ashamed for being both hibakusha and urban people. Rather than remain there, her family returned to Hiroshima where they lived in a one-room house made of thin boards and zinc sheets. Keloids are a form of disfiguring scar tissue which have become a symbol of Hibakusha identity.

...Now I am the mother of two children, and I am teaching students...I have to face up to the atomic bombing. Touching the scars from burns, my children ask, "What happened to your body?" Looking at the A-bomb Dome, they ask, "Why was it destroyed so badly?" I cannot evade such questions. And, as a teacher of Hiroshima, I cannot keep silent during summer. I have to challenge my hurting scars...I want to live my life, ruminating on the phrase, "The error shall never be repeated"[25]

Wilfred Burchett, the first foreign journalist to witness the devastation wrought on Hiroshima, has since described the courage of the hibakusha as the second lesson of Hiroshima: "the indestructibility of human resistance." In spite of suffering, censorship, cover-ups, and ostracism, many hibakusha became "the most stalwart and militant of peaceniks. Through them and their on-going struggle, the *urgency* of Hiroshima is transmitted to all of us."[26]

The scars, sensitivities, and anger of the politically engaged hibakusha have been most deeply aggravated and torn by the use of Japan as an "unsinkable aircraft carrier for the United States." To this day, many of the more than one hundred U.S. military bases and installations spread across Japan provide the technological infrastructure for nuclear warfighting. U.S. bases provided training and logistical support for U.S. forces during the Vietnam War, when the U.S. was again at war against "Oriental people with yellow skin."[27] Again, during the 1991 Gulf War, ten thousand U.S. troops and nuclear capable weapons were dispatched from their bases in Japan to be used against the people of Iraq in the Desert Storm war.

Little has changed since Suzu Kuboyama, the widow of Aikichi Kuboyama, the *Lucky Dragon's* radio operator, said in 1955, "Atomic artillery and rockets are brought into Japan though everyone opposes this. What do those eager to wage an atomic war think? Atomic weapons are brought to Japan that has suffered the damage from atomic bombs three times. How insulting it is for the people of Hiroshima and Nagasaki and my husband!"[28] Thirty years after Suzu Kuboyama's speech, when I first visited physics professor Shoji Sawada in Nagoya, where he teaches, he was intent on making sure that I saw the "elephant cages"— telecommunications installations built by the U.S. military for use in launching nuclear war.

The U.S. war in Vietnam was opposed by mass demonstrations and other protest actions in Japanese cities and at U.S. bases. As a result of what was for Japan the Fifteen Year War in Asia and the Pacific (1931–45) and the U.S. military occupation, the majority of Japanese had learned to detest militarism and war. As I describe in Chapter 4, Japanese identification with the Vietnamese victims of the U.S. war became intense. How could they not identify with another Asian people suffering massive aerial bombardments and other atrocities? In Japan, as in the United States, many feared that the United States "would use any means whatsoever to win the war, " including nuclear weapons.[29] This is precisely what the Joint Chiefs of Staff considered during the 1967 North Vietnamese siege of Khe Sanh and what President Nixon and his National Security Advisor Henry Kissinger threatened in 1969.

Chieko Watanabe, speaking from her wheelchair, expressed the thoughts and fears of many Hibakusha:

> All my feelings go to the people of Vietnam whose lives and lands have been mercilessly destroyed by the American intervention. I can share with them in their infinite despair and distress because I am also a war victim...the people of Vietnam [and] Cambodia have not suffered A-bombs so far. Nevertheless, they are constantly exposed to the menace of nuclear weapons today. In this sense, they, as well as the rest of the world, are close to suffering the same fate as I did.[30]

Although many in Japan, including hibakusha, regarded most of the Cold War era Middle East wars as "ethnic wars or religious wars, which seemed so distant and out of reach,"[31] this was not the case when the United States moved its troops based in Japan to the Persian Gulf and threatened the people of Iraq with nuclear weapons. Takeshi Ito, then the co-chairperson of Hidankyo, wrote to the U.S. president:

> Forty-six years ago, in the hell-like situation caused by the atomic bombing, hundreds of thousands of people were brutally killed. Those who barely survived are still suffering from the incurable wounds both physically and in mind. Our experience is evidence that proves the absolutely evil and devilish nature of nuclear weapons, which cannot be justified for whatever reasons.

> We feel even more painful when we see the war in the Gulf region escalating and causing serious damage day by day, with the increasing danger of weapons of mass-destruction being used...Richard Cheney, U.S. Defense Secretary, even declared that it was a right decision that 'he (Truman) used the bomb on Hiroshima and Nagasaki.' It was also suggested that there is a possibility of U.S. retaliation with nuclear weapons, if Iraq uses poison gas. You, too, did not exclude the possibility of using nuclear weapons, saying on February 5 that it would be better for the U.S. not to say whether or not it would use its nuclear weapons.

> These remarks, which tried to justify the use of nuclear weapons, not only desecrate more than 400,000 of those who died and 350,000 surviving A-bomb victims, but also amount to a blatant challenge to the whole human community. We cannot condone these outrageous remarks and arrogance. We strongly urge you and the U.S. Defense Secretary to withdraw these remarks...We call on you to stop the war without delay.[32]

Many hibakusha envision the possibility of life and the global order free of nuclear weapons, nuclear threats, and the dangers of nuclear holocausts.

Increasingly in recent years they have been joined by scientists, strategic analysts, and activists who understand that arms "control" cannot provide security or prevent the continuing proliferation of nuclear weapons. Although nuclear weapons cannot be disinvented, like chemical and biological weapons it is both necessary and possible to abolish them.

More than most of us, hibakusha are confronted by their physical limitations, as well as by the challenges of the material and political worlds we share. Unlike many of us, they have created and drawn on reserves of personal will to achieve a vision and reality that many have thought to be utopian: the abolition of nuclear weapons. Senji Yamaguchi, some of whose suffering is described in the following chapter, personified this commitment and vision when he addressed a U.S. nuclear disarmament conference in 1993, only days after yet another hospital confinement:

> We, the atomic bomb survivors at Nihon Hidankyo, are continuing daily in our efforts to completely ban nuclear weapons and to create an international treaty which would outlaw all nuclear weapons. We should not allow another Hiroshima or Nagasaki to happen anywhere on earth again.[33]

Vision, will, and spirit can challenge what appear to be the most powerful, repressing, and damning physical and political realities, including vested interests that maintain and reinforce their power through nuclear weapons and terror.

Practicing Atomic Diplomacy

With the hibakusha and the human consequences of nuclear war in the foreground of our thinking, we move to the second dimension of this reframing of Hiroshima and Nagasaki: considering why the Truman administration bombed these cities when it knew the Japanese government was suing for peace. This is painful material, and it is closely related to the history and self-perception of the people of the United States. With the revealing lights of the historical record, my purpose here is to further delegitimize the mythology that continues to protect the reputations of elected and appointed leaders, that has pacified people in the United States and much of the world, and—most importantly—that has legitimized the stockpiling and threatened use of nuclear weapons. As long as we, and here I refer to the people of the United States, remain ignorant of our history and identity, there can be no serious reflection, no option for truthfulness, no making amends, no change of consciousness that will serve to increase our security and well being. In this regard, we can learn something from modern German history.

I have joined Gar Alperovitz and Martin Sherwin, scholars of the Roosevelt and Truman administrations' atomic diplomacy, and a host of students of Japanese wartime decision-making, in challenging two myths manufactured to defend the indefensible. These consciously created myths, that "the atomic bombs dropped on Hiroshima and Nagasaki...saved a million [US] casualties,"[34] and that no one close to President Truman ever pressed him to consider alternatives to the bombings[35] have been repeated ad nauseam until they became the received and blinding wisdom of our political culture. These conscious deceits and their repetition have protected the careers and reputations of President Truman and many of his advisors. More importantly, they have legitimized the use of nuclear weapons and the global hierarchy of power based on nuclear extortion and the possible nuclear annihilation of the human species.

As described in considerable detail in Chapter 2, "The consensus among scholars is that the bomb was not needed to avoid an invasion of Japan...[and] it is clear that alternatives to the bomb existed and that Truman and his advisors knew it."[36] Admiral Leahy, the chairman of the Joint Chiefs of Staff and a special advisor to President Truman, understood that "a surrender of Japan can be arranged with terms that can be accepted."[37] Intelligence reports informed Truman that the Japanese government was attempting to surrender to the Soviet Union, a possibility which Truman noted in his diary and discussed with Stalin prior to the bombings.

As their diaries, memoirs, and declassified memoranda demonstrate, President Truman was guided by Secretary of War Stimson, Acting Secretary of State James Grew, and Secretary of State Byrnes toward the use of nuclear weapons to force an almost unconditional Japanese surrender before the Soviet Union fully joined the war in Asia. The influences of revenge, racism, and electoral politics cannot be denied, but Truman's conscious and articulated goal was to preclude Soviet influence in Japan, Manchuria, China, and Korea. He also hoped that by demonstrating U.S. nuclear capabilities and the will to use them, the Soviet sphere of influence in eastern Europe, recognized by Franklin Roosevelt and Winston Churchill at Yalta, could also be diminished.

These goals were not unique to Truman. By 1943 the potential of nuclear weapons in the postwar world had become central to the strategies being developed by Roosevelt and Churchill. In 1944 Roosevelt and his secretary of war "spoke of using the 'secret' of the atomic bomb as a means of obtaining a quid pro quo from the Soviet Union."[38]

Having juxtaposed what Michel Foucault would describe as "localized truths", the actions and experiences of people in Hiroshima and Nagasaki against those in Washington and Potsdam, new questions arise which I hope to explore more deeply in the future. To what extent should Michiko

Yamaoka's memories and suffering be differentiated from those of Primo Levi, Elie Wiesel, and other survivors of the European Judeocide? How do we differentiate the moral and political culpabilities of Hitler and Eichmann from those of Truman and Conant (the president of Harvard University who recommended the targets of the atomic bomb be vital war plants, closely surrounded by workers' homes)? What do these coexisting realities tell us about the nature of our society and the moral and political responsibilities we face?

The Deadly Connection

The second purpose of this book is to go beyond the "consensus among scholars" that Hiroshima and Nagasaki were in large measure destroyed to "stop the Russians in Asia, and to give them sober pause in eastern Europe."[39] Using Cold War and post-Cold War case studies, I describe how the crimes of Hiroshima and Nagasaki served as models for continuing U.S. nuclear extortion and atomic diplomacy. Focusing on the Cuban Missile Crisis, Nixon's "madman" theory of atomic diplomacy used unsuccessfully against Vietnam, Henry Kissinger's DEFCON 3 nuclear alert in the closing hours of the 1973 Middle East October War, and the more recent nuclear blackmail practiced by Presidents Bush and Clinton, is not without precedent. Richard Betts, Barry M. Blechman, Daniel Ellsberg, Michio Kaku, Stephen S. Kaplan, and others, including myself, have explored what Blechman and Kaplan called "Force Without War" and what I have termed the "Deadly Connection" between nuclear war and U.S. intervention.[40] *With Hiroshima Eyes* goes further by naming the continuity between Truman's bombing of Hiroshima and his reported 1946 threat to annihilate Moscow to ensure continued U.S. dominance of the Middle East. It explicitly links the atomic bombing of Nagasaki with the atomic diplomacy and nuclear blackmail practiced by Truman's successors. I have also diverged from those who have preceeded me by replacing the more commonly-used term *nuclear blackmail* with *nuclear extortion.* The latter is the more accurate term because it refers to the use of coercion, threats, and intimidations to achieve ends that are not limited to money.

While much of the historical record remains in classified government files, the memoirs of presidents and their aides, the public record, and the painstaking research of other scholars has revealed a damning and little explored history of U.S. nuclear extortion. Among the low points of this history were President Truman's threat to use nuclear weapons early in the Korean War; President Eisenhower's threats and preparations to initiate nuclear war during crises in Asia, the Middle East, and Latin America; the Cuban Missile Crisis; and Presidents Johnson's and Nixon's preparations and threats to use nuclear weapons in Vietnam and during Middle East wars. The Carter Doctrine, which threatened the use of "any means necessary" to retain U.S. control of the oil-rich Persian Gulf, remains a lasting legacy of the Carter presidency, a threat that was reiterated by Ronald Reagan shortly after his inauguration.

Confronting the Taboo

To explore the Deadly Connection, the prohibition against the use of the term and concept *imperialism* must be confronted. *Imperialism* is defined as "the relationship of a ruling or controlling power to those under its dominium. Empire is a state of affairs even when the imperialist power is not formally constituted as such."[41]

That "the words *empire* and *imperialism* enjoy no easy hospitality in the minds and hearts of most contemporary Americans"[42] cannot erase the realities they describe, be they U.S., Soviet, or Russian imperialism. The taboo, which serves as both external and internalized censor, limits people's ability to think, and thus the ability to create, strategize, and act. The taboo is a kind of lie, and as the philosopher Elizabeth Minnich observed, "one critical reason not to lie to ourselves…is that you cannot think well when there are things you cannot allow yourself to think about, and you cannot communicate with others when you have stopped being able to communicate with yourself."[43] The scholar, activist, and Belsen extermination camp survivor, Israel Shahak, explained it this way: ideological influences "tend to be more influential the less they are discussed and 'dragged into the light.' Any form of racism, discrimination, and xenophobia," and I would add imperialism, "becomes more potent and politically influential if it is taken for granted by the society which indulges in it. This is especially so if its discussion is prohibited, either formally or by tacit agreement."[44]

The taboo has been reinforced by the denial, on the part of the political right in the United States, that the country has an empire. The argument of many on the left that "because the United States has the largest empire, it must be the worst country" has also contributed to the disrespect accorded the words and concepts *empire* and *imperialism*.[45] In truth, as Walter Russell Mead has written, nations and their empires "have been shining and stinking since the start of recorded history."[46] This is as true of the United States today as it was of Britain, China, Rome, and Greece in centuries past.

A variety of euphemisms have been used to circumvent the taboo. As the Second World War drew to a close, the Council on Foreign Relations concentrated on planning for the management of "The Grand Area."[47] More frequently, we have heard the terms "the free world" and the "U.S. sphere of influence." Zbigniew Brzezinski, an author of *Discriminate Deterrence*, founding director of the Trilateral Commission, and Jimmy

Carter's national security advisor, ignored the taboo when he found it necessary to refocus the thinking of the U.S. foreign policy establishment in the closing days of the Cold War. He began his article, "America's New Geostrategy" in *Foreign Affairs*, with the words "The rumors of America's imminent imperial decline are somewhat premature."[48]

Almost a century earlier, before the Bolshevik Revolution contributed to the creation of the linguistic taboo, descendants of the pilgrims of Plymouth Colony organized the New England Anti-Imperialist League as part of their efforts to put an end to President McKinley's war against the people of the Philippines.[49] We live with a paradox: both imperialism and anti-imperialism are essential to the U.S. identity and national heritage.

In many U.S. schools young people are taught that Rome was to Athens as the United States is to Britain. Left unstated is that "what the experience of Athens suggests is that a nation may be relatively liberal at home and yet totally ruthless abroad…An entire nation is made into mercenaries, being paid with a bit of democracy at home for participating in the destruction of life abroad."[50]

From Saudi Arabia to Singapore, much of Pax Americana was, in fact, built on the ruins of Pax Britannica. Like the British, U.S. governments "have excelled in discovering reasons that obligated them to conquer the world."[51] This U.S. destiny has been manifested through the Monroe, Truman, Eisenhower, Nixon, and Carter doctrines; Mexican-American, Spanish-American, and Desert Storm wars; and military interventions from Tokyo to Tangiers, that are too numerous to name here.[52]

The British and other Europeans have not been nearly as linguistically inhibited. Years ago, when I hitchhiked between London and the Lake District with an English lorry driver, he bemoaned the loss of empire and the resulting increase in the price of a cup of tea. Unlike the English, we have rarely been taught that the primary purposes of empire are to gain advantages through privileged access to raw materials, labor, markets, and technology and to contribute to the military security of the imperial state.[53] Similarly, when we study the Lend Lease Agreement and the Anglo-American alliance of the Second World War, we rarely concentrate on the fact that Britain was saved by the United States at the expense of its empire.

The course of empire has its costs. People are killed, often brutally and in great numbers. Racism is often reinforced, and hatreds, sometimes enduring for generations or centuries, are created. Economies can be devastated and distorted, as well as benefited, when imperial nations prepare for or initiate war. Values and individual freedom are also usually casualties of war. It was no accident that the Vietnam War marked both the pinnacle and the decline of U.S. economic power. Similarly, as Jonathan

Schell described in detail in *The Time of Illusion*, it was predictable that President Nixon used the covert infrastructure that he created to protect the secret of the U.S. aerial bombardment of Cambodia ("the plumbers"), to invade the offices of the Democratic National Committee, thus further undermining the structures of democracy and precipitating the constitutional crisis called Watergate.[54]

U.S. support for military, dictatorial, and authoritarian regimes that routinely repress their peoples' freedom and human rights, is not an accident. George Kennan, the principal architect of U.S. foreign policy in the latter half of the twentieth century, described the framework and goals of the U.S. empire in 1948 when he served as the head of the State Department's policy planning staff:

> We have about 50 percent of the world's wealth, but only 6.3 percent of its population...In this situation, we cannot fail to be the object of envy and resentment. Our real task in the coming period is to devise a pattern of relationships which will permit us to maintain this position of disparity...We need not deceive ourselves that we can afford today the luxury of altruism and world-benefaction... We should cease to talk about vague and...unreal objectives such as human rights, the raising of the living standards and democratization. The day is not far off when we are going to have to deal in straight power concepts. The less we are then hampered by idealistic slogans, the better.[55]

Kennan's memorandum was marked *top secret*. The U.S. *imperium*, like the nuclear threats that have reinforced its power, has been most successful when it has been invisible to people within and outside the United States. Like its European predecessors, in most cases the U.S. Establishment has hidden the structures of power beneath veils of secrecy, ideology, and rhetoric while it has employed "local figures as functionaries... allowing the conquered to continue their daily lives." As Walter Russel Mead has explained, like other successful empires, "the American empire," when possible, is "ruled by consent and cooperation... benefits of empire [are] scattered widely, if unevenly, around the globe...its allies and dependencies ...arrayed in three tiers."[56]

With the end of the Cold War, the rise of the Pacific economy, and the information revolution that links global elites,[57] the structures of the U.S. empire are in transition. Nonetheless, the broad outlines described by Mead remain largely intact. The first tier of nations (some combination of which may, over time, replace the U.S. as the predominate global power) share in the benefits and costs of Pax Americana as junior partners. They include Japan, other G-7 nations, and the European liberal democracies whose "opinions on important issues are usually solicited—if not always deferred to." In the second tier are countries "whose economic and political situations hover between first- and third-tier conditions": Saudi

Arabia, Singapore, Korea, Greece, and Brazil, for example. They "enjoy much less freedom from external intervention in their domestic affairs" and are "more vulnerable to economic coercion" by the U.S. and first tier nations. At the bottom of the pyramid are the countries of the Third and Fourth Worlds including El Salvador, East Timor, Mozambique, Afghanistan, Haiti, Egypt, and Kuwait. They have "minimal representation in the councils of empire" and their "national governments in many cases are solely the representatives of foreign powers."[58]

Empire and Nuclear Weapons

There has been, and continues to be, an element of "nuclear deterrence" or "Mutual Assured Destruction," in the U.S.-Soviet (now U.S-Russian) rivalry since Moscow began assembling a nuclear arsenal in 1949. Nuclear weapons have, however, been more essential to the maintenance of the U.S. empire than to "deterrence". The Soviet (now Russian) empire was relatively compact and easily accessible to Moscow's "conventional" military forces. The United States, on the other hand, has frequently found it necessary to reinforce its conventional forces by threat of nuclear attack in order to maintain control over the distant extremities of its empire. This, not deterrence, has been the principle use of the U.S. strategic arsenal since the attacks against Hiroshima and Nagasaki. Noam Chomsky explained it this way:

> Our strategic nuclear weapons system provides us with a kind of umbrella within which we can carry out conventional actions, meaning aggression and subversion, without any concern that it will be impeded in any fashion...Harold Brown, who was the Secretary of Defense under Carter... said that this is the core of our security system. He said that with this system in place, our conventional forces become 'meaningful instruments of military and political power.' That means that under this umbrella of strategic nuclear weapons...we have succeeded in sufficiently intimidating anyone who might help protect people who we are determined to attack. So...if we want to overthrow the government of Guatemala ...or send a Rapid Deployment Force into the Middle East, or if we want to back a military coup in Indonesia...if we want to invade Vietnam...we can do this without too much concern that we'll be deterred because we have this intimidating power that will threaten anyone who might get in our way.[59]

President Eisenhower was more succinct in his memoirs:

> It would be impossible for the United States to maintain the military commitments which it now sustains around the world...did we not possess atomic weapons and the will to use them when necessary.[60]

Thus Harry Truman threatened to destroy Moscow in 1946 unless the Soviets withdrew from northern Iran. Thus Dwight Eisenhower threatened to attack China and Russia with nuclear weapons unless North Korea ended the war on U.S. terms. Thus the United States invaded Vietnam. In other cases, U.S. presidents aimed their nuclear threats directly at third tier nations: Vietnam in 1969, Iraq in 1991, and Korea in 1994. Military doctrines were revised accordingly: from Eisenhower's "Massive Retaliation" to Kennedy's "Flexible Response," and from the Nixon and Carter Doctrines to the still reigning "Discriminate Deterrence."

Despite widespread popular misconceptions, the U.S. government has yet to adopt a doctrine of no first use of nuclear weapons. As William Dyess, assistant secretary of state in the Carter administration, explained it, "the Soviets know that this terrible weapon has been dropped on human beings twice in history, and it was an American president who dropped it both times. Therefore, they have to take this into consideration in their calculations."[61] And, as Daniel Ellsberg wrote:

> In none of these cases [U.S. nuclear threats], any more than in 1945, was there apprehension among U.S. officials that nuclear war might be initiated by an adversary or needed urgent deterring. In most of them, just as against Japan, the aim was to coerce in urgent circumstances a much weaker opponent that possessed no nuclear weapons at all.[62]

Partial Listing of Incidents of Nuclear Extortion[63]

1946   Truman threatens Soviets regarding Northern Iran.

1946   Truman sends SAC bombers to intimidate Yugoslavia following downing of U.S. aircraft over Yugoslavia.

1948   Truman threatens Soviets in response to Berlin blockade.

1950   Truman threatens Chinese when U.S. marines are surrounded at Chosin reservoir in Korea.

1953   Eisenhower threatens China to force end to Korean war on terms acceptable to U.S.

1954   Eisenhower's Secretary of State Dulles offers France three tactical nuclear weapons to break the siege at Dien Bien Phu, supported by Nixon's public trial balloons.

1954   Eisenhower uses nuclear armed SAC bombers to reinforce CIA-backed coup in Guatemala.

1956   Bulganin threatens London and Paris with nuclear attacks, demanding withdrawal following their invasion of Egypt.

1956   Eisenhower responds to Soviet nuclear threat against Britain and France while demanding that it's allies retreat from Egypt.

1958   Eisenhower orders Joint Chiefs of Staff to prepare to use nuclear weapons against Iraq, if necessary to prevent extension of revolution into Kuwait.

1958   Eisenhower orders Joint Chiefs of Staff to prepare to use nuclear weapons against China if they invade the island of Quemoy.

1961   Kennedy threatens Soviets during Berlin crisis.

1962   Cuban Missile Crisis

1967   Johnson threatens Soviets during Middle East War.

1967   Johnson threatens a nuclear attack against Vietnam to break the siege at Khe Sanh.

1969   Brezhnev threatens China during border war.

1969-72 Nixon threatens Vietnam.

1970   Nixon signals preparations to fight nuclear war during Black September War in Jordan.

1973   Israel threatens use of nuclear weapons October 9.

1973   Kissinger threatens Soviet Union in last hours of the October War in the Middle East.

1980   Carter Doctrine announced.

1981   Reagan reaffirms Carter Doctrine.

1990   Pakistan threatens India during confrontation over Kashmir.

1990–91 Bush threatens Iraq during Gulf War.

1993   Clinton threatens North Korea.

Notes

1. *New York Times*, April 20, 1994.
2. Leonard Cohen, "Anthem," Strange Music, Inc. BMI.
3. Haruko Taya and Theodore F. Cook, *Japan At War: An Oral History*, New York: The New Press, 1992, p. 435.
4. Nihon Hidankyo, "1994 Campaign Policy—Draft," Tokyo, translated by Andrew Junker.
5. *Far Eastern Economic Review*, July 22, 1993.
6. *Far Eastern Economic Review*, September 16, 1994.
7. "U.S. Nuclear Weapons Stockpile," *Bulletin of the Atomic Scientists*, July/August, 1994.
8. *Discriminate Deterrence: Report of the Commission on Integrated Long-Term Strategy*, Washington, D.C.: U.S. Government Printing Office, 11 January 1988. See also Bill Clinton's responses on military questions during his publicly televised debates with George Bush; and Bill Clinton and Al Gore, *Putting People First: How We Can All Change America*, New York: Times Books, 1992, pp. 131–132.
9. "U.S. Strategy Plan calls for Insuring No Rivals Develop," *New York Times*, March 8, 1992.
10. Michael R. Gordon, "U.S.-North Korea Accord Has a 10-Year Timetable," *New York Times*, October 21, 1994.
11. Henry L. Stimson's diary, cited in Gar Alperovitz, *Atomic Diplomacy: The Use of the Atomic Bomb and the American Confrontation with Soviet Power*, New York: Vintage, 1965, p. 11.
12. From the trascript of an interview with Daniel Ellsberg prepared during the filming of *The Last Empire*, Cambridge: Cambridge Documentary Films, 1985.
13. Daniel Ellsberg, "Call to Mutiny," in Joseph Gerson, ed., *The Deadly Connection: Nuclear War and U.S. Intervention*, Philadelphia: New Society Publishers, 1984, p. 11.
14. The term "crime against humanity" is used thoughtfully. The best summary of the criminality of the use of nuclear weapons appears in Deith Motherson, *From Hiroshima to the Hague: A Guide to the World Court Project*, Geneva: International Peace Bureau, 1992. pp. 65-86. It draws on treaties banning poison and poisonous weapons, prohibiting the

causing of unnecessary, superflous, and aggravated suffering, and prohibiting indiscriminate damage to harmless people, violating neutral nations, causing severe damage to the natural environment and to valuable civilian objects.

15. Noam Chomsky, *American Power and the New Mandarins*, New York: Vintage, 1969.

16. Wilfred Burchett, *Shadows of Hiroshima*, London: Verso, 1983, p. 120.

17. Graham T. Allison, Albert Carnesal, and Joseph S. Nye, Jr., *Hawks, Doves & Owls: An Agenda for Avoiding Nuclear War*, New York: W.W. Norton, 1985.

18. Cook, op. cit. pp. 384–386.

19. Paul Joseph, "Individualism and Peace Culture," *Peace Review*, Fall, 1994.

20. Norma Field, *In the Realm of a Dying Emperor: Japan at Century's End*, New York: Vintage, 1993, p. 140.

21. Robert Lifton, *Death in Life: Survivors of Hiroshima*, New York: Random House, 1967, p. 209.

22. Lawrence S. Wittner, *One World or None: A History of the World Nuclear Disarmament Movement Through 1953*, Stanford: Stanford Univ. Press, 1993, p. 48. Memo from U.S. Secretary of State Christian A. Herter to Chairman of the Atomic Energy Commission John A. McCone, December 12, 1960. It is worth noting that philosophers ranging from Michel Foucault to Sissela Bok have observed that extremely repressive structures of power require lies. See Sissela Bok, *Lying: Moral Choice in Public and Private Life*, New York: Vintage, 1989, and Michel Foucault, *Power/Knowledge: Selected Interviews & Other Writrings 1972–1977*, edited by Colin Gordon, New York: Pantheon, 1977.

23. A Citizens Group to Convey Testimonies of Hiroshima and Nagasaki, *Give Me Water: Testimonies of Hiroshima and Nagasaki*, Tokyo, 1973.

24. Ibid.

25. Junko Kayashige, "I Cannot Keep Silent During Summer," Hiroshima, 1994.

26. Burchett, op. cit. p. 120

27. Junko Kayashige, letter to the author, April 18, 1994.

28. Translation provided by Japan Council Against Atomic and Hydrogen Bombs (Gensuikyo).

29. Kayashige, op. cit.

30. A Citizens Group, op. cit.

31. Mitsuo Kojima quoted in letter from Rieko Asasto, July 9, 1994.

32. Nihon Hidankyo, "Appeal From the A-bomb Victims," Tokyo, February 2, 1991.

33. Joseph Gerson and Andrew Junker, eds., "New Contexts, New Dangers: Preventing Nuclear War in the Post-Cold War Age," Cambridge: American Friends Service Committee, 1993.

34. A letter to Secretary Adams of the Smithsonian Institution written by twelve members of Congress on August 10, 1994, and "… and why we should remember the men in the Pacific, too," Bernard E. Trainor, *Boston Globe*, June 15, 1994. See also the capitulation of the Smithsonian Institution to the demands of critics, *New York Times*, August 30, 1994.

35. McGeorge Bundy, *Danger and Survival: Choices About the Bomb in the First Fifty Years*, New York: Random House, 1988, p. 97.

36. Cited in Gar Alperovitz, "The Hiroshima decision: a moral reassessment," *Christianity & Crisis*, 1 February, 1992.

37. Cited in Gar Alperovitz, "Why the United States Dropped the Bomb," *Technology Review*, August/September 1990.

38. Martin Sherwin, *A World Destroyed: The Atomic Bomb and The Grand Alliance*, New York: Vintage, 1977, p. 5.

39. William Appleman Williams, *The Tragedy of American Diplomacy*, New York: Delta, 1962, p. 254.

40. Richard K. Betts, *Nuclear Blackmail and Nuclear Balance*, Washington, D.C.: The Brookings Institution, 1987; Barry M. Blechman and Stephen S. Kaplan, *Force Without War: U.S. Armed Forces as Political Instruments*, Washington, D.C.: The Brookings Institution, 1978; Michio

Kaku and Daniel Axelrod, *To Win a Nuclear War: The Pentagon's Secret War Plans*, Boston: South End Press, 1987; and Joseph Gerson, *The Deadly Connection*, op. cit.

41. George Lichtheim, *Imperialism*, New York: Prager, 1971, p. 4.

42. William Appleman Williams, *Empire as a Way of Life*, New York: Oxford, 1980, p. viii.

43. Elizabeth Minnich, "Why Not Lie," *Soundings*, Winter 1985, Vol. 68, No. 4, p. 497.

44. Israel Shahak, *Jewish History, Jewish Religion: The Weight of Three Thousand Years*, London: Pluto Press, 1994. p. 3.

45. Walter Russell Mead, *Mortal Splendor: The American Empire in Transition*, Boston: Houghton Mifflin Co., 1987, p.4.

46. Ibid.

47. Noam Chomsky, *The Chomsky Reader*, edited by James Peck, New York: Pantheon, 1987, p. 317–318.

48. Zbigniew Brzezinski, "America's New Geostrategy," *Foreign Affairs*, Spring 1988.

49. Daniel Boone Schirmer, *Republic or Empire: American Resistance to the Philippine War*, Cambridge: Schenkman, 1972.

50. Howard Zinn, *Declarations of Independence: Cross-Examining American Ideology*, New York: Harper Collins, 1990, p. 73.

51. Mead, op. cit., p. 9; Walter LaFeber, "An Inclination to Intervene," *Boston Globe*, May 16, 1993, and "Somalia Leads Where?" *Boston Globe*, December 13, 1992.

52. Williams, op. cit., pp. 73–76, 103–110, 136–142, 165–167. See also,Richard J. Barnet, *Intervention and Revolution: The United States in the Third World*, New York: World Publishing Co., 1968.

53. Mead, op. cit., p. 5.

54. Jonathan Schell, *The Time of Illusion*, New York: Vintage, 1975.

55. Noam Chomsky, *The Chomsky Reader*, James Peck, ed., New York: Pantheon, 1987, p. 318.

56. Mead, op. cit., p. 6.

57. Jacques Attali, *Millennium:Winners and Losers in the Coming World Order*, New York: Times Books, 1991.

58. Mead, op. cit., pp. 19–22.

59. From an interview with Noam Chomsky, Cambridge Documentary Films, op. cit.

60. Dwight D. Eisenhower, *Mandate for Change*, New York: Doubleday, 1963, p. 181.

61. Ellsberg, op. cit., p. 50.

62. Ibid., p. 41.

63. In addition to references cited in note 40, see also references in chapter 2 and Seymour Hersh, "On the Nuclear Edge," *The New Yorker*, March 29, 1993; Seymour Hersh, *The Samson Option: Israel's Nuclear Arsenal and American Foreign Policy*, New York: Random House, 1991; and Walter Isaacson, *Kissinger: A Biography*, New York: Simon and Schuster, 1992.

CHAPTER TWO

The Atomic Bombings of Hiroshima and Nagasaki
Playing the Master Card

> We don't know anything about my younger brother. He was six years old... Even when people were burned to death you could usually find the bones and at least say, this is my house, so this must be them, but we found nothing. They must have been blown away somewhere.
> — Yasuko Kimura[1]

> Not only the conclusion of the war but the organization of an acceptable peace seemed to depend — for Byrnes, Stimson, and Truman, as well as for Conant, Oppenheimer and Teller — upon the success of the atomic attacks against Japan.
> — Martin Sherwin[2]

THE WORDS *Hiroshima* and *Nagasaki* have become symbols. For many they represent the instantaneous destruction of cities more than the cities themselves or their people. *Hiroshima* and *Nagasaki* convey the images of devastated cities of death, agony, and cinders, locked in time—August 1945. They are moments in our collective past and nightmares of our possible future.

Today there is much to shock visitors to Hiroshima and Nagasaki. Perhaps most disorienting is their apparent normalcy. In Hiroshima, with the exception of the A-Bomb dome, the Peace Park, the open sense of space, and the distant hills, there is little that immediately differentiates the city from other late-twentieth-century Japanese metropolitan centers. Downtown Hiroshima is dominated by department stores, neon signs, and corporate office buildings. Several times an hour, bullet trains stop briefly at a railway station that could easily be mistaken for a shopping mall. The stark lines, lights, and amplifiers of the hometown baseball stadium, in this case the Hiroshima Carp, assert themselves against the city's architecture. Even on August 6, shops and businesses are open. So complete is the reconstruction, celebrated by Hiroshima's hosting the Asian Games in 1994, that some hibakusha have committed themselves to preserving the remnants of the 1945 holocaust. They fear that the world will forget what happened, that their suffering and history will be distorted and possibly denied.

Yet, as the historian David Lowenthal wrote, "The past is everywhere...Each particular trace of the past ultimately perishes, but collectively they are immortal...the past is omnipresent."[3] Even as one is momentarily distracted in downtown Hiroshima, forgetting what happened in that city fifty years ago, *Hiroshima* remains. The A-bomb dome haunts the city and the world. Testimonies of the hibakusha, the physical images and evidence assembled in the Peace Museum, the cenotaph and the statuary of the Peace Park, and, most importantly, the persistence of memory, are staggering.

Hiroshima is omnipresent. The atomic bombings of that city and of Nagasaki continue to shape our understandings of the present and existential limits of the world within which we live. These holocausts have become abstracted universal symbols shaping our responses to peoples and governments. Those who are responsible for military and foreign policies of the world's governments, and those of us who labor to influence and change those policies, are all fundamentally influenced by our understanding of Hiroshima and Nagasaki.

Ian Buruma observed that "It is even harder to imagine what happened in Hiroshima than it is at Auschwitz for the horror of Hiroshima was compressed into one singular event, which left hardly a visual trace."[4] After seeing film footage of the bombings and reading about the nuclear attacks, it is not uncommon for students in the United States to respond that it is difficult to believe that this kind of destruction really happened.[5] Others, equally sheltered, numbly repeat that people were killed instantly and others burned to death as fire swept Hiroshima. They invoke the official statistics: 78,150 people killed, 13,983 missing, 37,425 injured, 62,000 of Hiroshima's 90,000 buildings destroyed, and 6,000 other buildings damaged beyond repair. Some will note that the City of Hiroshima's official estimate was the higher figure of 200,000 killed.

How did those who died suffer, and how much? What has the loss of their lives meant to those who suffered and survived? What does "13,983 missing" in the first, primitive, atomic bombing mean? Were they murdered, vaporized, or transformed into shadows, mushroom cloud, or black rain? Were they high school students, children, mothers, or grandfathers, reduced to memory, to physical and emotional voids? Are they now only numbers, transformed into disembodied specters for reasons of state?

For the hibakusha, those who have visited Hiroshima and Nagasaki, and for some others, the devastation wreaked upon the people of Hiroshima and Nagasaki is not beyond imagination. It does, however, remain beyond comprehension.

Fifty years later, coexisting with awe of the first atomic bombings, questions survive. What, for example, was the relationship between the atomic bombings and the emerging post-war hierarchy of power? Why were the bombs, "Little Boy" and "Fat Man," used against civilians? These questions, in turn, lead to others about the meanings of our lives, the world in which we live, and what is required for survival and security—for ourselves, our children, and future generations.

The comforting answers fabricated by the Truman administration and its apologists served, and continue to serve, their political purposes. U.S. and global public opinion were pacified by President Truman's initial statement that "the first atomic bomb was dropped on Hiroshima, a military base. That was because we wished *in this first attack* to avoid, insofar as possible, the killing of civilians."[6] The bombings were justified as punishment for Japanese aggression and to save a million U.S. casualties.[7] This rationalization was reinforced by an initial cover-up that limited popular understanding of the unprecedented devastation caused by the atomic bombings.[8] The Truman administration's propaganda, repeated by politicians, intellectuals and the media until it became the accepted and defining myth, smoothed the way for the consolidation of the United States postwar imperial domain.

The decisions to devastate the cities of Hiroshima and Nagasaki, and to incinerate, annihilate, and irradiate the people who lived there, had less to do with bringing the war in Asia and the Pacific to a close, than it did with establishing the rules of the game for the Cold War era that had already begun. The cities were attacked with nuclear weapons to ensure that the United States would not be required to share influence with the Soviet Union in Japan, a devastated, but technologically advanced nation, and to minimize Soviet influence in Korea, Manchuria, Mongolia, and northern China. President Truman and his closest advisors also sought to communicate to Joseph Stalin that the Yalta agreement could no longer serve as "the settlement of the Polish, Rumanian, [and] Yugoslavian...problems." The people of Hiroshima and Nagasaki were sacrificed to ensure that "the Soviets would be more accommodating to the American point of view" in the Cold War era.[9] The message was clear: We have the ability and the will to do this to human beings. Twice now. Beware.

Thus the atomic bombings of Hiroshima and Nagasaki marked the conscious debut of new forms of warfare, atomic diplomacy, and nuclear extortion as tools of modern imperial practice. This is state terrorism in its purest and least complicated form, and it has since been practiced repeatedly to maintain U.S. global hegemony and its spheres of influence.

As painful and disorienting as it is for people in the United States to consider, the similarities between the nearly simultaneous holocausts of Europe, Hiroshima, and Nagasaki are ignored at a cost. This difficult reflection is essential not only to our understanding of the increasingly distant past, but to comprehending who and what we, the U.S. nation, society, and government, have become. It was McGeorge Bundy, who served as ghost writer for Henry L. Stimson's defense of the atomic bombings and as national security advisor for Presidents Kennedy and Johnson, who wrote: "I do not myself find Hiroshima more *immoral* than [the firebombings of] Tokyo or Dresden, but I find the *political* question more difficult." Stimson himself was morally torn by the saturation bombing of Japanese cities and told President Truman that he "did not want to have the United States get the reputation of outdoing Hitler in atrocities," and that he "was a little fearful that before we could get ready, the air force might have Japan so thoroughly bombed out that the new weapon would not have a fair background to show its strength."[10] Robert Jay Lifton framed it well in the preface to *The Genocidal Mentality: Nazi Holocaust and Nuclear Threat*. Some will be offended by the necessity of drawing analogies between the U.S. and Nazi models, but the analogies must be explored.[11]

Truman was not Hitler. Auschwitz and Bergen Belsen were different from the firebombings of Dresden and Tokyo and the atomic bombings of Hiroshima and Nagasaki. The United States, like Germany and Japan, opted for the morality of total war. There was thus an element of truth in French war criminal Paul Touvier's answer to a question about the *principle* of crimes of humanity. "I can tell you about other horrors," he said, "Hiroshima, Nagasaki."[12] There are disturbing similarities in the devaluation of human life, in the racism which permitted such devaluation, and in the routinized industrialization of terror and murder, hence Lifton's *Genocidal Mentality* and Arendt's concept of the banality of evil.[13] There are similarities, too, in the cynical and near limitless use of state power in the pursuit of ideological and imperial goals.

The question posed by Joseph Sitruk, the chief rabbi of France, during the war crimes trial of Paul Touvier in 1994, challenges us as we reconsider the atomic bombings of Hiroshima and Nagasaki: "Shall we bury history, or shall we have the courage of carrying out the reflection to the very end?"[14]

Nuclear Holocausts As Personal Experiences

During the past decade, the question of why Hiroshima and Nagasaki were attacked when there was no military necessity for the bombings has become a personal question, as well as a profoundly important, abstract political one. While in Japan I have learned from politically engaged hibakusha. Some of these people, who became colleagues and friends, have stayed in my home and have addressed conferences and meetings that I have organized. Why they were callously, arbitrarily, and totally immersed in death has thus become more than an abstraction to me.

Junko Kayashige teaches in the Noboricho Junior High School, where Sadako Sasaki, whose story of a thousand paper cranes has so touched the world, was a student.* In Kayashige-*sensei's* classroom there is a banner that reads in English, "Never Give Up!" Junko was six years old on August 3, 1945, when her mother returned to Hiroshima with her and four of her sisters: the infant Toshiko, three year-old Fumie, Michiko who was in the fourth grade, and Katsuko, who was in the sixth grade. Her father had stayed in the city, though he worked in a neighboring prefecture, as had her two oldest sisters. Eiko worked in a steel factory, and Hiroko helped to demolish buildings to create fire lanes in the city. An older brother was in the military in distant Yamaguchi prefecture. Junko's mother had details to attend to in Hiroshima and, like many others, thought the city might be spared the bombing that had devastated so many other Japanese cities.

Early on the morning of August 6, Junko's mother took the baby and left to visit an aunt in nearby Itsukaichi. Junko's older sister, Michiko, rode off on a bicycle to buy ice for the icebox, and Junko and her younger sister, Fumi, went to an uncle's house nearby. Junko remembers being with her sister and cousins listening to a record, as her aunt cleaned the room they were in. She and a cousin were sitting on the window sill, and watched the Enola Gay as it flew over the city and dropped its bomb. Later she recalled:

---

*Sadako Sasaki was a toddler when Little Boy was dropped on Hiroshima. As a sixth grader in 1954, like thousands of other hibakusha, she fell ill with radiation disease. As part of her therapy she began folding paper cranes. A Japanese folk tradition teaches that if you fold one thousand paper cranes, you will live a long life. Sadako Sasaki died the next year, after she had folded 569 cranes. Her teacher, Tsuyoshi Nomura, helped her surviving students deal with their grief by completing Sadako's thousand cranes. Working with Ichiro Kawamoto, an inspired hibakusha, a national campaign was launched to build a memorial to Sadako in the Hiroshima Peace Park and thus to teach about the danger of nuclear weapons and the necessity of nuclear disarmament. Folding paper cranes, a traditional Japanese symbol of life, thus became a means of talking and teaching about peace in Japan and throughout the world, and an international symbol of peace.

I do not know how much time passed. I found myself lying on the ground under the window, inside the house. The house escaped from collapsing, but the desk, chairs, bookshelves, tatami mats, and flooring boards were gone. My sister, cousin, and aunt, having also been blown on the ground, were raising themselves when I saw them. We went outside. All our neighbors' houses were crushed to the ground...an old woman in our neighborhood was crying for help, trapped under the stone wall. Her daughter-in-law strove to get her out, but the wall was too heavy. My aunt gave her a hand too... We small children stood there watching. Houses around us were not on fire yet, but we became frightened when they started to catch fire. Trying to take three children with her, my aunt went back in the house to get a string which she thought to use for tying them on her back. I waited outside for her to come back, but I could not bear to stay there any longer. I finally ran away by myself.

Junko was seriously burned on her face, arms, and legs, portions of her body not covered by her white dress that reflected radiation.

I went walking on the roofs of the houses which were smashed flat on the ground...there were people staggering...I could not tell men from women. The skin of their bodies and even their faces had peeled off and [was] dangling, looking like seaweed. Everyone was heading toward the mountain, so I followed...I came to the riverside after passing over the Nakahiro Bridge...When I looked back behind me, the bridge I had just walked across was in flames, burning terribly on both sides...

All I could do was follow...Many people were crossing the river, so I tried to do the same, but the river was too deep for a little child to cross. A middle-aged woman who was ahead of me carried me by her side and across the river. She had some cucumbers. I thought of using the cucumbers to heal my burns on my face and arms. Remembering the cucumber tells me that I already knew that I had been burned.

I came across my uncle, whom my mother intended to visit. This was a crucial event that eventually saved my life.[15]

Junko's sister, Michiko, who had left on her bicycle to fetch ice, disappeared in the explosion. Her aunt died the next day. After days of searching, Junko's father found her oldest sister, Hiroko, who had been demolishing buildings, amidst the dead and dying in the remains of a school. He carried his daughter home on boards attached to a bicycle. Hiroko was severely burned and unable to move. As they travelled,

People put their hands together and said the words of Buddhist prayer, thinking she was already dead. My sister said to my father "I am not dead yet." Even...hurt, she was able to say "I am home!" loud when she arrived, which made all of us so glad and relieved. But whenever she was sleeping or awake, maggots were very active. We kept picking them off her body, using tweezers, but they crawled into her flesh and caused her pain...

> I can never forget the day my sister Hiroko died. That was the 17th of August, 1945. Those who had enough strength…were having a meal… Then, "Mama, could you come for a second?" …My mother told her to wait for a moment. A little later she went to see my sister. With the voice of my mother crying "Hiroko! Hiroko!" we realized something was wrong. When we rushed to her bedside she was already dead. The sound of her voice, "I am home!" and "Mama, could you come for a second?" never leaves my ears. I feel I can still hear her voice.[16]

Years later, as we drove across thoroughly modern and reconstructed Hiroshima en route to visit Junko's mother, we stopped at a dusty and somewhat neglected playground set amid blocks of apartment buildings. While I glanced, confused, at the lonely swing set and climbing structure, Junko told me that this was where her childhood home had stood. The rest was left to my imagination.

Professor Shoji Sawada teaches physics at Nagoya University. When I first met him at the 1984 World Conference against Atomic and Hydrogen Bombs in Hiroshima I was struck by how infrequently he smiled.

Professor Sawada was thirteen years old on August 6, 1945. When the bomb exploded over Hiroshima, he and his thirty-six-year-old mother did not see the brilliant flash. They were sleeping. He recalls:

> When I became conscious, I found myself crushed by lots of plaster and timbers. I managed to crawl out. My mother could not be seen, but I heard her voice. She said she could not move because her legs were caught by a big pillar. I tried to pull out the broken pillar. I pushed…as hard as I could, but it was no use. I asked passers-by to help us, but they couldn't because they were all injured and thoroughly occupied in trying to save themselves. When the fire came close to us, my mother said, "Don't care about me. Hurry up. Run Away!" Terribly broken-hearted, I said, "I'm sorry mum."[17]

The adolescent Shoji Sawada turned and made his way over the debris of the city, through devastated woods, and swam across the Enko river to a dry river bed from which he watched the city burn.

Hiroshima and Nagasaki were experienced individually. Each death, agony, pain, and memory was unique and remains singular. No one experienced the entirety of either holocaust. They and we can only intimate and imagine them. As John Dower wrote, the hibakusha do share the experience of Hell—a Buddhist as well as a Western concept of a "fiery inferno peopled with monsters and naked, tormented bodies." Hell is "almost exactly what witnesses of Hiroshima and Nagasaki saw—a raging inferno; streets full of monstrously deformed creatures; excruciating pain, without medicine and without surcease…'It was like Hell' is the most common refrain" of the survivors. "Many other scenes," Dower wrote, "also were imaginable only in hell. Outlines of bodies were permanently etched as white shadows in black nimbus on streets or walls, but the bodies themselves had disappeared...there were innumerable corpses without apparent injury. Parts of bodies held their ground, like two legs severed below the knees, still standing. Many of the dead were turned into statues, some solid and others waiting to crumble at a touch."[18]

Naomi Shohno, a hibakusha who, like Professor Sawada, was driven to understand the atomic bombings and became a physicist, explained that

> at the moment of the explosion a fireball with a temperature of *several million degrees centigrade* and an atmospheric pressure of several hundred thousand bars was formed at the burst point...Buildings were smashed to pieces and incinerated by the blast and thermal rays, and it was the great quantities of dust from the destroyed buildings, carried by the winds, that cast the city into pitch-darkness just after the bombing. The violent winds also tossed people about... As the fireball disappeared, the vacuum around the burst point pulled in dust, air, and the evaporated materials of the bomb, causing a mushroom cloud to rise... because of the combined effects of the blast, thermal rays, fires, almost all buildings within about 2 kilometers of the hypocenter in Hiroshima, and within about 2.5 kilometers in Nagasaki, were completely razed and consumed by fire *in an instant*...conflagrations occurred within about 3 kilometers of the hypocenter in Hiroshima and within about 3.5 kilometers in Nagasaki.[19]

The city and people of Hiroshima (and three days later Nagasaki) were devastated by the succession of the intense heat of the bomb's thermal rays, the force and winds of the blast, fires, firestorm, radiation poisoning, and the trauma of painful, immobilizing, and disfiguring wounds. For the "lucky" ones there was also the agony of survivors' guilt. No one emerged unscathed.

Wilfred Burchett, the first foreign journalist to view Hiroshima after it was devastated, described it this way:

> In Hiroshima, thirty days after the first atomic bomb destroyed the city...people are still dying, mysteriously and horribly...from an unknown something which I can only describe as the atomic plague.

> Hiroshima does not look like a bombed city. It looks as if a monster steamroller has passed over it and squashed it out of existence...The damage is far greater than photographs can show...you can look around for twenty-five and perhaps thirty square miles, you can see hardly a building...There is just nothing standing except for twenty factory chimneys—chimneys with no factories. A group of half a dozen gutted buildings. And then nothing...

> In these hospitals I found people who, when the bomb fell, suffered absolutely no injuries, but now are dying from the uncanny after-effect...Their hair fell out. Bluish spots appeared on their bodies. And the bleeding began from the ears, nose, and mouth...They have been dying at the rate of 100 a day.[20]

Origins of Atomic Diplomacy

Like the myth that Christopher Columbus discovered America, the fiction that President Truman used atomic bombs against the people and cities of Hiroshima Nagasaki to save American lives has become the received truth, the common wisdom, in the United States and much of the world, despite the overwhelming evidence to the contrary.

As the historian William Appleman Williams wrote thirty-five years ago, "The United States dropped the bomb to end the war against Japan and thereby to stop the Russians in Asia, and to give them sober pause in eastern Europe."[21] The official historian of the U.S. Nuclear Regulatory Commission, J. Samuel Walker, also observed that, "The consensus among scholars is that the bomb was not needed to avoid an invasion of Japan...It is clear that alternatives to the bomb existed and that Truman and his advisers knew it."[22]

General Eisenhower told Secretary of War Stimson that he opposed the use of nuclear weapons against Japan. "The Japanese were ready to surrender, and it wasn't necessary to hit them with that awful thing."[23] The chairman of the Joint Chiefs of Staff in 1945, Admiral Leahy agreed, "The use of this barbarous weapon at Hiroshima and Nagasaki was of no material assistance to our war against Japan."[24] Former Secretary of State Byrnes, President Truman's most trusted advisor, confirmed this conclusion on the fifteenth anniversary of the bombings when he said "We wanted to get through with the Japanese phase of the war before the Russians came in."[25] These criticisms and this reasoning were not completely unknown at the time and were factors in the U.S. Federal Council of Churches 1946 call for "active penitence" and for the reconstruction of "the two murdered cities."[26]

Competition for Asian Empire

To understand why the people of Hiroshima and Nagsaki were sacrificed primarily for geostrategic purposes, it is helpful to understand why the war was fought in the first place. The post-war U.S.-Japanese military alliance and the myths of the Cold War have obscured the underlying continuity of U.S. foreign and military policy: the expansion and maintenance of empire in the Pacific and Asia. It was this commitment to empire, to maximizing the reach of "The Grand Area," that provided the strategic rationale for the decision to bomb Hiroshima and Nagasaki.

Japan, like Germany, Italy, and to a lesser extent the United States, came late to building empire and establishing colonies. When Admiral Perry forced Japan to "open" in 1854, after two hundred years of Tokugawa-imposed isolation, the Japanese elite (like the authors of the U.S. constitution) believed they faced the clear choice of being colonized like their neighbors, or becoming a colonizer, like the Western nations that dominated the Asia/Pacific region.

As the long-censored Japanese historian Saburo Ienaga wrote, "In China, Japan competed with the West for a place at the imperial table and a slice of the Chinese melon."[27] U.S. support for Japanese conquest and expansion began with the 1895 Sino-Japanese War and the 1904–05 Russo-Japanese War. The 1905 Portsmouth Treaty, engineered by Theodore Roosevelt, included U.S. recognition of Japanese hegemony in Korea in exchange for Japanese recognition of U.S. colonization of the Philippines. It was when U.S. and Japanese imperial ambitions collided in the 1930s that war began to appear unavoidable.

The U.S.-Japanese confrontation had its origins in the Great Depression, the Japanese chapter of which began in 1927. In Japan, the disorientation of the economic crisis and growing protectionist barriers limiting its international trade reinforced the drive to conquer and colonize China. As Ienaga observed, "The attitude was identical with the European and American conviction that control of colonies in Asia, the Pacific, and Africa was 'manifest destiny.' A national consensus approved of an imperialist policy toward China, but there were sharp disagreements and differing emphases over the implementation."[28] Moderate imperialists, including Ambassador Yoshida Shigeru, favored expansion, investments, and opening markets for Japan in China in cooperation with Britain and the United States. Their rivals, who seized power through a series of contrived military incidents in China and assassinations and coups in Tokyo, preferred to initiate war in pursuit of what they saw as limitless resources in China. They believed the government would be careless to allow these resources to fall to Britain or the United States.[29] They moved to suppress Chinese nationalism and to drive Britain and the U.S. from the Asian continent.[30]

The Arab oil embargo of 1973, the Iranian Islamic Revolution in 1979, and the U.S. Desert Storm war against Iraq in 1990–91 have helped us to understand the centrality of oil throughout the twentieth century, yet many people continue to be surprised to learn that those in power in Tokyo formally decided on war against the United States as a result of an oil embargo. The embargo was imposed as a severe sanction against Japan, following its 1940 conquest of French Indochina. With its troops deployed and fighting from Vietnam to Manchuria and confronting a limited supply of oil, a stark choice was forced on the Japanese government: end the war with concessions and humiliating loss of face, or attempt to break the blockade through the conquest of oil-rich Indonesia and war against the United States.

Many in the Japanese leadership knew that with a gross national product only one-tenth that of the United States, the island nation could not prevail. The military scenario for their defeat in a prolonged island-hopping war and siege was anticipated by Admiral Yamamoto, the architect of the attack on Pearl Harbor. He understood that "Tokyo will probably be burnt to the ground."[31] Immediately after the September 6, 1941, Imperial Conference at which the decision to attack the United States and Britain was made, Prime Minister Konoe resigned, thus postponing the day of attack, because he knew "a tragic defeat" awaited Japan.[32] The hope of the doctrinaire and desperate men leading the government in Tokyo was that the destruction of the U.S. Pacific fleet in Pearl Harbor would buy them time. If Germany won the war in Europe, the United States would not be in a position to reassert its hegemony in the Pacific. If Germany lost, Japan's emperor and the militarists who surrounded (and to some extent controlled) him gambled the United States would prefer negotiation of a new Asian/Pacific *modus vivendi* to the bloody campaign that would be required to defeat Japan.[33]

How were the Japanese people mobilized to support a futile war? The reasons were multiple.[34] The Japanese were trying to survive a devastating and disorienting economic crisis, and like people in other countries at the time, many were willing to believe powerful men with simple solutions. The education system, centralized since the Meiji Restoration in the 1860s, had long served as a powerful vehicle for socialization of the young, and thus the society as a whole. The system taught reverence and sacrifice for the emperor, patriotism, trust in militarism, Japan's manifest destiny to create the "liberating" Greater East Asia Co-Prosperity Sphere, racist disdain for the previously colonized Asians and for the West, and the painful price of nonconformity. Japan had gradually became a police state, in which no dissent was tolerated. Press censorship closed the last opening for competing ideas and information. Members of the Japanese Communist Party, the only group to attempt organized resistance to Japanese militarism, were imprisoned and tortured.

Rationales

The dominant beliefs and values of a modern society are often reflected in books written for children. Thus we turn to the American Heritage Junior Library for an uncompromised statement of the myth of the bombings of Hiroshima and Nagasaki:

> Even if the Russians invaded Manchuria and the British attacked Malaya in August as planned, no one expected the invasion of Japan to be anything but a slaughter. Before the Japanese mainland could be secured, American casualties would amount to as many as one million men; and

the Japanese were expected to sacrifice twice that number in defense of their homeland. Then, on July 16, the bright glow of the Trinity test raised hopes that the war could be ended without an invasion.[35]

This theme was repeated in the politically charged and surreal debate over the Smithsonian Institution's proposed exhibit on the eve of the fiftieth anniversary of the Hiroshima and Nagasaki bombings. The exhibit was canceled even after museum officials subjected their exhibit script to "historical cleansing" under intense pressure from right-wing members of Congress and veterans groups. Excised were text and photographs that had been unanimously endorsed by the museum's advisory board of historians. Statements by General Dwight Eisenhower, Admiral William Leahy, General George Marshall and other senior officials expressing reservations about the atomic bombings were removed, as was the description of the firebombing of Tokyo as the "single most destructive non-nuclear attack in human history." Just six pictures of people maimed by the atomic bombings were retained, as was one that included an image of one person killed in the holocausts. Repetition of the mythology that the Japanese government was "not willing to surrender," that Truman ordered the atomic bombings primarily to "save lives," and that "if atomic bombs did not force Japan to Surrender...[U.S.] casualties could have risen to as man as a million" did not satisfy militarist critics. As a museum spokesman said before the exhibit was canceled, "things that are easy for historians are not so easy for us."[36]

A more nuanced and generous traditional interpretation appeared in William Johnston's introduction to the English language edition of Dr. Takashi Nagai's 1946 book, *The Bells of Nagasaki*. This book, initially censored by U.S. occupation forces in Japan, was one of the first widely distributed and detailed descriptions of what the people of Hiroshima and Nagasaki suffered.

> While Truman took full responsibility for the decision, there was a sense in which he did not make it. He was carried along by the tide of events. Two billion dollars had been spent on the atom bomb project, years of research had gone into it; many people were working with the assumption that the bomb would be used. Churchill took it for granted. Stalin, hearing about the new weapon, expressed the hope that Truman would make good use of it against the Japanese. There was the additional fact that the collective unconscious of the time, conditioned by years of war, was thirsty for blood, clamoring for revenge, impatient to see the end. Only by a heroic act of will running counter to the spirit of the times could Truman have stopped the dropping of that bomb. In a certain sense he was the pawn, the instrument, the victim.[37]

What William Johnston wrote was true. Yet, as the historian Barton Bernstein has written, "The intimidation of the Soviets" was at the very least the confirming rationale for the decision to attack Hiroshima and Nagasaki.[38]

In fact, President Truman and his advisors were quite cynical in their calculations. For them the atomic bomb was the master card, which would trump the Soviets in anticipated postwar confrontations. The Potsdam summit of The Big Three (Truman, Stalin, and Churchill) was postponed by Truman, to ensure that he had an atomic bomb in his negotiating hand when they gathered to further structure the postwar world.[39]

When *The Bells of Nagasaki* was written, it was not widely known that in the spring and early summer of 1945 President Truman was receiving reports from his chairman of the Joint Chiefs of Staff that "the Japanese were already defeated and ready to surrender,"[40] that Truman had discussed and dismissed Emperor Hirohito's efforts to surrender before and during the Potsdam summit, or that in the view of the U.S. Strategic Bombing Survey prepared by Paul Nitze, "certainly prior to 31 December 1945, and in all probability prior to 1 November 1945, Japan would have surrendered even if the atomic bombs had not been dropped, even if Russia had not entered the war, and even if no invasion had been planned or contemplated."[41]

The documentation is massive. U.S. and British intelligence projected that "when Russia came into the war...the Japanese would probably wish to get out on almost any terms short of the dethronement of the Emperor."[42] By June 1945 the Joint War Plans Committee of the Joint Chiefs of Staff had reported that an invasion of Kyushu and Honshu (politically and strategically the most important of Japan's four main islands) would cost the lives of 40,000 U.S. troops, and that the invasion of Kyushu, at a cost of 7,500 U.S. lives, might "well prove to be the decisive operation which would terminate the war."[43] The invasion of Kyushu was scheduled for November and of Honshu for early in 1946. This left months to negotiate the details of Japan's surrender, including the much-discussed possibility of a demonstration bombing of an uninhabited atoll to impress Japan's rulers with the seriousness of the moment.

Political decisions, including decisions relating to war and peace, are rarely made for a single reason. The forces that shape major decisions are many and complex. Johnston's observations that the decision to bomb Hiroshima and Nagasaki reflected the momentum of the atom bomb project, the desire to bring the war to an early conclusion, and the demand of the collective unconscious for revenge, are proably all true. So, too, is Martin Sherwin's conclusion that four assumptions, shared by President Truman and the Interim Committee (which made the formal recommendation to use the bombs against Japan), underlay the decision. They were: that the atomic bombs were legitimate weapons, which would have been used by the Nazi government had Germany won the race to build the bomb; that the atomic bombings would have a "profound affect" on Japan's leaders; that the U.S. public would want the bombs used; and that the bombs would have "a salutary effect on relations with the Soviet Union."[44]

Other factors also contributed to the decision, not the least of which was abiding racism against Asians in general and the Japanese in particular, which had been deepened by wartime rhetoric. A Pentagon publication compared Japanese to lice and explained that "before a complete cure may be affected...the breeding grounds around the Tokyo area must be completely annihilated."[45] Hollywood depicted Japanese as "degenerate, moral idiots...Stinking little savages" who should be "wipe[d] off the face of the earth."[46] President Truman's racism was evident two days after the bombing of Nagasaki when he wrote, "When you have to deal with a beast, you have to treat him as a beast."[47]

A more humanitarian rationale was devised for the use of the bombs against the Japanese people by James Conant, the president of Harvard University, who initially conceived and recommended the targets. He argued that the bombing would "awaken the world to the necessity of abolishing war altogether."[48]

It was, however, the fourth assumption identified by Sherwin, the diplomatic dimensions, that dominated strategic thinking at the highest levels of government in Washington.

Geostrategy and Nuclear Terror

There is little that is truly new or original, and this applies to Truman's use of nuclear terror as a means of diplomacy. The intense secrecy that surrounded "S-1" or the "Tube Alloy" effort, code words for the Manhattan Project, allowed President Roosevelt to monopolize decision-making about the atomic bomb and its uses. His scientific advisors and the secretaries of war and state were allowed input when Roosevelt deemed it necessary. However, in Martin Sherwin's estimation, while Roosevelt turned to Vannevar Bush and James B. Conant for advice, "on matters of broad policy...he never allowed control to slip from his grasp. The president at times made decisions on atomic energy in consultation with Churchill without the advice or knowledge of his advisers...he felt no obligation to keep Bush, Conant or anyone else apprised of his own actions."[49]

As early as the August 1941 Atlantic Conference, Roosevelt, in consultation with Churchill, had begun designing the post-war global hierarchy of privilege and power. Despite his later advocacy of the United Nations, from the beginning he ruled out an international organization as the guarantor of global law and order. An American-Anglo international police force would be more effective, he told Churchill. By 1942 Roosevelt recognized the political debt the U.S. and Britain would owe the Soviet Union for its sacrifice in defeating Nazi Germany. The concept of two "policemen" thus became four, and was expanded to include the Soviet Union and France. Nations which violated the post-war order enforced by the Big Four "would be quarantined...if they persisted...[they would be] bombed at the rate of a city a day until they agreed to behave."[50]

The following year, when Roosevelt and Churchill met in Quebec, is now seen as the point at which Roosevelt "began to deal with atomic energy as an *integral* part of his general diplomacy, linking and encompassing both the current wartime situation and the shape of postwar affairs."[51] As Churchill's aide, Lord Cherwell, had explained to the President's men, the British government considered "the whole [atomic energy] affair on an after-the-war military basis." For Churchill the atomic bomb was all that would lie "between the snows of Russia and the white cliffs of Dover... It would never do to have Germany or Russia win the race for something which might be used for international blackmail."[52]

With the Manhattan Project approaching probable success, Roosevelt became clearer about the United States taking "full advantage of the bomb's potential as a postwar instrument of Anglo-American diplomacy. There could still be four policemen, but only two of them would have the bomb."[53]

As it became evident to the scientists who had initiated the race to build the atom bomb that there would be no German bomb, several sought to further influence the president's thinking. Niels Bohr pressed Roosevelt and his advisers to include Moscow in preparations for postwar planning in order to prevent a disastrous arms race.[54] Leo Szilard, who actually drafted the 1939 letter from Albert Einstein to Roosevelt that led to the Manhattan Project, feared that armed force would be necessary in the postwar world to control the sources of uranium and thorium. He argued that "it will hardly be possible to get political action along that line unless high efficiency atomic bombs have actually been used in this war and the fact of their destructive power has deeply penetrated the mind of the public."[55] Szilard later regretted this recommendation and sought to reverse it. If anyone other than Churchill influenced Roosevelt it was Stimson, who was deeply concerned about repression in Russia and growing Soviet domination of Eastern Europe. Stimson viewed the secrets related to the manufacture of atomic bombs as a possible reward to the Soviets and "as a diplomatic instrument for shaping the peace."[56]

Roosevelt opted for the recommendations of Stimson and Szilard and for Churchill's vision of an anti-Soviet U.S-British nuclear monopoly. This was codified in the June 1943 Agreement and Declaration of Trust signed in Quebec, "specifying that the United States and Great Britain would cooperate in seeking to control available supplies of uranium and thorium ore both during and after the war."[57] Roosevelt and Churchill also signed an *aide-memoire* in Quebec that stated, "When a bomb is finally available, it might perhaps, after mature consideration, be used against the Japanese, who should be warned that this bombardment will be repeated until they surrender."[58] As Sherwin noted, at the time of Roosevelt's death in April 1945, "the question of the use of the bomb against Japan was more clearly settled than was general policy."[59]

Harry Truman might best be classed with Ronald Reagan and George Bush in his blunt and brutal use of military power and atomic diplomacy. Roosevelt died on April 12, and Truman assumed office alone, insecure, and relatively ignorant of foreign policy and military matters. He was unusually dependent on "trusted friends" and Roosevelt's advisers.[60] While serving in Congress and as vice president, Harry Truman concentrated on domestic policy. Roosevelt kept him ignorant of the "Tube Alloy" effort and related war and postwar planning.

The image of Secretary of War Stimson lingering behind after the new president's first cabinet meeting has passed into the lore of U.S. political history. Sensitive to the politics of transition, Stimson informed the new president that while it was best to leave the details for another time, he should know that "a new explosive... with almost unbelievable destructive power" was under development. A fortnight later Stimson explained to the president in greater detail that the atom bomb would be "decisive" in the postwar era.[61] Stimson's suggestion that the president create a "select committee" to consider the bomb's long-term implications led to the creation of the Interim Committee, which was recommending targets for U.S. atomic bombs in Japan before spring turned to summer.

Anti-communism in Washington and opposition to Russian dominance of Eastern Europe reinforced planning to use the nascent atomic bombs. Although Roosevelt and Churchill had agreed at the Yalta summit that Poland's postwar government would be "friendly" to the Soviet Union, and despite consistent counsel from Secretary Stimson and Admiral Leahy that Moscow consistently lived up to its commitments,[62] the newly installed president quickly fell under the influence of Averill Harriman, the ambassador to Moscow, outgoing Secretary of State Edward R. Stettinius and Winston Churchill. They opposed Soviet domination of Poland, which for them symbolized East-West relations in their entirety.[63]

They fed the president's fears with reports that Stalin had violated agreements and could not be trusted.[64]

On his second day as president, Truman began his confrontation with Moscow in a private meeting with Soviet Foreign Minister Molotov. Truman went "straight to the point."[65] In anything but diplomatic language, he demanded that Moscow respect the Yalta agreement and create a Polish government that represented all the Polish people. Molotov, who later complained that he had "never been talked to like that in my life," responded that "It [was] a matter of honor" for the Soviet Union to implement the Yalta agreement.[66] Truman had launched what became "a powerful foreign policy initiative aimed at reducing or eliminating Soviet influence from Europe."[67]

With the military defeat of Germany imminent, Churchill and Stalin were anxious for a summit meeting with Truman to plan the last stages of the war against Japan and to resolve their differences over the structure of the postwar international order. Truman, uncertain in his diplomatic skills and with no guarantees that he would have a working atomic bomb in his negotiating hand, was in less of a hurry. He thus appreciated, and accepted, Secretary of War Stimson's suggestion that the Potsdam summit be postponed until after the Trinity test was conducted in Alamogordo in July. As Stimson said at the time, the way to deal with the Russians was to "keep our mouths shut and let our actions speak for words…The Russians will understand them better than anything else… I call it a royal straight flush and we mustn't be a fool about the way we play it." Truman was less diplomatic: "If it explodes, as I think it will, I'll certainly have a hammer on those boys."[68]

Related considerations fed the planning for Potsdam and the decision to bomb Hiroshima and Nagasaki. Of central importance was a debate that emerged in Washington: would the Soviets join the war against Japan, and was it in the U.S. interest for them to honor the commitments they had made to join the war?

General Marshall initially feared that the Soviets would sit out the Asian phase of the war, leaving the "grinding" work and bleeding to U.S. forces. However, once Germany surrendered, on May 8, and assurances were given that the Soviet Union would declare war against Japan on or about August 8, pressure began to build in Washington to prevent the Soviets' entry into the war, and thus limit Soviet influence over Manchuria, China, Mongolia, Korea, and ultimately Japan itself. As Ambassador Harriman advised, once Moscow joined the war against Japan, "Russian influence would move in quickly and toward ultimate domination…There could be no illusion about anything such as 'free China' once the Russians got in...[Russia] will in the end exercise control over whatever government may be established in Manchuria and Outer Mongolia."[69]

Why this concern? Since the early years of the Meiji Restoration, Japan and Russia had competed for influence in Manchuria, northern China, and Korea. With Japan's approaching defeat, U.S. planners feared the creation of a north Asian military and political vacuum, which Russian forces would fill—adding rich and strategically important assets (and possibly a quarter of the world's population) to Soviet Cold War resources. Less widely understood was Japan's strategic importance for the coming confrontation with the Soviet Union. Former ambassador to Japan Joseph Grew and other planners understood that Japan could serve (as it has now for the past fifty years) as the keystone of U.S. power in Asia and the Pacific.

Geography was one of the two strategic assets that made Japan's inclusion in the Grand Area a preoccupation for U.S. planners. In the wake of the war, the Pacific would become an "American Lake." Control of Japan would allow the United States to complete the encirclement of the Soviet Union and enable the U.S. fleet to block Soviet naval access to the Pacific. To this day, the U.S. maintains more than one hundred military bases and installations in Japan, from Okinawa in the south to Hokkaido in the north.

Second, although much of Japan's industrial capacity had been and would be destroyed, the intellectual base upon which it had been built and its potential for the future were seen as strategic assets that U.S. planners did not want to fall into the Soviet sphere. Just five years later the United States would return to war, this time in Korea, largely to protect Japan's strategic flank, ensuring that Japan would not pass into the Soviet orbit and thus tilt the Asian and global balances of power.[70]

In May 1945, as President Truman waited for news from Alamogordo, former Ambassador Grew added to the debate over how to end the war with Japan while serving briefly as acting secretary of state. Convinced that a future war with Russia was certain, he raised four critical questions: How much pressure should be exerted on the Soviet Union to ensure that they honored their commitment to join the war? Was Soviet involvement in the war of such importance to the United States, that it should not risk efforts to gain from Moscow strategic concessions in Asia before their declaration of war? Should the concessions made to the Soviet Union at Yalta regarding their influence in Asia be reconsidered? "If the Soviets demanded to participate in the Occupation of Japan, should the U.S. acquiesce?"[71]

Grew's questions, passed along to Stimson, crystalized the secretary of war's understanding of the diplomatic potential of the atom bomb. "Once its power was demonstrated,"he observed, "the Soviets would be more accommodating to the American point of view. Territorial disputes could be settled amicably."[72]

Germany's surrender made it undeniably clear to the government in Tokyo that time was running out to negotiate a deal with Washington. The combined resources of the Allies would soon be arrayed against an already devastated Japan. Moscow had signalled its intentions when it announced that its nonaggression pact with Tokyo would not be renewed. In April, the Okinawan death toll, climbing to 150,000 civilians and 100,000 Japanese soldiers, made it apparent that the effort to buy time for the emperor and the home islands was drawing to a close. Before the end of the month General MacArthur reported to Washington that "the Japanese fleet has been reduced to practical impotency. The Japanese Air Force has been reduced to... uncoordinated, suicidal attacks against our forces...Its attrition is heavy and its power for sustained action is diminishing rapidly."[73] Japan "was running out of food, fuel, planes and raw materials of all kinds. Her major cities were in ruins, millions of her people were homeless and starving."[74]

Even before the Supreme War Guidance Council in Tokyo began formal discussions about the possibility of an "honorable" end to the war, peace feelers were communicated throughout Europe and were communicated to Truman. Japan's minister in Switzerland sought to "arrange for a cessation of hostilities." The Japanese ambassador in Portugal "declared that actual peace terms were unimportant so long as the term 'unconditional surrender' was not employed." The March 10 firebombing of Tokyo, which had claimed an estimated 100,000 lives and was repeated on March 26, had created the fear that "all of their wood and paper houses [would] be destroyed."[75]

These offers came as no surprise to the Allied leaders. A year earlier Churchill had observed that, once Russia declared war on Japan and it faced a three-part alliance, it would move to surrender. An invasion might not be necessary.

In May 1945 Secretary of War Stimson reported that a Russian declaration of war would have a "profound effect." By early July, the Combined Intelligence Committee confirmed Stimson's belief, reporting that "an entry of the Soviet Union into the war would finally convince the Japanese of the inevitability of complete defeat."[76]

In Japan, immediately following Germany's defeat, the Supreme War Guidance Council (the prime minister, the Foreign, Navy, and Army ministers, and the chiefs of staff) held a series of meetings that led the emperor to order the council to "immediately work out specific measures to end the war and implement them quickly."[77] Although the Japanese leadership was intensely anti-communist, the imperial government turned to the Soviet Union to mediate an end to the war. With most of China, Manchuria, and Korea under its control, the emperor and his government had strategic resources that could be offered to Moscow in exchange for peace. They had nothing left to offer the United States.

The United States had broken Japanese codes before the bombing of Pearl Harbor. As the Potsdam summit approached, U.S. intelligence monitored the Japanese efforts to surrender. Admiral Leahy, chairman of the Joint Chiefs of Staff and a special advisor to Truman, understood that "a surrender of Japan can be arranged with terms that can be accepted by Japan and that will make fully satisfactory provision for America's defense against future trans-Pacific aggression."[78] The Soviets, however, stalled, and the emperor, despite opposition from hard-liners in the military, grew increasingly desperate. Truman's knowledge of the emperor's effort to surrender is reflected in an entry in his diary: "telegram from Jap Emperor asking for peace."[79]

On the eve of the Potsdam summit, Japan's foreign minister cabled his emissary in Moscow that "unconditional surrender is the only obstacle to peace." Japan would surrender if Hirohito and the emperor system could be preserved. U.S. intelligence relayed the message to the president,[80] who feared peace might break out before he could play his master card.

As the State Department concentrated on post-war planning and as preparations for the earliest possible use of the U.S. nuclear weapons also continued apace, General Marshall recommended on May 29 that "these weapons might first be used against straight military objectives such as a large naval installation, and then if no complete result was derived...we ought to designate a number of large manufacturing areas from which people would be warned to leave—telling the Japanese that we intend to destroy such centers."[81]

Two days later the Interim Committee met. Without ever discussing whether the atomic bombs should be used, a decision was taken to make a "profound psychological impression on as many Japanese as possible." The committee accepted, without opposition, Harvard University President James Conant's suggestion that the best target would be a "vital war plant employing a large number of workers and closely surrounded by workers' homes." It was agreed that two weapons should be available for use in early August. The bombings of Hiroshima and Nagasaki thus resulted from a single decision.[82] Hiroshima, Kokura, Niigata, and Nagasaki all met this description and were chosen as the potential targets.

On July 16, shortly after the Potsdam summit convened, Secretary of War Stimson passed a note to President Truman saying "It's a Boy," a code that informed the president that the test at Alamogordo had been successful. As Churchill observed it, "Truman was evidently much fortified...and...he stood up to the Russians in a most decisive manner...He told the Russians just where they got on and off and generally bossed the whole meeting."[83]

None of the officials in Potsdam could understand the sense of awe and fear Robert Oppenheimer had experienced as he watched the first atomic explosion across the New Mexico desert. A sentence from the Hindu scriptures had immediately occurred to him: "Now I am become Death, destroyer of worlds."

Two brief exchanges at Potsdam are particularly revealing in relation to the "diplomatic" use of the first atomic bombs. The first relates to Japanese efforts to surrender to the Russians. Having been thoroughly briefed about the emperor's efforts to end the war, the president raised the subject with Stalin. The Soviet leader responded by reporting that the Soviets would launch their attack against Japanese-occupied Manchuria in early August. He then asked the president how the Soviets should respond to the Japanese request that former Japanese Prime Minister Konoe be invited to Moscow to initiate negotiations. Truman was noncommittal, and Stalin reassured the president that he would continue stalling.

The terms of surrender offered by the imperial government in Tokyo were nearly identical to those later formulated and accepted after the atomic bombings of Hiroshima and Nagasaki. The foreign policy establishment in Washington was inclined to retain the emperor on the Chrysanthemum Throne as a figurehead to facilitate the U.S. military occupation. Nevertheless, Potsdam's final declaration undermined the efforts of those in Tokyo's imperial court who were laboring to arrange Japan's surrender. The Big Three proclaimed that there would be "no alternatives" to the elimination of the authority and influence "of those who have deceived and misled the people into embarking on world conquest" (which would include the emperor). They warned that "stern justice shall be meted out to all war criminals," removing any incentive for "war criminals" to surrender unconditionally.

The second exchange came on July 24, as the summit drew to a close. At Churchill's suggestion, Truman "casually mentioned" to Stalin that the United States "had a new weapon of unusual destructive force." Stalin's calm response that "he was glad to hear it and hoped we would make 'good use of it against the Japanese'"came as a surprise to the president, who, by sharing the news, had unintentionally "used the bomb as a threat."[84]

The Soviet chief of staff, Marshall Georgi Zhukov, who met with Stalin shortly after the exchange, understood Truman's words as "political blackmail" and as a "psychological attack against ...Stalin." When

Molotov told the Russian dictator that Truman was "trying to raise his price," Stalin answered "Let him raise it. We must speak again with Kurchatov and tell him to get a move on with our work," meaning the Soviet Union's nuclear bomb project.[85]

The "Signal" is Sent

At eight a.m. on August 6, 1945, the people of Hiroshima felt relatively safe. Rumors had been circulating to explain the city's good fortune of not having been bombed as other Japanese cities had: Hiroshima was a beautiful city, and the Americans were saving it for their villas; there were important foreigners in the city, possibly including President Truman's mother; the city was not on U.S. maps. Less reassuring was the rumor that the Americans were preparing something "unusually big" for the city. Scientists had even discussed the possibility that an atomic bomb might be used against the city, but most thought it impossible.[86]

Another factor added to the false sense of security, and perhaps to the number of casualties. There were two air raid alerts during the night of August 5–6, and a third when the bombing mission's weather plane passed uneventfully over the city. At 7:32 the all clear was sounded. On a hot, bright, and beautiful morning, people were at work or making their way to work. "Housewives were completing after-breakfast chores." It was "early morning wartime routine."[87]

Little Boy, the *Enola Gay's* uranium bomb, exploded on target, 1,800 feet above the Shima Hospital. The heat, the force of the explosion, and the resulting firestorm completely destroyed the city, which stretched across a flat plain, broken previously only by rivers. According to the City of Hiroshima, an estimated 100,000 people died that day, and another 100,000 died soon thereafter from burns, injuries, and radiation.[88] The city's hospitals were immediately destroyed, as were most of the city's doctors, nurses, and other medical resources.

Among the victims were tens of thousands of Koreans, most of whom had been brought from Korea to serve as slave laborers in Japan's factories, mines, and work gangs. Several of the bomb's victims were U.S. prisoners of war.

President Truman could have, but did not, intervene to halt the U.S. military's momentum. The decision to bomb a second Japanese city had been made previously. Initiative for implementation lay with the bomber command in the Pacific. New orders, which the president did not issue, would have been required to prevent the bombing of Nagasaki.[89]

In Tokyo it took time for the government to reach agreement on the wording of its revised surrender proposal. Capitulation was inevitable. On August 9, as Soviet troops poured into Manchuria, and as Nagasaki was

devastated by the second atomic bomb dropped on Japan, the Supreme War Guidance Council was still arguing formally over the terms of surrender it would offer.

For a variety of reasons, less attention has been devoted to Nagasaki than to Hiroshima since the bombings. Nagasaki has long been one of the two major port cities of Kyushu. During Japan's two centuries of isolation from the world, the shoguns in Tokyo permitted the maintenance of a Dutch trading fortress on Dejima Island in the distant city's harbor, in order to create a tiny opening to developments in the rest of the world.

As U.S. forces bombed many of Japan's major cities and tightened its encirclement of the island nation, the children of Nagasaki were not forced to evacuate to the countryside. Most of the city's children remained in the city. Teenagers worked in factories and elsewhere as members of the students' "patriotic troops." As in Hiroshima, air raid alerts were frequent and blared several times on the night prior to the bombing. At 11:02 a.m., when the plutonium bomb Fat Man exploded over Nagasaki's largely Christian Urakami district, people were hard at work or beginning to prepare their midday meal.

Fat Man, named for Winston Churchill, was more powerful than the Hiroshima bomb. It is estimated that it killed 74,000 people, injured 75,000, and poisoned another 120,000. Sixty-six thousand houses were burned or damaged. The Urakami district was annihilated, but the devastation of the city was mitigated because the bomb fell off target. It exploded behind a mountain that, in turn, sheltered much, but not all, of the city center from the heat, the blast, and the firestorm. Wind patterns concentrated the radioactive black rain on the Nishiyama district, about three kilometers from the epicenter.

In both Hiroshima and Nagasaki, people who did not immediately die were immersed in death. In Hiroshima, Misao Nagoya was in the front of her home on August 6, 2.3 kilometers from the hypocenter. Years later she remembered:

> In an instant, red and yellow dust covered the world...and I was knocked to the floor by the terrific blast as if the earth was going to be destroyed. Though I was outside the house, I was blown inside, and pillars and roof fell on me. I narrowly escaped as the house caught fire. The young lady next-door was also caught by the falling house, but unfortunately, she could not escape. She was burned alive...

> That night, I stayed in the class-room of the school, which was used as a shelter. The hair of victims stood up. Their skin was dangling from their bodies. The patterns of their dresses were branded on them by the heat rays...Almost all of these victims died toward the dawn, asking desperately for water...

My sister who was in her first year at a girl's school, left home...for war-time mobilization...dismantling a building near to the center of the explosion. I have never heard of her again. She left not even a sign in this world. Was she just vaporized at the moment of the atomic explosion? Or was she washed out to sea, seeking water without enough energy to tell her name? All her class died at the same time...

We victims lived in fear for a long time. And soon the fear turned into a reality when I got married and became a mother. In July 1965 my son, four years old then, was diagnosed as suffering from leukemia...My son died on February 22, 1968.[90]

Sumiteru Taniguchi, then sixteen years old, was in Nagasaki on August 9, 1945. He told me his story forty-eight years later, and as we parted he gave me his calling card, half of which is a grotesque photograph of what remained of his body a month after the bombing. In an interview published before we met, Taniguchi-san explained:

I was riding my red bike down a road in Sumiyuoshi on August 9...It was two years since I had become a telegram delivery boy...

My eyes were blinded by a dazzling light and a burning wind... [It] threw me three meters forward, twisting my bicycle like a candy bar. Strangely, I was not bleeding, and there was no pain. I managed to drag myself into the basement of a munitions factory 300 meters ahead and suddenly an agonizing cramp started in my back and spread throughout my body.

I lay groaning in that basement for three nights. Finally on the fourth day a rescue crew came and took me to the Isahaya Public School...Instead of medicine, our treatment consisted of having a mixture of newspaper ashes and grease applied to our burns. A month later I was brought to Shinkozen Rescue Center where American soldiers must have filmed me...

"Kill me!!" I must have yelled again and again. The pain from my burns and the hopelessness all around me made me wish again and again that I were dead. Now when I look at this rotting blood and skin I seethe with these thoughts.[91]

Chieko Watanabe, who became an almost sainted figure of the nuclear disarmament movement in Japan, was a sixteen-year-old student worker at the Mitsubishi Electrical Machinery Factory on August 9, 2.5 kilometers from the Nagasaki hypocenter. She worked there with her classmates making parts for searchlights. At ten minutes to eleven she and her friend Ayako Yamashita stopped work to seek out an engineer. When the girls saw the flash of the atomic explosion, they ran frantically for the air raid shelter behind the factory. They didn't get far. Chieko was thrown by the force of the explosion, felt an intense pain, and fainted.

A little later, recovering consciousness, I looked around to find myself buried under a huge steel frame bent and twisted out of shape...My body was bent over, so that my legs were on my head. Because the steel frame pressed upon my back and head, I could not free myself...I have never been able to get back on my feet since.[92]

Chieko's back was broken, never to heal. Her body was so injured that she could not walk, stand, or, for many years, even sit.

Maybe it was the effects of the radiation, but as one week passed...and then a second week, the flesh on my hip and leg began to rot. In one big spot, the flesh rotted away as I watched; it became a hole as large as the palm of my hand. And at the bottom of the hole I could see my own bone.[93]

For years Chieko Watanabe was confined to her bed, unable to move the lower half of her body, suffering one disease after another. Like many hibakusha, she wanted to die. Only with the aid of her mother did she regain strength and the will to live. Her mother, too, struggled with despair, and once became so hopeless that she tried to strangle Chieko.

Like Sumiteru Taniguchi and Chieko Watanabe, Senji Yamaguchi was also in Nagasaki on August 9, 1945. He was fourteen years old and worked in the Mitsubishi Arms Manufacturing Works, 1.2 kilometers from the epicenter of the Nagasaki explosion.

I was working outside with my shirt off. The heat rays from the explosion, about 3,300 Fahrenheit, scorched my upper body. The heat rays vaporized some people, while burning others into charcoal-like remains.

I witnessed the shock wave from the explosion crush a pregnant woman against a wall and tear apart her abdomen. I could see her and her unborn baby dying. The blast instantly knocked down many homes and buildings as well. Mothers and children were trapped beneath the burning wreckage. They called out each other's names, and the mothers would cry out, pleading for someone to save their children. No one was able to help them, and they all burned alive. The people who came to rescue the immediate survivors or clear away the rotting dead bodies contracted radiation sickness. They died later, one after the other...

People started suffering from illnesses caused by the atomic radiation shortly after the bombing. They developed various kinds of cancers, such as breast and liver cancers, and pregnant women gave birth to deformed babies.[94]

When Senji Yamaguchi was well enough to resume daily life, his scars were so severe that children ran from him shouting "Here comes the Red Demon!" Depressed by recurrent illnesses and operations to remove keloids caused by radiation, he attempted suicide many times before the movement for the abolition of nuclear weapons, and his ability to contribute to it, gave him reason and will to live.

Fearing that a third atomic bomb might be exploded over Tokyo, on August 9 Emperor Hirohito asserted his authority and ended the political and procedural debates within the Supreme War Guidance Council. He informed the Council that "the time has come to bear the unbearable. I give my sanction to the proposal to accept the Potsdam declaration."[95] Within hours the cabinet drew up a communiqué that was sent to Washington, London, Moscow, and Chongqing (Chungking). Contrary to the emperor's explicit instructions, they accepted Potsdam's terms with the caveat that "the said declaration does not comprise any demand which prejudices the prerogatives of His Majesty as a Sovereign Ruler." In response, the Truman administration signaled its willingness to spare the emperor and to accept less than an unconditional surrender.[96]

As the suffering in Nagasaki continued, and while the imperial court awaited Washington's response to its offer of surrender, President Truman explained one meaning of the bombings. "Rumania, Bulgaria, and Hungary," he wrote, "are not to be spheres of influence of any one power."[97] Soon thereafter the president halted all lend-lease shipments to the Soviet Union, including food and transport equipment that were desperately needed for civilian relief in Russia.

In October, President Truman moved to mobilize the people of the United States for the confrontation with the Soviet Union. Using his Navy Day speech to gain wide public attention, the president was unequivocal that there could be "no compromise with the forces of evil…atomic bombs which fell on Hiroshima and Nagasaki must be a signal."[98]

To this day, people in Japan ask how many died to save the emperor system. In the United States we have yet to ask why so many innocent Japanese were killed and made to suffer for limited strategic advantage and to send "a signal" to the Soviet Union.

The Witness of the Hibakusha

Like the survivors of Auschwitz, Bergen Belsen, Dresden, and Birkenau, the survivors of the Japanese holocausts, the hibakusha, their memories and physical presence, are a stubborn, disturbing testimony to monstrous crimes of the past, and to the potential cruelty of which humans (in this case Americans) are capable. More hopefully, the lives and commitments of many hibakusha are testimonies to the possibilities of human courage, compassion, and of a life-affirming future.

To understand the context in which the hibakusha and other Japanese peace activists have labored for the last half century, it is important to be aware that "Japan has been obsessed with the United States." Japanese life and politics during the postwar period have been largely defined by relations with the United States and the self-interested and independent actions of the "colossus across the Pacific."[99]

After the multiple catastrophes of the Fifteen Year War came the U.S. military occupation of Japan. U.S. occupation forces used Japanese Marxists as "foot soldiers for democracy," to break down the enduring feudal and militaristic structures of Japanese society. The Left was purged in the late 1940s "reverse course," as the confrontation with the Soviet Union deepened. General MacArthur imposed a pacifist constitution which "renounc[ed] war as a sovereign right" and "foresw[ore] the existence of Japanese military forces." Soon, however, the Truman administration regretted this decision and pressed demands that Japan create a military.

U.S. occupation forces censored publication and broadcast of information about the atomic bombings of Hiroshima and Nagasaki, even as it organized war crimes trials in Tokyo. The Mutual Security Treaty, imposed on Japan in 1951 by the Truman administration in exchange for an end to the occupation, ensured that Japan would serve as the keystone of U.S. power in the Pacific, by legitimizing the continued presence of U.S. military bases within Japan. At great social, environmental, and political cost to Japan, these bases have served since as essential elements in the United States' global infrastructure for nuclear warfighting and conventional wars of intervention, from Vietnam to Iraq. So complete was the U.S. militarization of Japan that, in the 1980s, Prime Minister Nakasone described Japan as "an unsinkable aircraft carrier" for the United States.[100]

Japan, which suffered such a sharp and painful fall from imperial power to occupied nation, became Washington's junior partner. It could not help but be preoccupied by the United States, *the* imperial superpower, armed at one point with more than thirty thousand nuclear weapons, some of which were regularly brought into Hiroshima prefecture.

When Wilfred Burchett reflected that "Hiroshima asserts the existence of a will to genocidal, absolute destruction," he also observed that it represents "the indestructibility of human resistance." Speaking for many who have been awed and moved by the courage of politically active hibakusha, as noted earlier, Burchett wrote that "despite their ordeals, the cover-ups, even the ostracism from 'normal' society, the hibakusha survivors have fought back, becoming the most stalwart and militant of peaceniks. Through them and their ongoing struggle, the *urgency* of Hiroshima is transmitted to all of us."[101]

Of course, not all hibakusha have been visibly heroic. The resources of most hibakusha were taxed to the limit in their efforts to endure physical and emotional pain, to confront their own deaths and those of loved ones, and to care for their families. According to one survey, more than a quarter of the hibakusha spent "the rest of their lives fighting against diseases" caused by the bombings.[102] Others were tortured by survivor's guilt and discrimination. For some, the trauma led to repression of memory, or efforts to escape their pasts.[103] Many attempted or committed suicide.

Yet there were also many obviously heroic responses. Doctors in Nagasaki and Hiroshima, like Takashi Nagai, appeared to ignore their own personal tragedies and worked to heal and to teach until their bodies failed them. Other people assumed authority that was not normally theirs, and worked to ensure the provision of "food, clothing, and whatever could be made available to keep people alive."[104] Some provided spiritual leadership or, like Ichiro Kawamoto, worked with orphaned children. As the Occupation's censorship was withdrawn, some began to teach the lessons of Hiroshima across Japan and globally.

It was U.S. arrogance and another nuclear atrocity that galvanized the modern Japanese peace movement and led the more courageous hibakusha to "seize upon their hibakusha identity and put it to public use." On March 14, 1954, the U.S. exploded a hydrogen bomb at Bikini atoll. That only briefly secret test poisoned 236 natives of Bikini, 26 Americans at weather stations on nearby islands, and the 23-man crew of the Japanese tuna trawler *Lucky Dragon Number 5* (*Fukuryu-maru*).[105]

The intellectual and political ground for the birth of the new movement had been manifesting itself in Japan since the end of the U.S. military occupation, two years earlier. With the demise of the occupation, the Press Code Order of 1945, forbidding Japanese publication or broadcast of any information relating to the atomic bombings, no longer enforced Japanese ignorance of what their occupiers had done. Documentary accounts of the atomic bombings circulated widely, augmenting what had been popular knowledge. It shocked the Japanese public.

The Korean War, during which Japan served as a forward base for U.S. operations and as a source of war materiel, also contributed to the developing Japanese anti-nuclear consciousness and commitment. In response to public U.S. threats to use nuclear weapons against North Korea and China, the World Peace Council's Stockholm Appeal was circulated widely across Japan. It stated:

We demand the absolute banning of the atom weapons, arms of terror and mass extermination of population.

We demand the establishment of strict international control to ensure the implementation of this banning measure.

We consider that any government which would be the first to use the atom weapon against any country whatsoever would be committing a crime against humanity and should be dealt with as a war criminal.

We call on all men of good will throughout the world to sign this appeal.[106]

In Japan, the highly publicized suffering and death in 1955 of Aikichi Kuboyama, the radio operator of the *Lucky Dragon*, led to extensive media coverage about the effects of radiation, the dangers of the continuing nuclear arms race, and the devastation of Hiroshima and Nagasaki. This fueled the emerging Japanese peace movement and helped it gather more than thirty-two million Japanese signatures on the Stockholm appeal.

The first World Conference against Atomic and Hydrogen Bombs, organized in Hiroshima on the tenth anniversaries of the bombings of Hiroshima and Nagasaki, and after Kuboyama's death, provided a forum for hibakusha and led to the founding of Nihon Hidankyo. More than 150 organizations, led by the Communist and Socialist parties, sponsored the conference. Organizers included Sohyo, the General Council of Japanese Trade Unions; the Japan Teachers Union; the National Railway Workers Union; and women's, youth, religious, and cultural organizations. More than twenty-five thousand people, including delegates from fourteen countries, participated in conference-related events in Tokyo and Hiroshima.

So broad was the conference's appeal and moral mandate, that revisionist right-wing Prime Minister Hatoyama found it necessary to send personal greetings, which were read to the conference.

The two hibakusha who addressed the conference, Akimoto Takahashi from Hiroshima and Misako Yamaguchi from Nagasaki, had a profound impact on the conference and, through it, on others in Japan and abroad. They also were moved deeply, and were reinforced by the support they received and by the movement to abolish nuclear weapons that manifested itself before them. Misako Yamaguchi and another member of the Nagasaki A-bombed Maidens Group later wrote:

> When we, two atomic victims, were elected delegates to the Hiroshima World Conference… we could not bear … our ugly features being exposed to so many people, and refused to come. But we were told that it was the only chance to give people an understanding of the suffering and agony of the atomic bomb victims…Moved by the earnest request and backed by the financial aid from our friends, we came to Hiroshima.[107]

> We knew that our ten years of struggle with agony ha[d] come to play an important role for peace, we felt nothing but joy and happiness. We felt very sorry that all the atomic victims of Nagasaki could not share in this delight.

When she formally addressed the conference, Misako Yamaguchi found it difficult to speak, but she conveyed her message:

> I extend my heartfelt thanks to all the people who made great effort and cooperated in organizing this conference. I was fifteen years old when the atomic bomb was dropped. I lost my mother and younger brother. I

wonder if people can fully understand the ten years of long and difficult days...At present my health is stable, and I work at a university hospital. But there are many people who lead their lives in constant fear—even today or tomorrow they might be struck by diseases. Also many victims suffer every day in sadness from injuries.

Please, dear friends... Those who lost their mothers by the A-bomb, or those who cannot support their lives if their mothers suddenly fall ill, often think of committing suicide...

However, if we end our lives now, who will be able to tell the world the real terror of the atomic bombs?[108]

Akimoto Takahashi placed his appeal more clearly within the hibakusha's call for the complete abolition of nuclear weapons:

Since the bomb was dropped, we have undergone many difficulties, physically, economically, and mentally. Only one atomic bomb cruelly massacred innocent people—elderly, children, women. A-bombs are the enemy of...humanity, [and] should not be allowed to exist. We must appeal to the world public for an international control of atomic energy and a total ban on the test and production of atomic and hydrogen bombs.

As you can see, I have scars of burns on my upper body, but there are many more people with more severe injuries in Hiroshima. We absolutely reject the repayment of terror. Taking this August 6 as a starting point, let us together pray for No More Hiroshimas, and for eternal world peace.[109]

For Misako Yamaguchi, Akimoto Takahashi and countless other hibakusha, like Holocaust survivors of Europe, the painful recounting of what they witnessed and endured has served as therapeutic relief and has provided the historical and spiritual frames of reference for the nuclear disarmament movement.

Suzu Kuboyama, the widow of radio operator Aikichi Kuboyama, also spoke at the 1955 conference. Addressing the hibakusha of Hiroshima and Nagasaki, she expressed her understanding of the pain they had endured and contrasted their suffering to the excellent medical treatment her husband had received under the glare of the Japanese and international media. Unlike the hibakusha of Hiroshima and Nagasaki, she and his mother "could attend his death bed and give him water."

After praying that the souls of the victims rest in peace, Suzu Kuboyama vented her rage, a rage shared by millions of Japanese and which fueled the *AMPO* (anti-Mutual Security Treaty) revolt when the U.S.-Japan Mutual Security Treaty was revised and renewed in 1960:

Atomic artillery and rockets are brought into Japan though everyone opposes this. What do those eager to wage an atomic war think? Atomic weapons are brought to Japan that has suffered the damage from atomic bombs three times. How insulting it is for people of Hiroshima and Nagasaki and my husband!

Please do not bring such weapons into Japan.

Please do not use the …weapons, and destroy them.

Please stop production and testing of such weapons…

When atomic war is gone, I think, the victims of Hiroshima and Nagasaki can …feel happy. To preserve peace, let us go hand in hand in the pursuit of one task, opposition to atomic war, over and above whatever differences we may have in our thinking and politics.[110]

One year later, following the second World Conference Against Atomic and Hydrogen bombs, Nihon Hidankyo was established. Nihon Hidankyo committed itself to building a movement for the abolition of atomic and hydrogen bombs, compensation from the Japanese government to the hibakusha and families of atom bomb victims, and medical treatment for the hibakusha. It sought to enable hibakusha to become self-supporting, or to guarantee sufficient income for those who were unable to work. Later, an additional fundamental demand was added: "a formal apology to the hibakusha, by acknowledging…that dropping of the atomic bombs on Hiroshima and Nagasaki was against all humanity and a violation of international law."[111]

Their founding proclamation, a "Message to the World," speaks for itself:

After eleven long years since the atomic bombing, we could at last meet here, [having come] for the first time from all over Japan. We, who were not killed at that unforgettable moment, finally set ourselves up and came to this first nationwide conference…Up until now we have kept our silence, hid our faces, scattered ourselves and led our lives that were left to us, but now, unable to keep our mouths shut, we are rising up, joining our hands…

We have, at today's gathering, commemorated the dead and talked of the inexpressible sentiments piled up in these long years. But unending talks of sorrow and anger, or of torture and distress accumulated deep in our hearts were not for getting consolation or relief for the time being. We have reassured our will to save humanity from its crisis through the lessons learned from our experiences, while at the same time saving ourselves. Here, we appeal to the world…Humanity must never again inflict nor suffer the sacrifice and torture we have experienced.

How can we, who have been confronted with fear of radiation sickness ever since the day of the atomic bombing, who have seen people dying due to the radiation in Hiroshima and Nagasaki…watch these H-bomb experiments that contaminate air and water with indifference…

If our ordeals and resurrection could serve as a fortress to protect the life and happiness of humanity in the atomic age, we would be able to express from the bottom of our hearts that "We are glad that we are alive."

Conveying our sincere gratitude and determination, we conclude this message...to the world. [112]

Their words were not simply rhetoric. Chieko Watanabe addressed the second World Conference Against Atomic and Hydrogen Bombs with her mother's help. When her mother died, Chieko Watanabe forged the will and found the means to live independently. Until she died in 1993, despite her pain, Chieko Watanabe traveled across Japan and internationally to address conferences from her wheel chair, telling her story and calling upon the world to "stop making these terrible bombs." Like many hibakusha, she identified with other victims of U.S. militarism and opposed U.S. preparations to precipitate nuclear war in Vietnam and Iraq. [113]

Senji Yamaguchi, the "Red Demon" whose visage had frightened children, has served as a leading spokesman of the hibakusha and became Nihon Hidankyo's cochairperson. As he explained to a 1993 gathering of U.S. disarmament organizers, "In 1955, the first World Conference Against A- and H- bombs took place in Hiroshima. Here I joined the movement to abolish nuclear weapons. I have lived with suffering from the atomic bomb for forty-eight years, and I believe my life's greatest mission is to abolish nuclear weapons." [114]

Sumiteru Taniguchi also joined Nihon Hidankyo in its first years, and has served as an inspiration for the Japanese peace movement by using his identity to encourage others to work for nuclear disarmament. He expressed his will and vision, and those of many other hibakusha, this way:

You who have seen my body, don't turn your face away. I want you to look again. I survived miraculously, but in the scars of my body is the need to curse the atomic bomb. I want so much to believe in the warmth and determination I see in your eyes as you sit stiffly, watching us...

I joined the peace movement...I [still] hated showing my deformed body...Of course I do not want to become an object of display even now. But that does not mean that we victims should hide in the shadow. We must not give in to just struggling with our own personal despair and not working for peace... Living and struggling for peace is my joy and consolation, but those of us who have walked forward out of Hell know that there has been enough suffering. [115]

The will and commitment of hibakusha have been repeatedly reinforced by U.S. leaders who were unable to apologize, who turned away without seeing, and who had no appreciation of the need for reconciliation with the hibakusha.

During a 1958 television interview, reported internationally, Harry Truman was asked if he had any regrets about the decision to bomb Hiroshima and Nagasaki. The retired president answered: "Not the slightest—not the slightest in the world." He went on to repeat the canard that without the bombs the U.S. invasion of Japan would have cost Americans half a million casualties, and that "when you have the weapon that will win the war, you'd be foolish not to use it…If the world gets into turmoil, it will be used. You can be sure of that."[116]

This assertion that he had no reason to be sorry led hibakusha to understand that the man most responsible for the atomic bombings and their suffering remained insensitive to the consequences of his actions. Their resentment deepened as subsequent presidents reaffirmed the morality of the atomic bombings of Hiroshima and Nagasaki, prepared for nuclear omnicide, and threatened to use nuclear weapons in the course of successive wars.

Notes

1. Haruko Taya and Theodore F. Cook, *Japan at War: An Oral History*, New York: The New Press, 1992, p. 397.
2. Martin J. Sherwin, *A World Destroyed: The Atomic Bomb and the Grand Alliance*, New York: Vintage Books, 1975, p. 220.
3. David Lowenthal, *The Past is a Foreign Country*, Cambridge: Cambridge University Press, 1993, p. xv.
4. Ian Buruma, *The Wages of Guilt: Memories of War in Germany and Japan*, New York: Farrar Straus Giroux, 1994, p. 93.
5. This and other references to students' reactions are taken from exam essays written by students at Regis College, May, 1994.
6. Howard Zinn. *Declarations of Independence: Cross-Examining American Ideology*, New York: Harper Collins, 1990, p. 95. Italics added.
7. See, among others, *New York Times*, February 1, 1958, cited in Robert Jay Lifton, *Death In Life: Survivors of Hiroshima*, New York: Random House, 1967, p. 333; Gar Alperovitz, "The Hiroshima Decision: A Moral Reassessment," *Christianity & Crisis*, February 3, 1992; Bernard E. Trainor, "…And Why We Should Remember the Men in the Pacific, Too," *Boston Globe*, June 5, 1994.
8. Wilfred Burchett. *Shadows of Hiroshima*, London: Verso, 1983.
9. Sherwin, op. cit. pp. 190–194.
10. McGeorge Bundy, *Danger and Survival: Choices About the Bomb in the First Fifty Years*, New York: Random House, 1988, p. 96.
11. Barton J. Bernstein, "The Atomic Bombings Reconsidered," *Foreign Affairs*, January/February 1995; Robert Jay Lifton, and Eric Markusen, *The Genocidal Mentality: Nazi Holocaust and Nuclear Threat*, New York: Basic Books, 1990, p. xii.
12. Ted Morang, "The Last War Criminal: The Trial of Paul Touvier," *New York Times Magazine*, May 22, 1994
13. Hannah Arendt, *Eichmann in Jerusalem: A Report on the Banality of Evil*, London: Penguin Books, 1964.
14. *New York Times*, April 20, 1994.
15. Junko Kayashige, "I Cannot Keep Silent During Summer," Hiroshima. A 1994 revision of a speech first given in 1970.

16. Ibid.

17. Shoji Sawada, Transcript, 1989 World Conference Against Atomic and Hydrogen Bombs, Tokyo, p. 55.

18. John W. Dower, *Japan in War & Peace: Selected Essays*, New York: New Press, 1993, pp. 244–245.

19. Naomi Shohno, *The Legacy of Hiroshima: Its Past, Our Future*, Tokyo: Kosei Publishing Co., 1986, pp. 15 and 56 (emphasis in original).

20. Burchett, op. cit. pp. 35–36.

21. William Appleman Williams, *The Tragedy of American Diplomacy*, New York: Delta, 1962, p. 254.

22. Alperovitz, *Christianity and Crisis*, op. cit.

23. Ibid.

24. Ibid.

25. Williams, op. cit, p. 254.

26. Alperovitz, *Christianity and Crisis*, op. cit.

27. Saburo Ienaga, *The Pacific War, 1931-1945*, New York: Pantheon, 1978, p. 58.

28. Ibid., p. 9.

29. Ibid., p. 68

30. Ibid., pp. 9–10; J.W. Dower, *Empire and Aftermath: Yoshida Shigeru and the Japanese Experience, 1878-1954*, Cambridge, Mass.: Harvard University Press, 1988, p. 167.

31. Edward Behr, *Hirohito: Behind the Myth*, New York: Vintage, 1990, p. 174.

32. Yoshitake Oka, *Konoe Fumimaro: A Political Biography*, New York: Madison Books, 1992, pp. 173 and 187.

33. Behr, op. cit., pp. 228 and 258.

34. In the West, refugees from Nazi and Fascist Europe, the Nuremberg War Crimes Trials, and a vast body of literature, film, and press accounts have made the lessons of Nazi and Fascist repression, and popular resistance to it, essential elements of our own culture. While there are compelling and demanding films and books (Kinoshita's "24 Eyes," Kurosawa's *Something Like An Autobiography*, Cook's *Japan At War: An Oral History*, Ienaga's *The Pacific War*, etc.) that make the Japanese experience accessible to the West, barriers of race, culture, and language, as well as cynical decisions, made during the U.S. occupation, to integrate Japan's wartime political and bureaucratic elite into the postwar system, have left us ignorant of critical historical and spiritual lessons. Among the additonal resources that make this political history available to us are: Behr, op. cit.; Cook, op. cit.; David Bergamini, *Japan's Imperial Conspiracy*, New York: Pocket Books, 1972; Dower, op. cit.; John. W. Dower, *Japan in War & Peace: Selected Essays*, New York: New Press, 1993; John W. Dower, *War Without Mercy: Race & Power in the Pacific War*, New York: Pantheon, 1986; Edwin P. Hoyt, *Japan's War: The Great Pacific Conflict*, New York: De Capo Press, 1986; Ienaga, op. cit.; Edwin O. Reischauer, *Japan: The Story of A Nation*, New York: McGraw-Hill, 1990.

35. Michael Blow, *The History of the Atomic Bomb*, New York: American Heritage Publishing Co., 1968.

36. Letter to Secretary Robert McCormick Adams of the Smithsonian Institution signed by Rep. Peter Blute and eleven other Congressmen, August 10, 1994; "The Last Act: The Atomic Bomb and the End of World War II," Smithsonian Institution, Washington, D.C., October 26, 1994; open letter of historians and scholars to Dr. Ira Michael Heyman, November 6, 1994.

37. William Johnston in the introduction to Takashi Nagai, *The Bells of Nagasaki*, Tokyo: Kodansha, 1949, 1984 edition.

38. Barton Bernstein, op. cit.

39. Sherwin, op. cit., pp. 167–168; Gar Alperovitz, *Atomic Diplomacy: Hiroshima and Potsdam*, New York: Vintage, 1965, pp. 98–100.

40. Gar Alperovitz, "Why The United States Dropped the Bomb," *Technology Review*, August/September, 1990.
41. Gar Alperovitz, *Christianity and Crisis*, op. cit.
42. Alperovitz, *Technology Review*, op. cit.
43. Ibid.
44. Sherwin, op. cit. p. 203.
45. John, W. Dower, , *Japan At War & Peace*, New York: New Press, 1993, p. 264.
46. Ibid., p. 39
47. Letter from President Truman to Samuel McCrea Cavert, General Secretary, Federal Council of Churches of Christ in America, August 11, 1945, Truman Library.
48. Sherwin, op. cit., p. 200.
49. Ibid., pp. 67–68.
50. Ibid., pp. 88–89.
51. Ibid., p. 84, (emphasis in original).
52. Ibid., p. 83.
53. Ibid., pp. 88–89.
54. Ibid., pp. 96–97.
55. Ibid., p. 118.
56. Ibid., p. 131.
57. Ibid., pp. 104–105.
58. Ibid., p. 111.
59. Ibid., p. 144.
60. Ibid., pp. 8–9, 148.
61. Alperovitz, *Atomic Diplomacy*, op. cit., p. 11.
62. Sherwin, op. cit., pp. 157–58.
63. Alperovitz, *Atomic Diplomacy*, op. cit., p. 12.
64. Daniel Yergin, *Shattered Peace: The Origins of the Cold War and the National Security State*, Boston: Houghton Mifflin, 1978, pp. 78–79.
65. Sherwin, op. cit., p. 157.
66. Ibid., p. 159.
67. Alperovitz, *Atomic Diplomacy*, op. cit., p. 13.
68. Alperovitz, *Technology Review*, op. cit.
69. Alperovitz, *Atomic Diplomacy*, op. cit., p. 95.
70. Joseph Gerson, "Japan: Keystone of the Pacific," in Gerson and Birchard, *The Sun Never Sets*, Boston: South End Press, 1991, p. 174; Edward A. Olsen, *U.S.-Japan Strategic Reciprocity: A Neo-Internationalist View*, Stanford: Stanford University Press, 1985, pp. 4–6.
71. Sherwin, op. cit., p 189; Alperovitz, *Atomic Diplomacy*, op. cit., p. 26.
72. Sherwin, op. cit., p. 190.
73. Alperovitz, *Technology Review*, op. cit.
74. Behr, op. cit., p. 292.
75. Alperovitz, *Technology Review*, op. cit.
76. Cook, op. cit., p. 340; Alperovitz, *Atomic Diplomacy*, op. cit., p. 109.
77. Oka, op. cit. pp. 210–211 (see note 32).
78. Martin S. Quigley, *Peace Without Hiroshima: Secret Action at the Vatican in the Spring of 1945*, London: Madison Books, 1991, pp. 121–131; Behr, op. cit., p. 213; Alperovitz, *Technology Review*, op. cit.
79. Alperovitz, *Technology Review*, op. cit.
80. Sherwin, op. cit., p. 235.
81. Alperovitz, *Technology Review*, op. cit.
82. Sherwin, op. cit., p. 209.
83. Burchett, op. cit., p. 32.
84. Sherwin, op. cit., p 227.
85. Burchett, op. cit., p. 76.

86. Lifton, op. cit., p. 16.

87. Ibid., p. 18.

88. Johnston, op. cit., p. xiii.

89. Sherwin, op. cit., p. 233.

90. Misao Nagoya, 16th World Conference Against Atomic and Hydrogen Bombs "Special Report By Mrs. Misao Nagoya" Tokyo: 1970.

91. A Citizens' Group to Convey Testimonies of Hiroshima and Nagasaki, *Give Me Water: Testimonies of Hiroshima and Nagasaki*, Tokyo, 1973, p. 52.

92. *Taiyo ga Kieta Ano Hi*, Missionary for Peace, Tokyo, 1993, translated by Andrew Junker.

93. *Heiwano Tabi eh*, Missionary for Peace, Tokyo, 1993, translated by Andrew Junker.

94. "New Contexts, New Dangers: Preventing Nuclear War in the Post-Cold War Age," Transcripts from the October 29–31 Conference, Cambridge: American Friends Service Committee, 1993, p. 12.

95. Behr, op. cit., p. 299.

96. Ibid., pp. 300–301.

97. Burchett, op. cit., p. 105.

98. Ibid., p. 104.

99. Dower, op. cit., p. 5.

100. Gerson, op. cit. pp., 167–198.

101. Burchett, op. cit., p. 120.

102. Nihon Hidankyo, "Atomic Bomb Victims Appeal 1988," Tokyo, p. 12.

103. Lifton, op. cit., p.35–41; Cooke, op. cit., p. 399.

104. Lifton, op. cit., p. 211.

105. Ibid., p. 209; *Lucky Dragon*, Tokyo: Sanyusha Publishing Co., 1986, p. 24.

106. *Documentary Photographs 1945-1985: For a World Free of Nuclear Weapons*, (English Translation) Tokyo: Japan Council Against A and H Bombs (Gensuikyo), 1985, p. 12.

107. Japan Council Against Atomic and Hydrogen Bombs, "Happiness will Come Back to Us," *No More Hiroshimas*, Tokyo: 1955.

108. Provided by Japan Council Against Atomic and Hydrogen Bombs, Gensuikyo.

109. Ibid.

110. Ibid.

111. "Atomic Bomb Victims' Appeal 1988 Document," Tokyo.

112. "MESSAGE TO THE WORLD: Proclamation at the Establishment Meeting of Nihon Hidankyo," Hiroshima, August 10, 1956.

113. See, for example, Chieko Watanabe's speech to the Eleventh World Conference Against Atomic and Hydrogen Bombs, 1965.

114. "New Contexts, New Dangers," op. cit.

115. "Give Me Water," op. cit., p. 53.

116. Lifton, op. cit., p. 333.

CHAPTER THREE

The Cuban Missile Crisis
For Reasons of Prestige and Power

Do not put a loaded rifle on stage if no one is thinking of firing it.
— Anton Chekov[1]

So long as we had the thumbscrew on Khruschev, we should have given it another turn every day. We were too eager to make an agreement with the Russians. They had no business there [in Cuba] in the first place.
— Dean Acheson, former Secretary of State[2]

In order to establish the principle that we have a right to keep missiles on their border, even missiles we don't want anymore, but [the Soviets do not] have the right to keep missiles on our border, these people were willing to face what they regarded as a probability of a third to a half of nuclear war. I don't believe that there's [been such a] moment of madness and lunacy in human history.
— Noam Chomsky[3]

ON MONDAY EVENING, October 22, 1962, President John F. Kennedy addressed the people of the United States and the world from the White House. I was a high school student; like others across the country, I had been following election year charges that the president was doing nothing while the Russians were secretly building nuclear missile bases in Cuba. I found it difficult to comprehend all that the president said that night, but his meaning and tone were clear: "We will not prematurely or unnecessarily risk the costs of worldwide nuclear war in which even the fruits of victory would be ashes in our mouth, but neither will we shrink from that risk at any time it must be faced."

U.S. surveillance flights over Cuba had, the president said, "established...that a series of offensive missiles sites" were being built on the "imprisoned island" of Cuba. Each of these missiles was capable of "striking Washington, D.C., the Panama Canal, Cape Canaveral, Mexico City, or any other city in the southeastern part of the United States...Central America, or...the Caribbean." This was "a definite threat to peace," because it broke the tradition of "great care" the United States and the Soviet Union had long exercised in "never upsetting the precarious status quo which insured that these weapons would not be used in the absence of some vital challenge...this secret, swift, and extraordinary build-up of Communist missiles, in an area well known to have a special and historical relationship to the United States...cannot be accepted if our courage and our commitments are ever to be trusted again."

President Kennedy informed those watching him, and those who would later learn of his speech, that he had ordered the navy to establish a limited "quarantine" around Cuba. U.S. military forces were being reinforced and were prepared "for any eventualities." If the Soviets launched their missiles based in Cuba, the United States would retaliate.[4]

We were at the brink of war, possibly nuclear annihilation, to maintain (if only temporarily) the predominance of U.S. nuclear power and hegemony in the Americas.

The crisis, whose origins lay in the preceding months, years, and decades, climaxed six days later, before most people could respond meaningfully. Mitsuo Kojima, a hibakusha who had served the wounded and dying in Hiroshima, reacted like many people in the United States, Japan, and other nations. Years later he recalled that Kennedy's speech and warning caught him totally by surprise, and the crisis climaxed and passed before he could fully comprehend had happened.[5]

The Cuban missile crisis briefly threatened human survival and became a defining moment in history. Then it passed, having fundamentally altered humanity's understanding of its precarious security.

On the morning of October 28, six days after President Kennedy threatened to respond with "whatever action is needed" to win the removal of Soviet missiles from Cuba, Soviet Premier Nikita Khruschev announced the Soviet Union's willingness to comply. His sole condition was that the United States provide assurances that Cuba would not be invaded. Khruschev's announcement also contained, in what was for most people inaccessible diplomatic phrasing, an understanding that the United States would withdraw its nuclear-armed Jupiter missiles from Turkey after extended and face-saving negotiations.

The United States and the Soviet Union went eyeball to eyeball in their game of nuclear chicken before both sides blinked and altered course. So close did we come to nuclear war, that at the height of the confrontation President Kennedy believed the chances of war with the Soviet Union were "somewhere between one out of three and even."[6] Dean Rusk, Kennedy's secretary of state, later remarked that the missile crisis was the "moment in history when we came closest to nuclear war," apparently forgetting the atomic bombings of Hiroshima and Nagasaki.[7] These apprehensions were mirrored in the stated and silent fears of ordinary people in the United States, the Soviet Union, Cuba, Japan, and many other nations. The Cuban novelist Edmundo Desnoes put it succinctly: we feared that "It's all over."[8]

The Kennedy administration's handling of the Cuban missile crisis was immediately hailed in the United States as a great diplomatic and political victory for the president and the nation. It became essential to the myth of the Camelot presidency. The crisis had not spread to Berlin, Turkey, or Asia, as many had feared, and it was widely believed that John Kennedy and his advisors had forced the Soviets to back down without the United States making concessions.

A decade later, in the 1970s, when the Soviet Union finally achieved the rough parity in nuclear weapons that Robert McNamara (John Kennedy's and Lyndon Johnson's secretary of defense) had long predicted was inevitable, and three decades later as the graying Fidel Castro continued to defend the accomplishments of the Cuban revolution, few people reflected publicly about the madness of policy makers in 1962. The pride and prestige of the United States and its president were indeed preserved as a result of the nuclear confrontation. The victory was achieved at the risk of a thermonuclear exchange that would have killed an estimated two hundred million people in its first hour, a thousand times the death toll of Hiroshima and Nagasaki,[9] and at the cost of dangerously accelerating the nuclear arms race. By the 1980s the United States and the Soviet Union had fifty thousand nuclear warheads between them, and they shared the dubious ability of being able to bounce the rubble that would survive the first cataclysms of a global nuclear war. From the perspective of history, the reckless endangerment of hundreds of millions of lives by the "Best and Brightest" leaders of the United States, and by the Soviet and Cuban leadership, appears as thoughtless and wrong-headed as it was criminal.

In the northern hemisphere, the Cuban dimension of the missile crisis has been too easily neglected and forgotten. Many people still believe that during the Cold War all United States military planning and resources were motivated by the confrontation with the Soviet Union. The lenses created to manufacture consent to the maintenance of empire distorted our vision, and continue to do so to this day. Through these lenses, Cuba, Vietnam, and the Middle East were incidentally related locales for U.S.-Soviet confrontations, disconnected from history. Robert F. Kennedy thus wrote his memoir of the Cuban missile crisis without a single reference to the disastrous 1961 CIA-sponsored Bay of Pigs invasion of

Cuba, or to the sixty years of U.S. conquest, occupation, and abuse of the strategically located "American plantation" that preceded it.[10]

The Kennedys were, in fact, preoccupied and almost obsessed by their failure at the Bay of Pigs[11] and by Castro's growing influence in Latin America. In the spring of 1962, at the behest of the White House, Brigadier General Edward Lansdale conceived and began implementation of Operation Mongoose, a plan to invade Cuba and to overthrow Castro.

Convinced that the United States was not simply seeking to isolate his government, but to destroy it, Fidel Castro increasingly turned to Moscow for protection. Khruschev, in turn, was "sure that the Americans would never reconcile themselves to the existence of Castro's Cuba" and worried that if Moscow lost Cuba, China's influence in the Third World and communist nations would grow at Russia's expense.[12] In May 1962 Nikita Khruschev came to the conclusion that the Cuban revolution could not be defended with conventional weapons, but he was painfully aware of the Soviet Union's nuclear inferiority. Khruschev gambled that he could resolve both challenges by deploying medium-range ballistic missiles in Cuba. With one bold stroke he sought to defend the Cuban revolution and to restructure the "correlation of forces" of the global balance of power. Within weeks the leadership of the Soviet Communist Party fell in line behind him, and orders were issued for the secret deployment of the missiles and their supporting units.[13]

Seen from this perspective, the Cuban missile crisis was a tragic example of U.S. nuclear warfighting doctrine as described by Noam Chomsky. In 1962 President John Fitzgerald Kennedy, his advisers, and his lieutenants used the U.S. nuclear arsenal to intimidate those who sought to "protect people we [were] determined to attack."

A Special Historical Relationship

In the fall of 1960, former United States ambassador to Cuba Earl E.T. Smith described the twentieth-century history of U.S.-Cuban relations in less than diplomatic terms. "Until the advent of Castro, the United States was so overwhelmingly influential in Cuba...the American Ambassador was the second most important man in Cuba, sometimes even more important than the President [of Cuba]."[14] Journalist Tad Szulc was more direct. Since granting Cuba its independence in 1902, Cuba has been more of "an appendage of the United States" than a sovereign country.[15]

Long before the Spanish-American War, Manifest Destiny and geostrategic considerations turned the United States' ambitions to the fertile island ninety miles from the Florida coastline. Cuba's harbors could serve or threaten U.S. dominance of the Caribbean Sea. In 1823, Secretary of State John Quincy Adams observed that Cuba had "become an object of transcendent importance to the political and commercial interests of our union." He ventured that "it is scarcely possible to resist the conviction that the annexation of Cuba to our federal Republic will be indispensable to the continuance and integrity of the Union itself."[16]

Cuba was then a Spanish colony. Although Spanish imperialism was a depleted force, an intense political conflict stood between the ambitions of Secretary of State Adams and President James Monroe, and the annexation of Cuba. The island had more slaves per capita than any other nation in the world, and the defining and immobilizing debate within the United States was whether newly annexed territories would enter the Union as slave or free states. Northern members of Congress opposed the immediate annexation of Cuba. Partially as a result of his political need to buy time for the annexation of Cuba, President Monroe enunciated the doctrine that still bears his name. All of the Western Hemisphere lay within the United States' sphere of influence. European nations, Britain and France particularly, were placed on notice not to challenge U.S. dominance (or ambitions) in this region.[17]

Official sanction has not always been required for political penetration or symbiotic union. By 1895, when the long-suppressed Cuban revolution for independence from Spain reignited, North American businesses and banks owned Cuban sugar plantations, mines, and other resources estimated to be worth $30 million.[18] When revolution came, the Spanish crown moved with determination, brutally repressing the Cuban people, interning Cubans by the hundreds of thousands in concentration camps. There they died in staggering numbers, from torture, neglect, starvation, and disease. On the mainland the yellow press reported the most agonizing accounts of Spanish atrocities and urged support for Cuban nationalists based in New York. Instead, President Cleveland chose neutrality, an option that required Spain to continue to protect U.S. property in Cuba.[19]

In the 1890s the United States was plagued by a severe economic depression, and access and exports to the Chinese market were seen as one of the few means of reviving the United States' economy. At the same time, control over Subic Bay in the Philippines (then also a Spanish colony) was understood to be essential, as a U.S. naval base and for the refueling of commercial shipping, if economic and political concessions were to be wrung from China and then exploited.

In January 1898, in apparent response to renewed fighting across Cuba, the U.S. naval cruiser *Maine* was sent to Havana as "a visible expression of United States' concern." Within days it was sabotaged by forces whose allegiance remains a mystery. Despite the failure to identify the saboteurs, the sinking of the *Maine*, with its resulting heavy loss of U.S. lives, fueled war fever in the United States. McKinley's response was a declaration of war against Spain. The United States sought, McKinley said, "to put an end to the barbarities, bloodshed, starvation, and horrible miseries" in Cuba, to right "the very serious injury to the commerce, trade, and business of our people... [the] wanton destruction of property and devastation of the island," and the "enormous expense" caused by the ongoing turmoil. Significantly, McKinley made no reference to the Cuban nationalists who had long struggled for independence. When the guns of the Spanish-American war finally fell silent in the Caribbean and the Pacific, hundreds of thousands were dead, and the United States had conquered, occupied, and colonized Cuba, Puerto Rico, the Philippines, and Guam.

Not satisfied with simply expelling the Spanish oppressors of Cuba, U.S. occupation forces remained until 1902, when the U.S.-sponsored government in Havana accepted the Platt Amendment. This was a U.S. law that effectively precluded Cuban sovereignty and transformed the island into a U.S. economic colony and political protectorate.[20] The amendment gave the United Sates the right to "intervene for the preservation of Cuban independence, the maintenance of a government adequate for the protection of life, property, and individual liberty," and the requirement that Cuba "sell or lease to the United States the land necessary for coaling and naval stations."[21] During the next six decades, successive U.S. administrations clearly demonstrated that the "preservation of Cuban independence," the "protection of life," and "individual liberty" were something less than policy priorities of the United States.

In this way the United States' naval base at Guantánamo Bay was secured. U.S. agents gained regular access to the economic, political, and personal secrets lodged in Cuban tax, banking, and public works records. U.S. ambassadors were recommended because they were "essential to the protection of American investments in Cuba."[22] While the Platt Amendment provided the legal rationale for repeated U.S. military interventions, the ideological framework was proclaimed by Theodore Roosevelt in his 1905 corollary to the Monroe Doctrine: "wrong-doing, or an impotence which results in a general loosening of the ties of civilized society, may in America...ultimately require intervention by some civilized nation." The "civilized nation" that would right wrongs would, of course, be the United States.[23]

During "the next twenty-five years, at least five attempted revolutions were suppressed or influenced by the presence of U.S. Marines." Countless other warnings from Washington or the U.S. ambassador had similar results.[24] The last gasp of this tradition of gunboat diplomacy came in the early days of Franklin Roosevelt's administration. Washington was unwilling to tolerate the economic reforms, proposed by the government of Ramon Grau San Martin, that would restructure Cuba's debts and affect the freedom of U.S. corporations to exploit Cuban labor and resources. Grau's government was indelicately deposed through a combination of diplomatic and military maneuvers.

In the 1930s, after a century of conquest, intervention, and imperial administration, "Lake Monroe" (The Caribbean Sea) and its environs had been secured. The United States had consolidated its control over the hemisphere. Roosevelt astutely moved to soothe simmering anti-U.S. sentiments with his Good Neighbor policy, which explicitly renounced the right of any nation to intervene in the affairs of others. With U.S. economic influence, military bases, and loyal elites assiduously assembled throughout Latin America, there was less to this policy than met the eye.

In this context the Platt Amendment was finally abrogated in 1934, although the Navy's lease of Guantanamo Bay was not. With its military base, its dominant role in the Cuban economy, its loyal dictators, and its powerful ambassadors in Havana, the United States continued to exert tremendous influence over nearly all aspects of Cuban life.[25]

The last of the United States' brutal minions in Havana was the dictator Fulgencio Batista, an army sergeant who consolidated his power within the military while ruling Cuba through elected proxies. In 1936 he overthrew his former ally, President Miguel Gomez, and, with U.S. support, terrorized Cuban politics for most of the next twenty-two years. Batista was not the stereotypical Banana Republic dictator. In the Americas, he was ahead of his time, understanding "the refinements of twentieth-century totalitarianism," keeping tight reign on labor unions, the universities, and the press. His regime thus had more in common with Spanish and Italian fascism and the military dictatorships of the 1970s and 1980s. Cubans were killed, tortured, or maimed by the thousands to maintain and finance Batista's hold on power. By 1958, when he was finally overthrown by the Cuban revolution, it was estimated that his regime had murdered twenty thousand of Cuba's seven million people.[26]

Fidel Castro was never "our man in Havana." Although he and the Cuban revolutionaries were widely viewed in the United States as the democratic alternative to Batista's repression, President Eisenhower provided weapons to Batista and his army until the spring of 1958, six months before the guerrilla forces victoriously entered Havana. It was thus understandable that as Fidel Castro came to power, he was convinced that Eisenhower would attempt to turn back the clock. He warned the North Americans, "If you send Marines, thousands of them will die on the beaches."[27]

Castro's economic policies soon alienated Washington. An estimated $1 billion worth of U.S.-owned Cuban assets were nationalized, including sugar plantations, oil refineries, and tobacco, tourist, and other real estate resources. Castro launched literacy campaigns, armed the populace, drafted doctors to serve the people, and "destroyed the oligarchy and curbed the bourgeoisie."[28] Many Batista loyalists were summarily tried and publicly executed. And, on December 19, 1960, Castro formally aligned Cuba with the Sino-Soviet bloc.

Eisenhower responded by breaking diplomatic relations with Havana and imposing limited economic sanctions. In quick succession, the newly inaugurated Kennedy administration escalated the one-sided confrontation by eliminating Cuba's sugar quota (depriving Cuba of access to its most important market) and succumbed to the pressures of the CIA and the out-going administration by approving the self-defeating Bay of Pigs invasion.[29] As the blame for the failed invasion was apportioned, the President pointed to the CIA. The CIA pointed to the Joint Chiefs of Staff. And the Joint Chiefs pointed to the president, who had forbidden the aerial bombardment designed to cover the invasion.

The Kennedy Context

The poetic vision can reflect the collective unconscious and be awesome in its prescience. Thus when the celebrated poet, Robert Frost, read his inaugural poem at "the beginning hour" of the Kennedy presidency, he reflected both the young president's persona and much of the nation's expectation:

> The glory of a next Augustan age
> Of a power leading from its strength and pride
> Of young ambition eager to be tried[30]

With these words the old poet anticipated the imperial identity, the militarism, hubris, and inexperience that paved the political paths to the Cuban missile crisis and the seemingly endless war in Indochina.

Two memories of the Kennedy inauguration remain clear from my adolescence: the old white-haired poet wrestling with his papers as he battled the brilliance of the snow-reflected light, and the awesome tanks and missiles moving past me as they proceeded up Pennsylvania Avenue toward the president's reviewing stand.

John Kennedy and his young tribe of East Coast can-do academics and aristocrats marked a generational transition from the Eisenhower era, but their arrival was less than the total break with the past that was presented to the public. Kennedy had long straddled both wings of the Democratic party: liberals loyal to twice-defeated Adlai Stevenson and hard-liners still clustered around Dean Acheson, a visionary and executioner of Harry Truman's confrontational Cold War foreign policies. David Halberstam was on target in his description of Kennedy as he assumed office: "there was ... an element of the hard-liner in him, as there was to almost everyone in politics at that point...He was the epitome of the contemporary man in a cool, pragmatic age, more admiring of the old, shrewd, almost cynical Establishment breed...than of the ponderous do-good types." Kennedy admired the "guts and toughness" of the aging "Wise Men" of the Establishment, men like Acheson, John McCloy, and Averill Harriman, all of whom served in Kennedy's administration or during its travails.[31]

Kennedy's inner circle was, however, dominated by younger men who were described as pragmatic rationalists. McGeorge Bundy came from Harvard where he was dean of a government department dedicated to ultra realism. Like many in the administration, Bundy was a veteran of the Second World War, but unlike his colleagues, he was an admirer of, an apologist for, and a collaborator with Henry L. Stimson, the secretary of war who played a significant role in the decision to bomb Hiroshima and Nagasaki. Robert McNamara brought the unsettling and profitable logic of systems analysis from Ford's offices in Dearborn, Michigan, to Pentagon and Cabinet counsels. Dean Rusk, who as assistant secretary of state had negotiated fine points of the U.S.-Japan Mutual Security Treaty for the Truman administration, returned to Foggy Bottom as secretary of state. Retired General Maxwell Taylor had written the best selling book *The Distant Trumpet,* which advocated a new strategic doctrine relying more heavily on counterinsurgency ground troops reinforced by threats of limited or general nuclear war. Taylor initially joined the inner circle as military advisor to the president in the wake of the Bay of Pigs disaster and soon moved to head the Joint Chiefs of Staff.[32]

U.S.-Soviet relations in the first years of the Kennedy presidency were dominated by aggressive rivalry, fear, and miscalculation. From Washington's perspective, Nikita Khruschev's Kremlin appeared to be constantly "taunting, scheming, pushing for advantage" in Berlin, in Southeast Asia and elsewhere in the Third World, in outer space, and in the technology of nuclear terror, where the Soviets claimed to be equal, if not superior to the United States. The Soviet Union seemed to be on the offensive as it attempted to ally itself with the wretched of the earth across the Third World, and even challenged traditional U.S. primacy in Cuba and elsewhere in the Western Hemisphere.[33]

Influenced by the thinking of Henry Kissinger, Maxwell Taylor, and, to a lesser extent, the then little known Pentagon advisor Daniel Ellsberg, the Kennedy administration broke with the Eisenhower-Dulles military doctrine of massive retaliation. Briefly, this doctrine asserted that U.S. presidents would respond to any Soviet conventional (non-nuclear) or nuclear attack "against the U.S. or its allies with a massive nuclear attack."

The doctrine was designed to prevent the Soviets from initiating or assisting military actions that challenged United States dominance within its global sphere of influence. It relied on the threat of nation killing, and on "linking local conflicts to the specter of a global war of annihilation."[34]

Massive retaliation was more than an arcane military concept. Truman relied on an earlier version of this doctrine during the 1946 and 1948 crises in Iran and Berlin, and when the United States was on the defensive in Korea in 1950. Eisenhower and his secretary of state, John Foster Dulles, relied on it frequently and conveyed its lessons to the ambitious vice president, Richard Nixon. Eisenhower and Dulles prepared or threatened to use the U.S. nuclear arsenal in Korea in 1953, in Guatemala in 1954, in the Middle East in 1956 and 1958, and against China in 1958 during the conflict over the offshore islands Quemoy and Matsu. In his memoirs Eisenhower described one way that he implemented the doctrine. He

> let the Communist authorities understand that, in the absence of satisfactory progress, we intended to move decisively without inhibition in our use of weapons, and would no longer be responsible for confining hostilities to the Korean Peninsula. We would not be limited by any worldwide gentleman's agreement. In India and in the Formosa Straits area, and at the truce negotiations at Panmunjom, we dropped the word, discreetly, of our intention. We felt quite sure it would reach Soviet and Chinese Communist ears.[35]

As the Kennedy administration came to office, the massive retaliation doctrine was losing its credibility. The Soviets had been assembling their nuclear arsenal for a decade and were popularly believed to be capable of launching a retaliatory attack following a U.S. first strike attack. Politicians, the public, and strategic analysts in the United States and elsewhere questioned the proportionality and credibility of threatening first strike nuclear attacks or a thermonuclear exchange in response to every conventional threat to U.S. power. Were Guatemala, Quemoy and Matsu, or Laos worth the cataclysms of nuclear war or the pariah status that would cohere to the United States if it initiated nuclear war during any but the most dire circumstances? Nonetheless, as presidential advisor Daniel Ellsberg later wrote, President Kennedy and his successors believed "that past and current threats [to use nuclear weapons] had succeeded, this was why... they and their successors kept making such threats and buying more and more first-use and first-strike nuclear weapons systems to maintain and increase the credibility and effectiveness of threats they expected to make in the future."[36]

Kennedy's response to the critique of maximum deterrence was Maxwell Taylor's concept of flexible response. This was a synthesis of Henry Kissinger's advocacy of threatening, and, if necessary, fighting, limited nuclear wars, with calls for increased reliance on counterinsurgency and ground forces. Kennedy's cutting edge weapons system was the Green Beret, an infantryman, reinforced by the theory of escalation dominance and a diversified nuclear arsenal that made it theoretically possible to trump the Soviets (or any other enemy) at every step in the ladder of military escalation.

Flexible response assumed that the leaders of the Soviet Union, and other potential adversaries, were ultimately rational. Instead of opting for suicide, they would, the doctrine asserted, back away from confrontations with the United States, leaving the field open to conventional U.S. ground forces. But, should the system be tested, "John Kennedy…was still willing to face the ultimate risk of nuclear war…He neither shrank from that risk nor rushed out to embrace it."[37]

During the 1960 election campaign, the centerpiece of Kennedy's strategy had been the charge that the Republicans had allowed the United States to fall behind Russia in the nuclear arms race. By the time he assumed office, many were convinced that the United States was vulnerable to the "missile gap" that had opened between the Soviets and the United States. This was not what Secretary of Defense McNamara and U.S. intelligence found upon further investigation. There was a gap, but not the imaginary one that Kennedy had propounded. Deputy Secretary of Defense Roswell Gilpatric publicly described the real missile gap in October 1961: the United States "has a nuclear retaliatory force of such lethal power than an enemy move which brought it into play would be an act of self-destruction."[38] The Soviets were estimated to have "fewer than fifty" intercontinental ballistic missiles (ICBMs).[39] The United States had 185 ICBMs and more than 3,400 deliverable nuclear bombs. According to a 1961 National Intelligence Estimate, "fewer than fifty" Soviet ICBMs were, in fact, four.[40]

A year after assuming office, Secretary of Defense McNamara revised the Single Integrated Operational Plan for nuclear war. U.S. nuclear weapons were targeted against "Soviet missiles, bomber bases, submarine tenders, air defenses…and control systems." In accordance with the doctrine of flexible response, McNamara was accepting the principles that nuclear weapons could be used in a limited nuclear war and that "the United States must be in a position to bring the war to a conclusion on terms favorable to Washington."[41]

With the strength, energy, and limited experience of younger men, Kennedy and many of his advisers were unaware of the deep fears that their rhetoric and activism engendered in Moscow. In spite of his recent diplomatic successes, Nikita Khruschev knew the weaknesses and limits of Soviet military power. He watched anxiously as the new administration accelerated its production of nuclear warheads and missiles. He could not ignore Kennedy's warning that the Soviet Union "should not rule out the possibility of a U.S. first strike" nuclear attack, and he deeply resented U.S. encirclement of the Soviet Union with nuclear weapons aboard Jupiter missiles in Turkey and Italy and Polaris submarines at sea. After the Bay of Pigs, Khruschev remained sure the U.S. would remain unreconciled to Castro's Cuba, receiving regular reports about Operation Mongoose, a Pentagon plan to overthrow his Cuban ally.[42]

Though powerful, the leadership of the United States was insecure and inflexible. Roy Medvedev, the dissident Soviet historian, was particularly perceptive about the the temper of those times:

> the abortive coup in Cuba [Bay of Pigs] coincided with the defeat of pro-American, right-wing forces in Laos...The pro-American Government of Ngo Din Diem was also finding it difficult to retain power in South Vietnam. Among Washington's ruling circles these indignities abraded a certain sensitivity, particularly in view of recent reversals in Middle East and Africa. American politicians were unaccustomed to such setbacks and were prepared neither to retreat nor to reconcile themselves to the prospect of a reduction of their influence over international politics.[43]

At the June 1961 superpower summit in Vienna, Khruschev judged Kennedy to be insufficiently bold, "an inexperienced young leader" who could be bullied, intimidated, and blackmailed.[44] He assumed, too, that Washington "had learned some lessons from [its] defeat" at the Bay of Pigs and "wouldn't refuse a chance to repeat their aggression."[45] The stage was thus set for further contention in Berlin and confrontation in Cuba.

More needs to be said about the Kennedy administration's obsession with Cuba. While the Kennedys continued to view Castro as "a reminder of deep humiliation and a target for revenge,"[46] it was Castro's commitment to free the nations of Latin America from United States influence that drove U.S. policy. Having removed Cuba from the U.S. imperial domain, Castro and his comrades sought to liberate other Latin American nations as well. Speaking in Havana on February 4, 1962, Castro "virtually declared war" on the American order in what later became known as the Second Declaration of Havana. He condemned the price of U.S. imperialism in the region, the "unending torrent of money flow[ing] from Latin America to the United States: some $4,000 per minute, $5 million per day...A thousand dollars per corpse." He declared "It is the duty of every revolutionary to make the revolution."[47] Two weeks later, Brigadier General Edward Lansdale presented his six-phase proposal for the U.S. destabilization and overthrow of the Cuban government.

The Kennedy administration was less concerned about Castro in impoverished Cuba than it was about the possibility of a rebellious Latin

America, then an important source of copper, oil, bananas, tungsten, and tin for the United States. Even before his inauguration, when he first called for an "Alliance for Progress" with Latin America, Kennedy conceived a campaign patterned after Roosevelt's Good Neighbor Policy, designed to serve as a political, economic, social, and military alternative to Castro's vision of people overcoming hunger through revolutionary communism. The design and proclamation of the alliance were slow in coming, partially owing to the fallout from the Bay of Pigs fiasco, but primarily because of the difficulties of crafting a credible proposal. The challenge was to conceive a program that would be seen as addressing "a life expectancy less than two-thirds of our own, a lack of schools and sanitation and trained personnel, runaway inflation in some areas, shocking slums in the cities, squalor in the countryside, and a highly suspicious attitude toward American investments." When it was launched at a special meeting of the Inter-American Economic and Social Council in Punta del Este, Uruguay, in August 1961, the United States promised $20 billion over the next decades if Latin American governments took "necessary internal measures." The proposal called for a 2.5 percent increase in the per capita incomes of Latin American nations, an end to illiteracy, increased availability of low-cost housing, price stabilization, potable drinking water, control of communicable diseases, and an increase in life expectancy.[48]

"Reality," as Kennedy biographer Theodore Sorensen later reflected, "did not match the rhetoric which flowed about the alliance on both sides of the Rio Grande." Kennedy's commitment to the program and to democratic governments in the hemisphere was limited. Like their predecessors, "the president and his advisers were less consistent... in their attitude toward military takeovers. Kennedy deplored the arrest of fellow presidents with whom he had visited, [and] the suspension of civilian rule," because they were self-defeating. Kennedy believed, however, that in many countries "the military often represented more competence in administration and more sympathy with the U.S. than any other group."[49] These attitudes were understood through much of Latin America. As one official at the Punta del Este council meeting said, "the United States is trying to stop Castro, nothing more. That it may do; money and guns can stop a man. But it will never stop Castroism."

While the State Department and the Agency for International Development offered carrots to Latin America, the Pentagon prepared sticks for Cuba. In the summer and early autumn of 1961 the Joint Chiefs initiated planning for a blockade and full-scale invasion of Cuba. In November the planning group was informed by Robert Kennedy that "higher authority wanted higher priority for Cuba." In late February 1962

Brigadier General Lansdale presented his plan for Operation Mongoose in "keeping with the spirit of Presidential memorandum of 30 November 1961."

By March, U.S. agents were to start moving into Cuba. Between April and July "operations inside Cuba for revolution" were to begin, while "political, economic, and military-type support" were provided from the United States. On August 1, the planning group was to receive authorization for future operations, to be followed immediately by guerrilla attacks within Cuba. A revolt, supported by substantial U.S. military force, was scheduled to begin two months later, in October. The revolt and invasion were to be followed by the establishment of a new Cuban government.[50]

The attitude in the Pentagon was that if the Soviets "picked up rumblings of these plans...So much the better." No effort was made to hide an Operation Mongoose military exercise in April that mobilized 40,000 marines and sailors from North Carolina to the Caribbean. The goal of this practice invasion was to unseat the mythical dictator "Ortsac" (Castro spelled backwards) and it culminated with an amphibious assault of Vieques, a Puerto Rican island.

Robert McNamara and McGeorge Bundy have since conceded that if they "had been in Moscow or Havana at that time, [they] would have believed the Americans were preparing for an invasion." They have argued, however, that despite Kennedy's decision in March 1962 to "respond promptly with military force to aid" the planned Cuban revolt, the purpose of Operation Mongoose was "not...stronger action but a substitute for it." Others close to the planning disagree. Pierre Salinger, Kennedy's press spokesman, for example, has been clear that the aim of Operation Mongoose "was to destabilize Cuba and bring down the Castro regime before October 20, 1962...Operation Mongoose brought together all the elements needed for a military overthrow of the Castro regime."[51]

Some essential elements, however, were lacking. Most critical was the inability of the agents Lansdale placed in Cuba to find popular support for a revolt, which later could be reinforced by the planned U.S. invasion. The operation bogged down and fell hopelessly behind schedule.

The operation's weaknesses were less visible from the outside than were its military mobilizations. When Khruschev traveled to Bulgaria in the spring of 1962, he had more on his mind than Eastern Europe. "[O]ne thought kept hammering away at my brain: what will happen if we lose Cuba?...We had to establish a tangible and effective deterrent to American interference in the Caribbean... The logical answer was missiles. The United States had already surrounded the Soviet Union with its own bomber bases and missiles." As General Anatoli I. Gribkov, who coordinated the unprecedented secret deployment of Soviet missiles and war materials to Cuba, recalled later, "Although Khruschev worried a great deal that the ratio of strategic weapons—300 on the Soviet side to 5,000 in the United States' arsenal—was heavily against the Soviet Union...his main purpose...[was] to help the young Cuban Republic defend the freedom it had won, to deter the U.S. aggression actively being planned against it." Castro's fear of the anticipated U.S. invasion led him to accept Khruschev's proposal for the secret deployment of the missiles, and a confidential agreement was reached in June.[52]

The Popular History

The popular lore of the Cuban missile crisis developed in the United States through President Kennedy's televised statements and uncritical press coverage at the time. Robert Kennedy's best selling memoir, *Thirteen Days*, a carefully researched and popular history of the crisis written by NBC's Elie Abel in 1966, the memoirs of trusted Kennedy associates, particularly Theodore Sorensen and Arthur M. Schlessinger Jr., and Nikita Khruschev's memoirs, rounded out the official history.

As Robert Kennedy portrayed it, "neither side wanted war over Cuba...but it was possible that either side could take a step that, for reasons of 'security' or 'pride' or 'face', would require a response by the other side...and eventually an escalation into armed conflict."[53] The scholars Richard E. Neustadt and Graham T. Allison precisely described, and reinforced, the popular perception in their afterword to Robert Kennedy's book: "Robert Kennedy...like McNamara...was haunted by the prospect of nuclear doom. Was Khruschev going to force the President into an insane act?"[54] The popular belief is that U.S. leaders are beneficent. If the United States precipitated a nuclear war, it could be only the Kremlin's responsibility.

With the exception of Khruschev's memoirs, the popular history paints a picture of a confrontation between two great powers with similarly destructive nuclear arsenals. For the most part, the Russians are depicted as being dangerously reckless, willing to force the U.S. president to take insane action. The Kennedy administration and its advisers are described as careful, deliberate, and courageous. The Soviets are presented as seeking to offset a slight nuclear inferiority, or perhaps even attempting to achieve superiority, through their outrageous deployment of missiles to Cuba. This version of events presents Fidel Castro as accepting the missile deployments because of his commitment to international communism, led by the Soviet Union.

Despite the president's tortured prose about a special historical relationship, from the popular perspective the missile crisis stood outside of history, having no relation to the legacy of U.S. intervention in Cuba or the rest of Latin America. The popular view of the crisis was a- or antihistorical, like so much of U.S. politics and culture. Nikita Khruschev's and Walter Lippman's highly publicized proposals made at the height of the crisis that the United States withdraw its Jupiter missiles from Turkey in exchange for the removal of Soviet missiles from Cuba, have never reframed popular understanding of the nuclear crisis.

The popular lore of the crisis has been concisely summarized by Neustadt and Allison:

September 6, 1962. Four months after Khruschev's decision, the Soviet Union lands nuclear capable missiles in Cuba.

October 14. A U-2 reconnaissance aircraft flying over Cuba photographs the missiles, beginning what U.S. policy-makers experience as a thirteen-day crisis.

October 22. President Kennedy initiates the public confrontation with his televised speech, during which he announces the presence of the Soviet missiles, demands their withdrawal, declares the military "quarantine" of Cuba, and places U.S. military forces on alert. Nikita Khruschev responds by placing Soviet forces on alert and threatening to "sink U.S. ships if they interfere with Soviet ships en route to Cuba."

October 24. At the climax of one of the two most harrowing periods of the confrontation, Soviet ships bound for Cuba stop short of the quarantine line, with some returning to the Soviet Union.

October 26. Nikita Khruschev sends President Kennedy a rambling, existential, threatening letter, proposing the withdrawal of Soviet missiles from Cuba in exchange for a U.S. pledge not to invade Cuba. This is followed the next morning, October 27, by a tougher letter demanding U.S. missiles in Turkey also be withdrawn.

October 27. President Kennedy indicates his willingness to accept Khruschev's offer to trade the Cuban missiles for a no-invasion pledge, and warns that if the withdrawal of the Soviet missiles does not begin the following day, a U.S. air strike or invasion would be launched on Monday or Tuesday, the twenty-nineth or thirtieth.

October 28. The confrontation climaxes when the Kremlin announces its missiles in Cuba will be withdrawn.[55]

Despite its limitations, there is much that is revealing and terrifying, if little remarked, in the official history. To begin with, while the freewheeling debate within Excom (the Executive Committee of the National Security Council)[56] has been praised for providing options and fluidity during the crisis, the division of Kennedy's advisors into roughly two camps has rarely been discussed. The majority, led by Robert Kennedy and Robert McNamara, believed that the Soviet leaders were rational and would back down in the face of the United States' theoretical ability to exercise escalation dominance, trumping the Soviets with overwhelming military force at every step up the ladder of escalation. They did fear, however, that for reasons of "prestige and power... neither side [w]ould withdraw without resort to nuclear weapons."[57]

One of the more likely escalation scenarios was described by Robert Kennedy: "If we carried out an air strike against Cuba and the Soviet Union answered by attacking ... Turkey, all NATO was going to be involved. Then...the president would have to decide whether he would use nuclear weapons against the Soviet Union, and all mankind would be threatened."[58] Similar scenarios began with fighting at sea following the sinking of a Soviet freighter or naval vessel attempting to break the U.S. blockade.

The escalation feared by Robert Kennedy assumed that Khruschev might have been unwilling or unable to withdraw Soviet missiles from Cuba following the President's October 27 warnings. With little political room of his own in which to maneuver, President Kennedy would then have approved air strikes against Soviet missiles, nuclear weapons bunkers, and Ilyushin bombers in Cuba. In response to the public humiliation of devastating U.S. air strikes against Soviet forces in Cuba, Khruschev would then have ordered the destruction of U.S. missile bases in Turkey. That, in turn, would have triggered U.S. and NATO attacks on the bases from which the Soviet attacks against Turkey were launched. Finally, fearing additional U.S. attacks and driven by the logic of "use them or lose them," Soviet leaders might have launched what remained of their nuclear arsenal against U.S. and European cities. The United States would have retaliated with its intercontinental ballistic missiles.[59]

The second, and less influential, camp within the Kennedy administration was dogmatic in its belief that the Soviets would respond rationally to the imbalance of forces and would play by the rules of game theory. This group, led by former Secretary of State Dean Acheson and Treasury Secretary Dillon, believed that the United States strategic and tactical military advantage was so overwhelming that if there was a risk, "it lasted only until our destroyers, troops and aircraft were deployed in the Atlantic and Florida." This explains Acheson's reflection that, "So long as we had the thumbscrew on Khruschev, we should have given it another turn every day." The values and commitments of this group were similar to the Joint Chiefs of Staff, one of whose members, General Curtis LeMay, told the President that "there would be no reaction from Moscow to a U.S. invasion."[60] General William Y. Smith, then on Maxwell Taylor's staff, later wrote that throughout the crisis the Joint Chiefs were "consistent and united in recommending the use of overwhelming military power against the Soviet and Cuban military on the island."[61]

Khruschev's memoirs confirm the obvious. With the attempt to deploy nuclear weapons in Cuba, the Soviet Union joined the United States in the criminal practice of nuclear extortion and atomic diplomacy. From his point of view, "the Americans would think twice before trying to liquidate our [Cuban] installations by military means…If a quarter or even a tenth of our missiles survived—even if only one or two big ones were left—we could still hit New York… an awful lot of people would be wiped out." He was giving the United States "a little bit of their own medicine."[62]

The Kennedy administration's response reflected its deep concerns about the domestic political implications of the Soviet action, and a commitment to maintain what nuclear superiority was possible. Throughout the crisis, the White House displayed its reliance on flexible response and escalation dominance. Committed to maintaining its image of power and prestige, it risked catastrophic nuclear war to preserve that image. At the height of the crisis, President Kennedy instructed Adlai Stevenson, the U.S. ambassador to the United Nations, that "the United Sates would not be shaken in its determination to get the missiles out of Cuba. There was to be no wobbling. The time had come to turn the screw."[63] The President's letter to Khruschev on the night of October 27 concluded with an ultimatum from which it would have been difficult to back down.

Perceptions, Prestige, and Escalation Dominance

The reflexive responses of Kennedy's advisors, and the divisions among them were manifest from the beginning, when they were shown the reconnaissance photos confirming Soviet construction of missile bases in Cuba. Seeing Cuba as "a pistol aimed at the Western Hemisphere," the initial consensus was that "an air strike against the missile sites could be the only course."[64]

After initially recommending a surprise attack against the missile sites, upon reflection Excom considered six options:

1) no action,

2) political and diplomatic pressure against the Soviets, including the possibility of linking withdrawal of U.S. missiles from Turkey to withdrawal of Soviet missiles from Cuba,

3) secret negotiations with Fidel Castro to sever his alliance with Moscow,

4) various kinds of blockades, or a naval "quarantine,"

5) air strikes against the missile sites and other military targets in Cuba,

6) an invasion of Cuba through which the U.S. would "take Cuba away from Castro."[65]

Before he became one of the leading advocates for a naval "quarantine" of military equipment bound for Cuba, Secretary of Defense McNamara won the general agreement of Excom that the Soviet missiles in Cuba would not significantly alter the global imbalance of power or increase "the potential megatonnage capable of being unleashed on American soil." The deployments reduced the warning time of a Soviet attack by several minutes, but it was not thought that this would seriously limit the ability of the United States to retaliate with a nation-killing second strike nuclear attack. From McNamara's perspective "the missiles...represented an inevitable occurrence: narrowing the missile gap between the United States and the U.S.S.R. It simply happened sooner rather than later." McNamara initially believed that it little mattered whether the United States had seventeen times more or fewer nuclear weapons than the Soviet Union. Either way the number of American casualties would be unacceptable.[66]

Ironically, it was Adlai Stevenson who moved McNamara and the balance of opinion within Excom toward a military response. The potential political impact of the deployment, not the military or existential implications, concerned Stevenson. "No politician," Stevenson argued, "could have missed the significance of Russian missiles in Cuba. We just had to get them out of there. This was the first time that the Latin Americans were also directly involved or threatened."[67] As Theodore Sorensen later recalled, the Soviet nuclear weapons in Cuba could not be tolerated "if our commitments [were] ever to be believed by either allies or adversaries."[68]

McNamara's rationalism wilted under the weight of these arguments. He conceded that the "political effect in Latin America and elsewhere would be large." The President concurred because he "was less concerned about the missiles' military implications than with their effect on the global balance...it represented a provocative change in the ...status quo. Missiles on Soviet territory or submarines were very different from missiles in the Western Hemisphere, particularly in their political and psychological effect on Latin America."[69]

Excom narrowed U.S. options to two: blockading Cuba or bombing the missile sites before their construction was complete (with the possibility of following the attack with an invasion to overthrow Castro). McNamara, joined by Robert Kennedy and George Ball, argued that a blockade was a form of "limited pressure, which could be increased as the circumstances warranted." The president could move up the ladder of escalation to air strikes, invasion, and, in a worst case scenario, war with the Soviet Union.[70]

Dean Acheson, Maxwell Taylor, and Paul Nitze argued for air strikes. They thought a blockade could not guarantee that the missiles would be withdrawn. Air attacks, they argued, would focus the confrontation on Castro and Cuba. A blockade could also lead to Soviet reciprocation in West Berlin and horizontal escalation of the crisis.[71] Challenging Robert Kennedy's doubt that air strikes could be entirely successful and his hesitancy to emulate Tojo's surprise attack against Pearl Harbor, Acheson hammered away with the Monroe Doctrine, which "made clear to all the world that the United States would not tolerate the intrusion of any European power into the Americas." The president, Acheson argued, had warned Moscow that the United States would be forced to act if they installed offensive weapons in Cuba, and Congress had publicly authorized the president to prevent such deployments "by whatever means may be necessary, including the use of arms."[72]

Initially the advocates of blockade, renamed "quarantine" to avoid a formal act of war, prevailed. They did so only because a blockade did not preclude the possibility of escalation. Within days, U.S. nuclear forces were placed on alert. Preparations for 2,000 aerial bombing sorties against Cuba were completed; 250,000 troops were mobilized for an invasion of Cuba, and the overseers of Operation Mongoose were ordered to "create a political office to plan for a post-Castro Cuban government." On the night of October 27, when Robert Kennedy met with Soviet Ambassador Dobrynin, he was clear that "We had to have a commitment by tomorrow that those bases would be removed...if they did not remove those bases, we would remove them."[73]

The Discriminatory Principle of Nuclear Inequality

From the beginning of the confrontation, Nikita Khruschev was preoccupied by the fact that the "United States had already surrounded the Soviet Union with its own bomber bases and missiles...American missiles were aimed against us in Turkey and Italy, to say nothing of West Germany."[74] Unknown to the U.S. public, considerable debate within Excom focused on these obsolete missiles and on maintaining the discriminatory principle that the United States could base nuclear missiles on the Soviet Union's borders, but that the Soviet Union could not reciprocate. At the height of the confrontation, nearly all the members of Excom preferred risking nuclear war to compromising this principle.[75]

The possibility of swapping the withdrawal of missiles in Turkey and Cuba was first raised by Adlai Stevenson on October 20, five days into the crisis. Unknown to most Excom members, prior to the crisis the President had twice issued instructions that the Jupiter missiles in Turkey be removed. They were "unreliable, inaccurate, obsolete, and too easily sabotaged." The Turkish government had objected to the withdrawal, and the President's instructions were subsequently lost in the diplomatic morass. The Joint Congressional Committee on Atomic Energy had recently revived the issue by recommending the removal of Jupiter and Thor rockets based in Turkey and Italy.[76] Despite this history, the president responded to Stevenson's recommendation with a blunt rejection. He would not withdraw the missiles in response to a Soviet threat.

Five days later debate over the fate of the Jupiter missiles in Turkey moved far beyond the secret councils of the White House. Walter Lippman, the dean of liberal journalists, opened the day with a politically explosive proposal in the *Washington Post*, which was read by President Kennedy and Soviet Ambassador Dobrynin.

As the United States and the Soviet Union approached the brink of nuclear war, Lippman advised that the President should seek a "face-saving agreement." Lippman was clear that he was not advocating a "'Cuba-Berlin' horse trade," because the two were not analogous. "The only place that is truly comparable with Cuba," he wrote, "is Turkey. This is the only place where there are strategic weapons right on the frontier of the Soviet Union." Lippman went on to describe a second similarity between the military bases in Cuba and Turkey. Both were "of little military value."

There was little focused discussion about Lippman's proposal in the White House or elsewhere in the media that day. Attention was focused on the first, uneventful interception of a Soviet ship within the "quarantine" zone.[77]

Two days later, as the Soviets were completing construction of their Cuban missile bases and as pressure in the White House and Congress mounted for an immediate invasion of Cuba, the fate of the missiles in Turkey moved to the center of the crisis. The Kremlin's tough and formal letter to President Kennedy on October 27, broadcast internationally, declared that the Jupiter missiles would have to be withdrawn from Turkey if the crisis was to be resolved peacefully. The Soviet leaders wrote:

> You are worried over Cuba. You say that it worries you because it lies at a distance of 90 miles across the sea from the shores of the United States. However, Turkey lies next to us. Our sentinels are pacing up and down and watching each other. Do you believe that you have the right to demand security for your country, and the removal of such weapons that you qualify as offensive, while not recognizing this right for us?[78]

Robert Kennedy later recalled that, "the proposal the Russians made was not unreasonable and did not amount to a loss to the U.S. or to our NATO allies." It was simply unacceptable. The proposal left the President feeling vulnerable, troubled, and angry. He continued to resist withdrawing the missiles from Turkey under Soviet threat, but at the same time "he did not want to involve the U.S. and mankind in a catastrophic war over missile sites in Turkey that were antiquated." Nonetheless, as Excom deliberated throughout the day, President Kennedy communicated his inclination to attack Cuba the following Monday or Tuesday.[79]

Within Excom, former Ambassador Thompson warned that the Soviet proposal "had a glittering symmetry," but that accepting it would be seen as proof of Washington's weakness. Rusk and Bundy agreed that despite the Jupiter's negligible military value, "If we appear to be trading the defense of Turkey for the threat in Cuba," the NATO alliance, and thus the global power of the United States, would be severely undermined. Robert McNamara and Douglas Dillon agreed that the missiles should not be withdrawn to reach a settlement. They advocated rendering the Turkish missiles inoperable as soon as it was decided to attack Cuba in order to minimize the possibility that the invasion would precipitate escalation to nuclear war.[80]

That Excom meeting ended with the shared belief that on the following day the President would probably order air strikes and an invasion of Cuba. Even as he feared that he might not live to see another Saturday, Robert McNamara reminded Robert Kennedy that they needed to organize a government for Cuba and to make plans to respond to the Soviet Union in Europe. Someone even joked that Bobby Kennedy should be appointed mayor of Havana.[81]

The members of Excom did agree to a last effort to avoid war, accepting a formula never formally proposed by the Soviet leadership. In a letter to Khruschev, the president agreed that if the Soviet Union would withdraw its missiles under United Nations supervision and pledge not to repeat the deployment of missiles to Cuba, the United States would "give assurances against an invasion of Cuba." The president made oblique reference to the Jupiter missiles. The withdrawal of Soviet missiles from Cuba, the president wrote, "would enable us to work toward a more general arrangement regarding 'other armaments' as proposed in your second letter, which you made public." Soviet failure to accept this proposal, Kennedy continued, "would surely lead to an intensification of the Cuban crisis and a grave risk to the peace of the world."[82]

Robert Kennedy was dispatched to meet with Ambassador Dobrynin to ensure that the Russians fully understood this proposal and that time was running out. When the attorney general returned to the White House later that night, the president ordered twenty-four Air Force Reserve troop-carrier squadrons to active duty. They would be needed for an invasion.

The Kremlin proved to be less willing to gamble with the lives of hundreds of millions of people than were the U.S. president and his advisers. The following morning Khruschev and the Kremlin blinked a second time. They "rationally" agreed to the humiliation of publicly withdrawing their missiles from Cuba in exchange for U.S. guarantees that Cuba would not be attacked and the anticipated "thoughtful appraisal of the international situation."[83]

Other Truths

Because the structures of power changed with the end of the Cold War, so too did the structures and content of knowledge. One manifestation of these changes was the Cuban Missile Crisis Project, which organized five conferences. These conferences, and related media events between 1987 and 1992, drew on Soviet and Cuban policy-makers of the Cuban missile crisis era and scholars of the crisis to discuss personal memories and official documents that might otherwise have remained secret. The project confirmed the details of much of the official history, and revealed that the dangers of escalation to nuclear war were far greater than most people understood at the time, including policy-makers.

Possibly the most surprising revelations were made by General Anatoli I. Gribkov at the 1992 Havana conference. Gribkov was the man responsible for coordinating the dispatch of Soviet missiles, troops, and other war materials to Cuba. His testimony shocked his audience in Havana, some to disbelief. According to Gribkov, the Soviet arsenal in Cuba included tactical (battlefield) nuclear weapons, which were to be used to repel a U.S. invasion of Cuba. Additionally, General Pliyev, the commander of Soviet forces in Cuba, was initially given the authority to use these tactical nuclear weapons without additional clearance from Moscow. [84]

According to Gribkov, only half of the R-12 medium-range ballistic missiles (MRBMs) deployed to Cuba were ready to be fueled (an eighteen-hour process) in the last days of the confrontation, and none of them had been targeted. None of the longer range M-14 MRBMs had reached this stage of readiness. Twelve Luna rockets and eighty FKR cruise missiles were, however "in place and targeted on likely beachheads and ocean approaches" of a U.S. invasion.[85]

Gribkov revealed that in July 1962, as Pliyev prepared to leave for Cuba, in the presence of Soviet Defense Minister Malinovksy, Nikita Khrushev "had personally given General Issa Pliyev, commander of the Soviet Group of Forces on Cuba, authority to use his battlefield weapons and their atomic charges if, in the heat of combat, he could not contact Moscow." Pliyev's authority to launch nuclear weapons without additional authorization from Moscow did not extend to the intermediate range missiles that could reach the U.S. mainland. General Gribkov carried a reconfirmation of these orders to Pliyev when he joined the Soviet forces in Cuba in early October.

Once war became an imminent possibility on October 22, Pliyev's orders were revised. He was ordered to "take immediate steps to raise combat readiness and to repulse the enemy together with the Cuban Army and with all the power of the Soviet forces, except for the MRBM's that could reach the United States and all of the Luna rockets, cruise missiles, four atomic mines and atomic bombs for the Ilyushin 28s." With the danger of war no longer only a theoretical possibility, Soviet leaders acted to lower the risk of nuclear war.[86]

The revision of Pliyev's orders did not remove the possibility that Soviet troops in Cuba would use their tactical nuclear weapons in the case of a U.S. invasion of Cuba (the invasion which Kennedy signaled was a distinct possibility in his October 27 letter to Khruschev). Gribkov believes that U.S. air strikes would have destroyed all the MRBM sites in Cuba and all the Ilyushin bombers. They would, he wrote, "have cut the Soviet and Cuban defense forces to pieces, disrupting communications on the island and severing contact with Moscow." He is less certain that the storage sites for the tactical nuclear weapons' warheads would have been found and destroyed. Because they were inspired by the spirit of the Cuban revolution and had orders to "fight independently...until the enemy was completely destroyed," Gribkov believes that "a desperate group of Soviet defenders, with or without orders from above [might] have been able to arm and fire" a Luna warhead or a more powerful cruise missile. "If such a rocket had hit U.S. troops or ships," Gribkov asked, "would it have been the last shot of the Cuban crisis or the first of a global nuclear war?"[87]

The Soviet decision to deploy tactical nuclear weapons in numbers that were "too few to assure the defeat of a full-scale American invasion," but sufficient to ignite escalation to a full-scale nuclear cataclysm, was so dangerous and irrational that some initially doubted Gribkov's testimony. The same was true of his description of Khruschev's delegation of authority to Pliyev. These claims have never been denied by a knowledgeable Soviet leader.[88]

The Cuban contribution to the intensity of the crisis and to Nikita Khruschev's decision to withdraw the missiles was also elaborated at the 1992 Havana conference. On October 27, as the crisis was intensifying, Cuban antiaircraft batteries were ordered to fire on U.S. reconnaissance planes. When the Cuban batteries began to fire, Soviet officers thought "combat had begun and that the previous restraints on Soviet forces had been superseded." Soviet gunners launched the surface-to-air missile that destroyed a U-2 spy plane and killed its pilot. Excom learned of this incident while it was still absorbing the shock of Moscow's new demand that U.S. missiles in Turkey be withdrawn. The initial response of most Excom members to the loss of the U-2 was that the United States had no option except launching air attacks against Cuba. President Kennedy wisely and skillfully sidestepped this pressure.[89]

More disturbing was the 1992 confirmation that Fidel Castro pressed Nikita Khruschev to launch a preemptive nuclear attack against the United States in the event of a U.S. invasion of Cuba. Castro approached the subject this way:

> We started from the assumption that if there was an invasion of Cuba, nuclear war would erupt. We were certain of that...Everybody here was simply resigned to the fate that we would be forced to pay the price, that we would disappear... Before having the country occupied—totally occupied—we were ready to die in the defense of our country. I would have agreed, in the event of invasion...with the use of tactical nuclear weapons...I wish we had had the tactical nuclear weapons. It would have been wonderful."[90]

In his memoirs, dictated after being toppled from power, Khruschev recorded what Castro's letter of October 26 advised:

> Aggression is almost imminent within the next twenty-four or seventy-two hours...If...the imperialists invade Cuba with the goal of occupying it, the danger that that aggressive policy poses for humanity is so great that following that event, the Soviet Union must never allow the circumstances in which the imperialists could launch the first strike against it...the imperialists' aggressiveness is extremely dangerous and if they actually carry out the brutal act of invading Cuba in violation of international law and morality, that would be the moment to eliminate such danger forever through an act of clear and legitimate defense, however harsh and terrible the solution would be, for there is no other.[91]

This helps to explain Oleg Troyanovsky's account of Khruschev's decision to end the confrontation. Troyanovsky, who played a key role in drafting Khruschev's letters to Kennedy during the crisis, reported at the Havana conference that Khruschev was told President Kennedy planned to address the U.S. public on October 28. "Everyone agreed that Kennedy intended to declare war, to launch an attack...Khruschev hurriedly drafted a message to Kennedy agreeing to withdraw Soviet missiles from Cuba. He did so without informing or consulting Fidel, and thus solved his own predicament without regard for Castro's."[92]

The third deeply disturbing revelation to emerge from the Cuban Missile Crisis Project came earlier. In 1987 Raymond Garthoff, a special assistant in the State Department during the Kennedy administration, reported something that "even Excom didn't know at the time." It had long been known that President Kennedy placed U.S. nuclear forces on a Defense Contingency (DEFCON) 3 alert prior to his October 22 speech. (The normal level of readiness is DEFCON 5.) On the night of October 24, the commander of the Strategic Air Command, General Thomas Power "sent out the 'DEFCON 2' alert instructions to all SAC units...*in the clear*, without authorization, just so the Soviets could pick it up... General Power had simply taken it upon himself to rub the Soviets' noses in their nuclear inferiority."[93]

October 24 was the day Soviet ships stopped dead in the water moments before sailing into the "quarantine" zone. With a military confrontation at sea at least postponed, President Kennedy had stressed to Secretary of Defense McNamara the importance of giving Kremlin leaders time and political space to think. The last thing he wanted was an unauthorized shot or unanticipated incident. With the Pentagon too calm to be trusted, McNamara had focused his attention on the Navy, not the Strategic Command.

Nor was General Power's unauthorized nuclear threat an isolated incident. In 1987 Robert McNamara recalled: "No matter how hard you tried, no matter how much rationality you tried to inject into the process, it just never turned out the way you anticipated."[94] This led him to craft "McNamara's Law" which he believed was as applicable to the war in Vietnam and conflicts in the Middle East as it was to the Cuban missile crisis: "It is impossible to predict with a high degree of certainty the consequences of the use of military force because of the risk of accident, miscalculation, inadvertence and loss of control."[95] He had learned his "law" from at least two incidents revealed prior to the Missile Project conferences.

The first has been recounted by both McNamara and his then deputy, Roswell Gilpatric. On the night of October 24, after President Kennedy had stressed the need to make certain that there was no shooting, McNamara became concerned that he was "not being well informed." He and Gilpatric went unannounced to the Flag Plot, the Navy's command center in the Pentagon that was a "naval sanctuary traditionally respected by the civilian command structure" (i.e., off-limits to civilians, including the secretary of defense). The two civilian officials crossed the threshold and questioned the duty officer before Admiral Anderson, the Navy's chief of staff, appeared and diverted McNamara's attention.[96]

McNamara had noticed a marker that indicated "a U.S. ship off in the ocean by itself, far from the quarantine line." He asked Anderson the significance of the marker, and was told that the marker indicated a U.S. ship monitoring a Soviet submarine. McNamara's questions became an interrogation of the Navy chief of staff. What was the U.S. ship doing there?

Was there a chance of a confrontation between the two ships? What were the ship commander's orders in the case that there was an engagement? Anderson's reply was near insubordination: the "Navy knew all there was to know about running a blockade since the days of John Paul Jones." McNamara's interrogation then became a lecture: "the object was not to shoot anybody but to communicate a political message to Khruschev. The operation must be run to avoid humiliating the Russians, if at all possible, otherwise Khruschev might start a war." Gilpatric marked the exchange as a turning point within the Pentagon. "From that point on they were submitting, asking approvals."[97]

After the missile crisis, but before he was banished from the Pentagon to Lisbon, where he served as U.S. ambassador to Portugal, Admiral Anderson more accurately described the meaning of the marker that aroused McNamara's curiosity. "The presence of many Russian submarines in the Caribbean and Atlantic waters," the admiral reported, "provided perhaps the finest opportunity since World War II for U.S. Naval anti-submarine warfare to exercise their trade, to perfect their skills and to manifest their capability to detect and follow submarines of another nation." During the crisis, six Soviet submarines were, in fact, harried "mercilessly" and forced to surface.[98]

While the Flag Plot incident demonstrated that, with diligence, the White House could maintain some control over its forces, the potential dangers of not fully controlling the military were revisited three days later, at the height of the confrontation on October 27. Already shaken by the news of the U-2 downing over Cuba, and struggling to determine the appropriate response to the Kremlin's demand that U.S missiles be withdrawn from Turkey, the president and Excom received news of another U-2 incident. A plane based in Alaska had inadvertently flown over Soviet air space while on an "air sampling mission." Soviet planes had unsuccessfully given chase. After concluding that the Kremlin was "unlikely to interpret the incursion as the prelude to an attack," the president remarked, "There is always some son of a bitch who doesn't get the word." Khruschev responded the next day: "Is it not a fact that an intruding American plane could easily be taken for a nuclear bomber, which might push us to a fateful step?"[99]

In fact, as General William Smith recounted during the 1992 Havana conference, the Joint Chiefs of Staff and the White House pursued both similar and different goals during the crisis. President Kennedy had one goal, the withdrawal of the Soviet missiles from Cuba. The Joint Chiefs shared that goal, but they also sought to use the crisis to oust Castro, to regain the respect of the White House, and to meet the parochial needs of the individual services.[100]

Fall Out

In the United States, the initial popular responses to the end of the Cuban missile crisis were relief that nuclear war had been averted and admiration for the president's victorious confrontation with the Soviet Union. Fears aroused by the crisis were in large measure stilled by announcing creation of a telephone hotline between the White House and the Kremlin, and by negotiating the limited test ban treaty, banning nuclear testing in the atmosphere and ocean. While these actions went a long way toward demonstrating that the superpowers had backed off from their brinkmanship, the crisis touched and marked humanity with the unavoidable lesson that Hiroshima, Nagasaki, and worse could indeed become our fate and future.

Although Nikita Khruschev was ousted in 1964 in part because of the costly miscalculations of attempting to base nuclear weapons in Cuba, his nuclear diplomacy did achieve one of its two goals. President Kennedy's assurances that Cuba would not be invaded were functionally implemented, thus helping to protect and consolidate the Cuban revolution.[101] In time the Jupiter missiles were withdrawn from Turkey, but this had minimal impact because they were, as Kennedy and the Congress knew, obsolete.

The crisis had at least three lasting and particularly dangerous legacies. First was an unexpected negative dimension of the logic of escalation dominance. Instead of accepting their nuclear inferiority and second class status, the Soviet leadership chose to invest whatever was required to eliminate its nuclear inferiority. By the early 1970s they achieved the rough parity with the United States that ensured MAD (Mutual Assured Destruction) would be the outcome, if not the goal, of a U.S.-Soviet nuclear war. This in turn spurred President Nixon's efforts to regain U.S. first strike capability.

Second, Fidel Castro's actions during the crisis, as described in Khruschev's memoirs, demonstrated that nuclear powers could not always expect their opponents to respond according to the "rational" rules of game theory. They might act "irrationally," seeking to protect their independence, power, and prestige at the risk of a devastating nuclear attack. In the late 1980s and early 1990s fear of this model became a driving force behind U.S. efforts to prevent proliferation of nuclear weapons in what Washington called rogue states, such as Iraq, North Korea, and Iran.

Finally, the popular perception in the United States, and a lesson learned by politicians and strategic analysts, was that U.S. nuclear threats and the practice of escalation dominance had forced the Soviet Union to back down. U.S. commitment to, and practice of, building and threatening to use its first strike nuclear arsenal was reinforced.

Notes

1. Gen. Anatoli I. Gribkov and Gen. William Y. Smith, *Operation ANADYR: U.S. and Soviet Generals Recount the Cuban Missile Crisis*, Chicago: edition q, inc., 1994, p. 5.
2. Elie Abel, *The Missile Crisis*, Philadelphia: J.B. Lippincott Co., 1966, p. 182.
3. From an unpublished interview conducted by the author for the film *The Last Empire*, 1984.
4. Robert F. Kennedy, *Thirteen Days: A Memoir of the Cuban Missile Crisis*, New York: W.W. Norton Co., 1968, pp. 153–159.
5. Quoted in a letter from Rieko Asato to Joseph Gerson, July 9, 1994.
6. Theodore Sorensen, *Kennedy*, New York: Harper & Row, 1965.
7. *Boston Globe* July, 29, 1994.
8. Edmundo Desnoes cited in James G. Blight, Bruce J. Allyn, and David A. Welch, *Cuba On the Brink: Castro, The Missile Crisis, and the Soviet Collapse*, New York: Pantheon Books, 1993, p. 15.
9. Robert McNamara, cited in Richard E. Neustadt's and Graham T. Allison's afterword to Robert F. Kennedy, *Thirteen Days*, op. cit., p. 111.
10. Kennedy, op. cit.; Maurice Zeitlin and Robert Scheer, *Cuba: Tragedy in our Hemisphere*, New York: Grove Press, 1963, p. 34.
11. CIA Assistant Director Ray Cline, cited in Gribkov, op. cit., p.90
12. Nikita Khruschev, *Khruschev Remembers*, Boston: Little, Brown and Co., 1970., pp.492–93.
13. Gribkov and Smith, op. cit., pp 12 and 167.
14. Zeitlin, op. cit., p. 30.
15. Tad Szulc, *New York Times*, April 24, 1960, citied in Zeitlin, op. cit., p.31.
16. Blight, et al., op. cit., pp. 324–25.
17. Ibid., p. 324.
18. C. Wright Mills, *Listen Yankee: The Revolution in Cuba*, New York: Ballantine Books, 1960, p. 20.
19. Blight, et. al., op. cit., p. 327.
20. See Zeitlin, op. cit., p. 34; and James Petras and Maurice Zeitlin, *Latin America: Reform or Revolution*, New York: Fawcett Library, 1968, p. 270.
21. Zeitlin, op. cit., p. 22.
22. Ibid., p. 38–39.
23. Blight, op. cit., p. 322.
24. Zeitlin, op. cit., p. 34.
25. Blight, op. cit., p. 322.
26. Zeitlin, op. cit., p. 50.
27. Ibid., p.52.
28. John Gerassi, *The Great Fear in Latin America*, New York: Collier Books, 1967, p. 394.
29. Blight, op. cit., pp. 335–36.
30. Arthur M. Schlesinger Jr., *A Thousand Days: John F. Kennedy in the White House*, Boston: Houghton Mifflin Co., 1965, p. 3.
31. David Halberstam, *The Best and the Brightest*, Greenwich, Ct.: Fawcett Publications, Inc., 1973.
32. See Halberstam, pp.19–65; and Tetsuya Kataoka, *The Price of a Constitution: The Origin of Japan's Postwar Politics*, New York: Crane Russak, 1991, pp.1 and 110.
33. Gribkov and Smith, op. cit., pp. 79–80.
34. Tony Palomba, "First Strike: Shield for Intervention," in *The Deadly Connection: Nuclear War and U.S. Intervention*, Joseph Gerson, ed., Philadelphia: New Society Publishers, 1984, p. 80.
35. Dwight D. Eisenhower, *Mandate for Change, Volume l*, New York: Doubleday, 1963, pp. 178–81.
36. Daniel Ellsberg, "Call to Mutiny" in Gerson, op. cit. p. 41.
37. Sorensen, op. cit., p. 512.

38. McGeorge Bundy, *Danger and Survival: Choices About the Bomb in the First Fifty Years*, New York: Random House, 1988, p.381.
39. Gribkov and Smith, op. cit., p. 86.
40. Heather A. Purcell and James K. Galbraith, "Did The U.S. Military Plan a Nuclear First Strike for 1963?" *The American Prospect*, Fall 1994; Gerson, op. cit., pp. 41–42.
41. Gerson, op. cit., pp. 81–82.
42. See Debora Shapley, *Promise and Power: The Life and Times of Robert McNamara*, Boston: Little, Brown, 1993, p. 168; and Khruschev, op. cit., pp 492–93.
43. Roy Medvedev. *Khruschev*, Garden City, New York: Doubleday, 1983, p. 177.
44. James Reston, *New York Times Magazine*, November 15, 1964, cited in Abel, op.cit., p. 37.
45. Khruschev, op. cit., p. 495.
46. Gribkov and Smith, op. cit., p. 81.
47. Blight, op. cit., p. 18.
48. See Sorensen, op. cit., pp. 534–35; and Gerassi, op. cit., pp. 251–52.
49. Sorensen, op. cit., p. 535.
50. Chang and Kornbluth, cited in Gribkov and Smith, op. cit., pp. 90–92.
51. See Bundy, op. cit., p. 416; and Pierre Salinger, "Gaps in the Cuban Missile Crisis Story," *New York Times*, Feb. 5, 1989.
52. See Khruschev, op. cit., p. 493; Gribkov and Smith, op. cit., p. 167; and Shapley, op. cit., p. 167.
53. Kennedy, op. cit., p. 41.
54. Ibid., p. 125.
55. Ibid., pp. 112–113.
56. Excom members included: Secretary of State Dean Rusk, Secretary of Defense Robert McNamara, Director of the CIA John McCone, Secretary of the Treasury Douglas Dillon, National Security Advisor McGeorge Bundy, Presidential Counsel Theodore Sorensen, Under Secretary of State George Ball, Deputy Under Secretary of State U. Alexis Johnson, Chairman of the Joint Chiefs of Staff Maxwell Taylor, and Assistant Secretary of State for Latin America Edward Martin. Others who participated in Excom meetings included Chip Bohlen, who left to become ambassador to France after the first day of the crisis and was replaced by former Ambassador to the Soviet Union Llewellyn Thompson, Deputy Secretary of Defense Roswel Gilpatric, Assistant Secretary of Defense Paul Nitze, Vice President Lyndon B. Johnson, Ambassador to the United Nations Adlai Stevenson, Special Assistant to the President Kenneth O'Donnell, Deputy Director of the USIA Don Wilson, and the former Secretary of State Dean Acheson.
57. Sorensen, op. cit. p. 680.
58. Kennedy, op. cit., p. 74.
59. Ibid., pp. 113–114.
60. Ibid., pp. 14, 36 and 117. LeMay led the firebombing of Tokyo and later ordered unauthorized flights over the Soviet Union during the Eisenhower administration, possibly to provide the *casus belli* for a preemptive war against the Soviet Union. Paul Lashmar, "Stranger than 'Strangelove'" *Washington Post National Weekly Edition*, July 11–17, 1994.
61. Gribkov and Smith, op. cit., 127.
62. Khruschev, op. cit., pp. 493–94.
63. Abel, op. cit., p. 173.
64. Shapley, op. cit., p. 167; Kennedy, op. cit., p. 27.
65. Sorensen op. cit., p. 683; see also Abel, op. cit., pp.60–63.
66. Chang and Kornbluth, cited in Gribkov and Smith, op. cit., p. 157; and Kennedy, op. cit., p. 124.
67. Abel, op. cit., p. 60; and Chang and Kornbluth, op. cit., p. 157.
68. Chang and Kornbluth, op. cit., p. 157.
69. Sorensen, op. cit., p. 683.

70. Kennedy, op. cit., p. 12; See also Shapley, op. cit., p. 173.

71. Ibid. p. 173. See also Kennedy, op. cit., p. 13; and Sorensen, op. cit., p. 687.

72. Abel, op. cit., pp. 64–65.

73. Gribkov and Smith, op. cit., p. 121; Kennedy, op. cit., p. 85.

74. Khruschev, op. cit., p. 493.

75. See Fred Kaplan, "Detailing JFK's stance during missile crisis," *New York Times*, October 21, 1987.

76. Abel, op. cit., p. 190.

77. Ibid., pp. 157-58.

78. Kennedy, op. cit., p. 72.

79. Ibid., pp. 72-73; Shapley, op. cit., p. 180.

80. Kaplan, *New York Times*, October 21, 1987; Kennedy, op. cit., p. 74.

81. Kaplan, op. cit.

82. Kennedy, op. cit., pp. 165–66; Abel, op. cit., pp. 197–98.

83. Kennedy, op. cit., p. 168.

84. Blight, et al., op. cit. p.61; Gribkov and Smith, op. cit., p. 4, 5, and 43.

85. Gribkov and Smith, op. cit., p. 63.

86. Ibid., pp. 43 and 63.

87. Ibid., pp. 6, 7, 53.

88. Blight et al., op. cit., p. 353.

89. Gribkov and Smith, op. cit., p. 67.

90. Blight, et al., op. cit., pp 251-52.

91. Nikita Khruschev, *Khruschev Remembers: the Glasnost Tapes*, Boston: Little, Brown and Co., 1990, p. 177; Blight, et al., op. cit., p. 481.

92. Blight, et al., op. cit., pp. 357–58.

93. J. Anthony Lukas, "Class Reunion: Kennedy's Men Relive the Cuban Missile Crisis," *New York Times Magazine*, August 30, 1987; see also Shapley, op. cit., p. 178.

94. Shapley, op. cit., p. 178.

95. Lukas, op. cit.

96. Abel, op. cit., p. 155.

97. Shapley, op. cit., pp 176–77.

98. Abel, op. cit., p. 155.

99. Gribkov and Smith, op. cit., p. 128; Abel, op. cit., p. 194.

100. Gribkov and Smith, op. cit., p. 144.

101. Kennedy's commitment to insure that Cuba was not invaded was not formally implemented because Fidel Castro prevented U.N. oversight of the missiles' withdrawal as provided for in Kennedy's proposal. To compensate for this diplomatic difficulty, Soviet forces suffered the further humiliation of having to submit to U.S. aerial surveillance of their ships as the missiles were withdrawn. President Johnson and Secretary of State Kissinger later gave equivalent assurances that Cuba would not be invaded.

CHAPTER FOUR

Vietnam

Failures of Nuclear Diplomacy

> Again we heard the voice of America threatening to use the atomic bomb. Out of the Occupation's oppression came a petition for peace: "the first government to use the atomic bomb will be considered guilty of a war crime." That argument for peace won and peace returned to Korea, but now new wars are raging in Laos and Vietnam.
> — Sumiteru Taniguchi, 1970[1]

> I call it the Madman Theory...I want the North Vietnamese to believe I've reached the point where I might do anything to stop the war.
> — Richard Nixon[2]

> I refuse to believe that a little fourth-rate power like North Vietnam does not have a breaking point.
> — Henry Kissinger[3]

IN AUGUST 1970 Mrs. Misao Nagoya addressed the World Conference Against Atomic and Hydrogen Bombs. Her words reflected broad Japanese opposition to the U.S. war in Indochina. Her words also carried her memories of Hiroshima, twenty-five years earlier, and the recent, probably related, death of her son from leukemia:

> Prime Minister Sato and President Nixon, can't you ever understand the suffering and pain of the A-bomb victims without you yourselves being thrown into the smelting furnace of the atomic bomb? We A-bomb victims can feel the agony of the people of Okinawa, Vietnam and Cambodia with our own bodies without going there. No atomic bomb should ever be dropped again anywhere on this earth. No one should encroach on other people's territory and destroy the wealth and peace of the people in other lands.[4]

93

Unknown to Mrs. Nagoya, and to all but a few people outside the most elite political circles in Washington, Moscow, and Hanoi, during the previous year President Nixon and his national security advisor, Henry Kissinger, had repeatedly threatened to escalate the war in Vietnam. Their threats and preparations included the possibility of nuclear attacks against North Vietnam. During the most intense period of the confrontation, twenty-nine days in October 1969, the Strategic Air Command was placed on a DEFCON 1 alert (the highest possible) to signal Nixon's intent to Hanoi via Moscow. B-52 bombers "were placed in takeoff duty on runways across the United States, fully armed, fueled, ready to fly attack missions." Elsewhere, including municipal airports in places like Atlantic City, F-106 interceptors sat on runways armed with tactical nuclear weapons.[5]

Nixon's "November ultimatum" was not the first Vietnam-related practice of nuclear extortion by a U.S. president. It was the third.

By the time Mrs. Nagoya spoke, the imminent danger of nuclear war in Vietnam had passed because of the determined antiwar protests of people much like herself. The October 1969 Moratorium in Washington, D.C., and in cities and towns from Cleveland, Ohio, to Tempe, Arizona, convinced Richard Nixon that the domestic political costs of savage attacks against Vietnam were simply too great.

The United States in Vietnam

Histories of the Vietnam War abound. Even as the Bush and Clinton administrations have been moving to normalize relations with Vietnam to gain access to its potentially valuable post-Cold War market, the history and meaning of the war continue to be intensely debated. Competing interpretations of the most divisive U.S. conflict since the Civil War echo through Congress, the media, schools and universities, movie theaters, community centers, and Veterans' Administration hospitals. Flag poles draped with POW/MIA banners are visible reminders of the unresolved debate. The Vietnam War Memorial in Washington perhaps best reflects the mainstream view: no glory, no honor, and starkly etched names of 58,132 American war dead. Vietnamese, Laotian, and Cambodian civilians and soldiers killed in the war are present only in their absence, as are the war dead of U.S. allies such as South Korea and Canada.

Presidents from Harry Truman through Richard Nixon engaged, deepened, and escalated the U.S. war in Vietnam. Their reasons were many, and they changed with time. *The Pentagon Papers*[6] stressed U.S. economic interests in Southeast Asia, the need of the United States to preserve the region as a market for Japan after having forbidden Japanese trade with the Chinese mainland, the anti-communism of the era, and the need to "preserve U.S. prestige" as principle reasons for U.S. engagement in and escalation of the war.[7] For many U.S. policy-makers, Vietnam was less a nation of people than a "test case of U.S. capacity to help a nation meet a Communist 'war of liberation.'"[8] Soon it became a war "to avoid humiliation."[9] President Nixon worried that if the United States abandoned the Saigon government, irredeemable damage "would be done to other nations' confidence in our reliability."[10] In essence it became a "war to teach people elsewhere the lesson that the United States had many weapons in its arsenal to destroy revolutionary movements and that revolutions don't pay."[11]

Presidents also feared the domestic political costs of withdrawal or defeat. As Daniel Ellsberg wrote, each of these presidents "aimed mainly to avoid a definitive failure, 'losing Indochina to Communism' during his tenure."[12]

Legacies of the war are carved deeply and intimately into the lives and memories of the war's Indochinese survivors. Of Vietnam's wartime population of forty million people, an estimated two million were killed between 1954 and 1975. Two million more were wounded; fourteen million people were made refugees.[13] After the 1973 Paris Peace Accords and the 1975 rout of the government in Saigon, war continued as peace. Successive U.S. governments isolated Vietnam and strangled it economically, "like a ripe plum," much as the United States has done to Cuba since 1960. Their goal was to achieve in peace what had eluded them in war. Even an Indian effort to reinvigorate Vietnamese agriculture with the shipment of one hundred water buffalo was prevented by threatened U.S. economic retaliation.[14]

Soon most Vietnamese, like growing numbers in the United States, will have been born since the war. These young Vietnamese have learned about the war from their families, from the scars of war that surround them, from museums, and in their schools. The predominant Vietnamese understanding of the war against the United States is that the war was but a moment in the thousand-year history of struggle for independence from China and, later, from France. The defeat of the United States was the culmination of a hundred-year struggle begun in resistance to French colonialism.

The twenty-year war also lingers in the land. Most of the 15,500,000 tons of bombs and munitions (five times the total dropped on all fronts during the Second World War) used by the United States during the war in Indochina were aimed at Vietnam, a nation the size of Massachusetts, Connecticut, and Rhode Island combined. Their destructive force was roughly that of 600 Hiroshima bombs.[15] In some Vietnamese provinces, the ground is still laden with the remains of old weapons. As Ngo Vinh Long described it,

> In the district of Ben Hai…in some villages there are about four hundred pounds of scrap metal per square yard. It is literally metal ground, but what is much more heart-rending is to see the tens of thousands of people who are crippled…carrying with them until their dying days the wounds of the Vietnam War. When you have met these people and talked with them, you realize that those who died, like the victims of Hiroshima…might have been luckier than they.[16]

Unexploded ordnance continues to kill and maim farmers and children on a daily basis.

Eisenhower, Nukes and Dien Bien Phu

The United States first prepared to attack Vietnamese with nuclear weapons during the final days of the French war of colonial reconquest. When Dwight D. Eisenhower became president, the United States was already sending thirty thousand tons of war materiel per month to French forces in Vietnam. By 1954, the U.S. had assumed eighty percent of the war's costs. Eisenhower had inherited this war from Truman, whose ambivalence about the French colonial war ended with the triumph of the Chinese Communist revolution in October 1949. From then on, U.S. policy was to provide "political, economic and military assistance and advice 'to areas threatened by communist aggression.'" Special attention was devoted to "the problem of French Indochina."[17]

U.S. money was not enough to defeat the Vietminh (Viêt Nam Dôc-Lâp Dông-Minh, League for the Independence of Vietnam). By 1954, French-controlled zones in Vietnam were limited to Hanoi and its immediate environs, and the interior of southern Vietnam bordering Laos and Cambodia. That winter the French commanding general, Navarre, encouraged the Vietminh to engage in a set piece battle at what the general thought was an impregnable fortress at Dien Bien Phu. It was a calculated gamble. Navarre believed the Vietminh's supply system and artillery were primitive, and that French forces would decimate the Vietminh with their superior technology.

General Navarre miscalculated badly. In March, the French airfield at Dien Bien Phu was destroyed. Thereafter, without reinforcements, three thousand French troops were isolated at the fortress and faced the prospect of starvation and deadly attrition.[18] French General Paul Ely was dispatched to Washington, where he requested direct U.S. intervention to break the siege.

This was the era of the doctrine of massive retaliation. Eisenhower's threatened use of nuclear weapons in Korea seemed to have worked, and Secretary of State Dulles saw the doctrine as "an easy way to conduct diplomacy."[19] The doctrine was marketed as the "New Look." U.S. "air power, and carrier-based air power with nuclear weapons or perhaps simply the threat of nuclear weapons would determine the global balance...an inexpensive Pax Americana."[20] The Pentagon and the White House answered General Ely's request accordingly.

In response to the French appeal, the Pentagon developed "Technical and Military Feasibility of Successfully Employing Atomic Weapons in Indochina," later modified to become the aptly-named Operation Vulture. The plan called for massive bombing of Vietminh positions by sixty B-29s to be followed by attacks with three atomic bombs.[21] With the exception of Army Chief of Staff General Matthew Ridgeway, the Joint Chiefs of Staff endorsed the proposal. Air Force Chief Nathan Twining argued that "You could take all day to drop a bomb, make sure you put it in the right place...and clean those Commies out of there and the band could play the Marseillaise and the French could come marching out in great shape."[22]

Secretary of State Dulles, Vice President Nixon, and Atomic Energy Commission Chairman Lewis Strauss all enthusiastically supported Operation Vulture, and with the support of the Joint Chiefs they won the president's conditional support for the proposal. Eisenhower's caveat was that France and Britain first endorse the nuclear attacks. To prepare the political and diplomatic ground, Senate Majority Leader Lyndon Johnson was consulted and his support for the offer secured. The president then enunciated his domino theory. If Vietnam fell, the rest of Asia, including, possibly, Taiwan and Japan, would soon follow.[23]

John Foster Dulles and Admiral Radford, of the Joint Chiefs of Staff, were sent to London and Paris where they proposed two options. One or two U.S. atomic bombs could be detonated in China to disrupt Vietminh supply lines, or two atomic bombs could be dropped on the Vietminh at Dien Bien Phu. Eisenhower's ambassadors "were stunned and disappointed" by the responses they received. Churchill did not believe British public opinion would support the use of atomic bombs in Vietnam, and he challenged the assumption that the loss of Vietnam would lead to the collapse of Western influence in Asia. The French were no more receptive to Dulles's arguments that nuclear "weapons must now be treated...as having become conventional." French Foreign Minister Bidault declined the U.S. offer, thinking it impossible to predict China's response, and understanding that "if those bombs are dropped near Dien Bien Phu our side will suffer as much as the enemy."[24]

Pentagon leaks that it was "definitely considering the use of small atomic bombs in that area" were not sufficient to entrap Churchill and Bidault, or to intimidate the Vietminh.[25] On May 7, after fifty-six days of desperate fighting, French forces at Dien Bien Phu were overrun. The French government sued for peace the next day in Geneva.[26] The Geneva

Accords provided for French military withdrawal, the establishment of "regroupment zones" north and south of the seventeenth parallel, a ban on the introduction of foreign military bases and alliances with foreign powers, and a general election to reunify the country in 1956. The Declaration of the Geneva Conference was endorsed by all but one of its participants. Only the United States did not join in the agreement.[27] The way was thus opened for the murderous twenty-year quagmire and at least two more spasms of nuclear blackmail.

In southern Vietnam the Vietminh abided by the accords and prepared to win the promised election. The elections were never held, because, as President Eisenhower later wrote, "had elections been held…possibly 80 percent of the people would have voted for the communist Ho Chi Minh."[28] By 1956 the U.S. Military Assistance Advisory Group was the only remaining foreign military presence in Vietnam. With the assistance of Michigan State University and other U.S. agencies, the United States organized the Civil Guard, a fifty-thousand-member South Vietnamese army.[29] By the late 1950s the United States, working through the government of Ngo Dinh Diem, had created a structure of repression which was implemented not by U.S. troops, but through the institutions it had created.

This apparatus was designed primarily to destroy the Vietminh, which in 1959 was still holding out for elections. They were conducting neither military operations nor defending their cadre with arms. In May of that year, as its members were being imprisoned and murdered by the South Vietnamese government, the Vietminh finally resorted to armed self-defense. Unexpectedly, the "whole Saigon government apparatus fell apart at once because it was…based on nothing but a monopoly of violence."[30] The repressive, corrupt Diem regime had a precarious hold on power, while the Vietminh, transformed into the National Liberation Front, or NLF, promised freedom, national independence, and economic justice.

John Kennedy assumed the U.S. presidency supporting Eisenhower's objectives in Vietnam. While he may have developed doubts about the U.S. role in Indochina late in his administration, all his public statements "emphasized the importance of taking a stand in Vietnam."[31] In the first days of his administration he warned of the threat of "international Communism" in Vietnam and Laos, and in May 1961 he secretly dispatched four hundred Special Forces (Green Berets) and another one hundred "advisors" to experiment with his much ballyhooed commitment to anti-communist counter-insurgency. Simultaneously, and with equal secrecy, Kennedy began a covert war against North Vietnam, training, assisting, and infiltrating South Vietnamese sabotage teams into North

Vietnam and neighboring Laos. Kennedy's war was primarily a U.S. war against South Vietnam. The only North Vietnamese presence was a minimum of materiel assistance that trickled down the Ho Chi Minh Trail. While Kennedy pressed the Diem regime to reform and to broaden its base, U.S. efforts in the early 1960s concentrated on defeating the NLF, referred to as the Vietcong by most people in the United States throughout the war.[32]

The administration's idealistic theory was that the U.S. military commitment could remain limited. U.S. forces would help Vietnamese to help themselves. Instead, the president's rhetoric and his repeated public rationales for U.S. intervention raised the profile of the war in U.S. political consciousness and "encourag[ed] the generals...to seek a greater share in shaping of policy."[33]

The NLF call for neutrality in 1962 and its growing support within South Vietnam led to panic in Washington. The Joint Chiefs of Staff successfully pressed for more troops, the freedom to use napalm (ostensibly for defoliation), and the creation of free-fire zones in which anyone was considered an enemy, and thus a legitimate target of U.S. firepower. Accepting Mao Zedong's dictum that in guerilla war the insurgents are fish nurtured by the surrounding sea of peasants, the Pentagon sought to drain the sea, leaving the guerilla fighters isolated, exposed, and vulnerable. Central to this strategy were "strategic hamlets," essentially internment camps, to which peasants were removed from their land.

By September 1962 the Diem government claimed that more than one-third of its rural population had been "resettled." French journalist and historian Bernard Fall described the strategic hamlets as "the most mammoth example of 'social engineering' in the non-communist world." Resettlement was imposed by coercion and terror and had profound and unanticipated consequences:

> the villagers were almost always resettled forcibly, sometimes being pushed at gunpoint into the 'security' of the hamlets. Areas surrounding the hamlets were declared 'open zones' where aerial and artillery bombardment served as an extra inducement to move into the hamlet and stay there.... Vietnamese peasants worshipped their ancestors and expressed their reverence by tending ancestral graves. The land where they lay was sacred and formed part of the peasants' social identity. When they were driven from that land, the links with their ancestors were snapped. They felt totally lost in a strange world... Their feeling of disorientation often produced results diametrically opposed to those intended.[34]

By the end of 1962 NLF forces had grown from 16,500 to 23,000 cadres, supported by an additional 100,000 militia forces. Early in 1963 the United

States estimated that, despite the strategic hamlets, half the people of South Vietnam supported the NLF.[35]

Repression, endemic to the Diem regime, and the assassinations of two presidents set the stage for further U.S. escalation of the war. Diem and his family were Catholic, and they discriminated against the Buddhist majority. In May 1963 South Vietnamese government forces attacked Buddhists protesting government restrictions that limited celebration of the Buddha's birth, killing nine people. Diem's regime refused to express regret or to provide compensation to the bereaved families, claiming that the NLF was responsible for the attack. The ensuing confrontation between the government and the Buddhists became a crisis when Thich Quag Duc, a Buddhist monk, immolated himself to protest Diem's repressive regime.

Thich Quag Duc's silent, motionless, and flaming body was filmed and broadcast internationally. Diem's response further stunned already shocked international opinion. He would, he said, be "glad to supply the gasoline" for others. His wife termed the monk's sacrifice "a barbecue." The Kennedy administration, warned by its ambassador of the deteriorating situation, pressed Diem to settle with the Buddhists. Diem's response came in early August with a coordinated raid against pagodas in Saigon, Hue, and other cities. Thousands of monks were arrested; some were killed, and many were brutally beaten.

This was Diem's final outrage. His foreign minister resigned, after shaving his head in symbolic solidarity with the Buddhist leadership. Generals approached Ambassador Henry Cabot Lodge, to learn if the United States would support a coup d'état. In mid-September Washington's commitments were clearly signaled, and the coup that followed on November 1 claimed the lives of Diem and his family. Three weeks later, as Ambassador Lodge was returning to the United States to consult about the chaotic situation in South Vietnam, President Kennedy was assassinated.

From the beginning of his administration, Lyndon Johnson was clear that "I am not going to lose Vietnam."[36] Within four days of Kennedy's assassination he "confirmed U.S. support for Diem's successors and requested plans for clandestine operations against the government in the North."[37] In February 1964 the president authorized Operation Plan 34A, which was directed against North Vietnam. The operation included surveillance flights, kidnapping North Vietnamese for intelligence purposes, infiltrating sabotage teams to blow up rail lines and bridges, and the bombardment of coastal sites from PT boats. The attacks were planned by the U.S. and South Vietnamese militaries, but they were carried out by the latter with assistance from Asian mercenaries and support from U.S.

forces. Bombing in Laos was also intensified in an effort to block North Vietnamese material assistance to the NLF.[38]

Robert McNamara traveled to Saigon the following month and found the new government unable to take the initiative. The NLF dominated key provinces and had destroyed many strategic hamlets. The situation had:

> unquestionably been growing worse...about 40 percent of the territory is under Viet Cong control or predominate influence. Large groups of the population are now showing signs of apathy and indifference...the ARVN [South Vietnamese army] and paramilitary desertions rates...are high and increasing...while Viet Cong are recruiting energetically and effectively....The morale of the hamlet militia and of the Self Defense Corps on which the security of the hamlets depends is poor and failing.

McNamara recommended increased aid to the South Vietnamese government, backed by an additional fifty thousand U.S. troops.[39]

In the following months, with Republican presidential candidate Senator Barry Goldwater communicating that he was "trigger happy," and General Curtis LeMay calling for "bombing Vietnam back into the Stone Age," Lyndon Johnson presented himself as the election year's "peace candidate." Secretly the "peace candidate" and his aides were planning the war's costly escalation. The plan that emerged focused on complementing escalation of fighting in the South with bombing of the North. The bombing, they schemed, would "get the North to use its influence to call off the insurgency in the South."[40] The intellectual foundation of this approach, if that is what it can be called, was the concept of diplomacy through violence, a derivative of escalation dominance theory.

In June 1964 word was sent to Prime Minister Phan Van Dong in Hanoi that "the United States patience was not limitless," and that it understood North Vietnam's control over the Vietcong. Should the United States find it necessary to escalate the war, "the greatest devastation would of course result for the D.R.V. itself."[41]

In August, Johnson prepared the political and legal ground for the anticipated escalation of the war. Seizing on confusion arising from the still-secret Operation 34A naval attacks against North Vietnam, the public and Congress were assaulted with a highly organized disinformation campaign. The president announced a nonexistent North Vietnamese attack against two U.S. destroyers in the Gulf of Tonkin, as U.S. planes were dispatched to "retaliate" against North Vietnam, A congressional resolution drafted months earlier by Johnson's war planners was forced through the Senate, with only two dissenting votes. The Tonkin Gulf Resolution authorized the president to take "all necessary measures to repel any armed attack against the forces of the United States...including the use of armed force." Lyndon Johnson later used the resolution as his declaration of war.[42]

A little more than a month after his landslide election victory, Lyndon Johnson began carrying out the threat communicated earlier to Phan Van Dong. U.S. forces were ordered to conduct "reprisal" attacks against NLF forces in the South, which were followed by a sustained air war against North Vietnam, code-named Operation Rolling Thunder.

In South Vietnam, General Westmoreland, commander of U.S. forces in Vietnam, continued the futile efforts to separate the NLF from the indistinguishable peasantry. Free fire zones proliferated. U.S. and South Vietnamese ground and air forces destroyed vast numbers of inhabited Vietnamese homes and populated villages with everything from cigarette lighters to napalm and B-52 bombers. Body counts became the measure of success. The related "official unconcern with Vietnamese lives and property" led to atrocities, from the common practices of "turkey shoots," "skunk hunting," and "popping dinks," to the use of villages for target practice, massacres at My Lai 4 and similar communities, and the reduction of the south's second largest city, Hue, to rubble during the Tet offensive. In the last years of the Johnson administration, the secret Phoenix program coordinated the undercover murder of tens of thousands of reputed members of the NLF.[43]

U.S. and ARVN soldiers were killed, wounded, and psychically scarred in ambushes, in attacks on their bases, while on "search and destroy" missions, and by anti-aircraft fire. However, the day-to-day rhythms of the war in the south, reflected in the thirty-three–to–one ratio of Vietnamese to U.S. deaths, were better described by Brigadier General William C. DePuy, the commanding general of the 1st Division at Lai Khe, and Clare Culhane, the administrator of a Canadian hospital in Quang Hay. The "solution in Vietnam," said DePuy, "is bombs, more shells, more napalm...till the other side cracks and gives up."[44] Culhane described:

> Endless cases of women and children being run down by tanks, of GIs picking off children as they swam out to pick up food cartons from an overturned supply truck, of pilots inviting passengers for human "turkey shoots."[45]

The air war against the north, Operation Rolling Thunder, was launched on March 2, 1965 with twenty B-52s and twenty-five F-105s bombing Xam Bong in North Vietnam. By April, 1,500 sorties were being flown each month.[46]

The air war was fought according to the doctrine of diplomacy through violence. Although North Vietnamese troops in South Vietnam numbered only four hundred at the beginning of the bombing campaign, the strategy was to "strike for the purpose of changing the North Vietnam decision on intervention in the south...[to] use selected and carefully graduated military force...on a very large scale from the beginning so as to maximize their deterrent impact and their menace."[47] The recommendation of Maxwell Taylor, chairman of the Joint Chiefs of Staff, was that "bombing was...to be given away at the negotiation table for something concrete in return, not abandoned beforehand merely to get negotiations started."[48] Between 1965 and 1969, 4,500,000 tons of bombs were dropped on North and South Vietnam, about five hundred pounds for every Vietnamese.[49]

The pilots' initial understanding of their missions was to disrupt and prevent the movement of supplies southward to the Vietcong. This "gradually broadened to include supply depots—fuel dumps, ammo dumps, etc.—where resupply material is collected." Other targets included oil refineries, communications centers, and transportation systems, particularly bridges which served as "choke points."[50] Fuel dumps, ammunitions dumps, oil refineries, communications hubs, and bridges were often located in or near populated communities, including cities. As early as 1966, *The New York Times* reported extensive bombing of civilian targets in Hanoi, Phy ly, and Nam Dinh, and across North Vietnam.[51]

Bombing and strafing missions against North Vietnam were flown by a multiplicity of fighter aircraft and bombers, capable of launching rockets, antipersonnel fragmentation bombs, and a variety of other bombs. Thousands of Operation Rolling Thunder sorties were flown by B-52 bombers, which also rained destruction across broad swathes of the south. Ngo Vinh Long described their capabilities:

> B-52s typically flew in formations of 4, 8 or 16 airplanes per mission. Each B-52 carried enough bombs to destroy an area half mile in width and a mile and a half in length. Since there was very little overlapping, the B-52s could destroy more than the nuclear bomb used over Hiroshima with much less political fall-out.[52]

Fragmentation bombs were used against Vietnamese in both North and South Vietnam. Journalist John Gerasi, who traveled to North Vietnam for the Bertrand Russell Foundation, described how they worked:

> The main fragmentation bomb is the...cluster bomb unit. It consists of a "mother bomb" filled with 640 "guavas", baseball-size secondary bombs... These guavas...explode on the ground sending 260 steel pellets about one-fifth of an inch in diameter...in all directions with great force... The pellets do no harm to concrete, to brick buildings or to weapons, but they tear into human or animal flesh...once inside a body it keeps boring, often travelling up legs or arms or through chests and stomachs, tearing the insides. These bombs are used mostly in the countryside.[53]

Each "mother bomb" contained approximately 166,400 steel pellets.

Quoting from an Air Force manual, Gerasi went on to explain the military's rationale for the use of such weapons:

> The Air Force distinguishes four kinds of targets: political, "psycho-social," military and economic. In an underdeveloped country such as Vietnam…political centers move around and may be hard to locate.…psycho-social (health installations, schools, churches) targets, however, are "of great importance to the underdeveloped country" and are easy to locate.[54]

Gerasi documented the consequences of thirty-three air raids on the city of Nam Dinh in 1965 and 1966:

> The Americans bombed and strafed many densely populated districts of the city like the workers' living quarters and so on. They bombed the textile complex when the weavers were working and blew up the dyke protecting the city. The U.S. went to the length of destroying hospitals, schools, nurseries, kindergartens and even churches and pagodas."[55]

The violence of Operation Rolling Thunder did not lead to the capitulation of North Vietnam as Secretary of Defense McNamara and General Taylor had anticipated. Instead, it deepened the loyalty of the North Vietnamese to their government and stiffened their will. Rather than press the NLF to withdraw from the battlefield, North Vietnam began augmenting its own forces in the south. By the end of 1967, 55,000 North Vietnamese soldiers were assisting the NLF's 240,000 armed cadre.[56] With the air war failing to change the course of the war, President Johnson covertly ratcheted up the numbers of U.S. troops in Vietnam from a commitment of 75,000 to 125,000 in July 1965, to 525,000 in August 1967.

It was a losing effort. The president had undertaken what was essentially a brutal and dirty colonial war with a conscript citizens army. Popular protest, leading to the creation of the most massive antiwar movement in U.S. history, and resistance within the ranks, increasingly limited the president's options.[57]

Although the death toll continued until 1975, Lyndon Johnson's war, and his presidency, effectively ended with the Tet Offensive that began on January 31, 1968. Between fifty and sixty thousand NLF troops, with the aid of hundreds of thousands more South Vietnamese, briefly occupied nearly every populated area of South Vietnam. Cities, provincial capitals, and district centers of all sizes were seized. In Saigon, even the U.S. Embassy was captured and occupied for a humiliating twenty-four hours.

Khe Sanh: No "Damn Dinbinphoo"

Lyndon Johnson was profoundly marked by his memories of Dien Bien Phu. In 1965, as he prepared to authorize the deployment of 200,000 troops to Vietnam, the president hesitated in response to questions from Assistant Secretary of State George Ball about the causes of the earlier French defeat. This led McGeorge Bundy to write what is reported to be the longest memorandum he ever prepared for the president, "specifically rejecting the Dien Bien Phu analogy for the Vietnam commitment."[58] Three years later six thousand U.S. troops at the old French fortress at Khe Sanh found themselves surrounded by an estimated forty thousand North Vietnamese.[59] General Westmoreland and the besieged U.S. forces were preparing for a battle that came to symbolize U.S. determination in Vietnam, and which led many to recall the battle at Dien Bien Phu.

Khe Sanh was a relatively isolated fortress of dubious military value. Built by the French in the mountainous area near the Demilitarized Zone (DMZ) and the Laotian border, it served as an observation post for monitoring North Vietnamese movements, and as a base for regional forays. It had the potential of serving as the jumping off point for a U.S. invasion of Laos to attack Vietnamese supply lines. General Westmoreland has argued there was a strategic reason for holding Khe Sanh, that the base barred North Vietnamese access to the coastal plains spreading to the east beneath the mountains. Yet before the 1968 battle, "Khe Sanh was never held in strength sufficient to keep the North Vietnamese from moving to the east."[60]

In mid-January 1968, having observed large movements of North Vietnamese forces toward Khe Sanh, and after discovering Vietnamese trenches in what was termed the surrounding "Indian Country," Westmoreland observed that the coming weeks would be active. The anticipated battle could, he predicted, become a turning point in the war. It appears that General Westmoreland believed that he could succeed, where General Navarre failed fourteen years earlier.

The president, some of his advisors, and many in the press agreed the battle could become a turning point, but in whose favor, it was not entirely certain. There was one thing about which the president was certain. He didn't "want no damn Dinbinphoo" at Khe Sanh.[61] The president accepted the Joint Chiefs of Staff's recommendation to join the battle at Khe Sanh on January 29, the day the North Vietnamese launched their first major attacks.

In the course of the seventy-seven day siege, with Khe Sanh fully encircled by Vietnamese trenches and tunnels, the isolated garrison endured barrages, mortar attacks, ambushes, and assaults. The U.S. attacked with B-52s and fighter bombers, raining nearly 100,000 tons of bombs, rockets, and napalm on Vietnamese positions. "Indian Country" was transformed into a terrifying mass of fire. Vietnamese forces were hit with the equivalent of a 1.3 kiloton nuclear bomb, or roughly six

Hiroshima-size bombs, every day of the siege, taking an estimated toll of fifteen thousand lives.[62] What the Vietnamese experienced was described in the last diary entry of Hoai Phong:

> Fifteen days after the siege began, things turned out to be more atrocious than ever and even by far fiercer than...Dien Bien Phu.... From the beginning until the sixtieth day, B-52 bombers continually dropped their bombs in this area with ever growing intensity and at any moment of the day. If someone came to visit this place, he might say that this was a storm of bombs which eradicated all living creatures.[63]

Despite the aerial barrage, the North Vietnamese maintained their pressure and at times threatened to overrun the U.S. garrison. When the scope and intensity of the Tet Offensive initially overwhelmed U.S. forces across Vietnam, Lyndon Johnson questioned whether U.S. troops at Khe Sanh were vulnerable and if they could be resupplied. He worried that he was facing a reenactment of Dien Bien Phu. On February 1, after reassuring the president, General Wheeler dispatched an "eyes only" cable to his commanding general in Vietnam. General Westmoreland was informed that there was "a considerable amount of discussion... comparing Khe Sanh to Dien Bien Phu" in Washington. On behalf of the Joint Chiefs, he inquired "whether there are targets in the area which lend themselves to nuclear strikes, whether some contingency nuclear planning would be in order, and what you consider to be some of the more significant pros and cons."[64]

The declared U.S. nuclear warfighting policy at that time was mutual assured destruction, but the Strategic Air Command was prepared for other contingencies.[65] In 1964, the National Security Council had advised the Joint Chiefs of Staff that the government of South Vietnam might not be defensible "unless North Vietnam and even China were defeated," and that "such a commitment...would almost inevitably involve a Korean-scale ground action and quite possibly the use of nuclear weapons at some point."[66] The following year Robert McNamara had made it clear that inhibitions against the U.S. use of nuclear weapons in Vietnam were not overwhelming, and that "We'd use whatever weapons we felt necessary to achieve our objective."[67] The war was being fought as the diplomacy of violence, and the violence of nuclear weapons might be necessary to achieve U.S. goals.[68] General Wheeler was asking General Westmoreland if this was the point at which nuclear weapons should be used.

Westmoreland's response was cautious and diplomatic: "the use of nuclear weapons should not be required in the present situation," but their use was not precluded. "Should the situation in the DMZ area change dramatically, we should be prepared to introduce weapons of greater effectiveness against massed force. Under such circumstances I visualize that either tactical nuclear weapons or chemical agents should be active candidates for employment."[69]

Only Westmoreland and Wheeler knew the degree to which the former was communicating between the lines. Later, in his memoirs, Westmoreland regretted that nuclear weapons had not been used to break the siege:

> Because the region around Khe Sanh was virtually uninhabited, civilian casualties would be minimal. If Washington officials were so intent on "sending a message" to Hanoi, surely small tactical nuclear weapons would be a way to tell Hanoi something, as two atomic bombs had spoken convincingly to Japanese officials during World War II and the threat of atomic bombs induced the North to accept meaningful negotiations during the Korean War. It could be that use of a few small tactical nuclear weapons in Vietnam—or even the threat of them—might have quickly brought the war to an end."[70]

The threat was made in the veiled manner that many previous nuclear threats had been communicated. In response to Westmoreland's cable, General Wheeler created a secret Pentagon planning group to study the possibility of using nuclear weapons at Khe Sanh. That secret was poorly kept. On February 9, in response to a question from Senator J. William Fulbright, Secretary of State Rusk "denied the existence of any plans for nuclear use or of stockpiles of nuclear weapons in Vietnam." The White House followed Rusk's testimony with a press statement that "no recommendations had been received for the use of nuclear weapons in Vietnam," implying that if recommendations were received their use was possible.[71]

The threats continued. Several days later General Wheeler reinforced fears of nuclear war by stating that he "did not think nuclear weapons would be required." His thinking and the requirements of the war could, it was understood, easily change. Finally, on February 16, in a statement ostensibly designed to end speculation about the imminent use of nuclear weapons in Vietnam, President Johnson said that "the president must make the decision to deploy nuclear weapons.... No recommendation has been made to me. Beyond that, I think we ought to put an end to that discussion." Johnson's statement quieted much of the media, congressional, and international debate, but it did not silence it. The president, some noticed, had not ruled out the possibility of a nuclear attack, something he could have done easily.[72] In Washington, as the Associated Press reported, the Japanese government quietly let "it be known...that any use of nuclear special weapons by the United States in the Vietnam conflict—in the defense of Khe Sanh, for example—would be a disaster for U.S.-Japanese relations.... the United States would lose

Japanese support overnight if nuclear weapons were used for a second time on Asian people. The memories of Hiroshima and Nagasaki still are politically potent.... the Japanese attitude has created other problems...that could delay the return of Okinawa."[73]

There is no evidence that the Johnson administration's veiled threats influenced the outcome of the battle at Khe Sanh. The siege and savage bombardments continued into March. On March 6th, General Westmoreland concluded that the North Vietnamese were turning their attention from Khe Sanh, and that the battle had been won, even if the fighting had not turned the direction of the war.

At least one intelligence analyst differed with Westmoreland about precisely when the North Vietnamese had turned their attention from Khe Sanh. He "found indications of withdrawals from Khe Sanh even before Tet" and evidence that units of at least one North Vietnamese division at Khe Sanh were involved in the Tet Offensive's fighting in Hue.[74]

This is entirely consistent with what is considered the authoritative Vietnamese interpretation of the decision to confront U.S. forces at Khe Sanh. According to General Tran Cong Man, the editor of *Quan Doi Nhan Dan* after the war, General Westmoreland would have done better to have trusted his initial suspicions that the North Vietnamese concentration was a feint to distract the Americans. "Westmoreland thought Khe Sanh was Dien Bien Phu. But Dien Bien Phu was the strategic battle for us. We mobilized everything for it. At least we had a chance to have a favorable balance of forces.... We never had that at Khe Sanh.... Our true aim was to lure your forces away from the cities, to decoy them to the frontiers, to prepare for our great Tet Offensive."[75]

The price paid by the Vietnamese at Khe Sanh was enormous, but as Nguyn Huu Vy, who fought with the Vietminh against the French and later against the United States, reflected, the casualties associated with the Tet Offensive were "not a very high price.... We wanted to make a political statement.... Without the Tet Offensive, the killing would have been greater."[76]

In traditional military terms, the Tet Offensive was a defeat for the NLF because of the thousands of casualties they suffered.[77] This was not, however, a traditional war. The offensive delivered an enormous political shock to the U.S. political landscape. The scope, intensity, and duration of the attack stunned the people of the United States, the political establishment, and even the Pentagon. The U.S. political and economic elite, mindful of the growing power of the antiwar movement across the United States, faced a stark choice: "Either...go to war like in the Second World War, or...pull out."[78]

General Westmoreland requested that another 200,000 U.S. troops be deployed to Vietnam. Instead, the policy review ordered by President Johnson concluded that an additional 200,000 troops would not win the war, and that such a deployment was capable of provoking "a domestic crisis of unprecedented proportions" across the United States.[79]

I can still remember watching President Johnson's televised address to the nation on March 31. As a student activist facing the choices of applying for conscientious objector status, emigration to Canada, or draft resistance leading to imprisonment, I was amazed and encouraged by the president's announcement that, with the exception of limited attacks immediately north of the demilitarized zone, the U.S. bombing of North Vietnam would cease. (I did, however, notice that his unstated implication was that the air and ground war in the south would continue.) Like almost everyone watching the broadcast, I was stunned by his announcement that he was withdrawing from the presidential election.

Three days later he announced that representatives of North Vietnam had agreed to meet with U.S. representatives in Paris to begin negotiations. The next stage of the U.S. war in Vietnam came with Richard Nixon's campaign promise that he had "a secret plan to end the war."

The Japanese Context

The Japanese relationship to the Vietnam War was deep, complex, and closely related to the strategic role and structures the U.S. military occupation imposed on Japan. The New Left antiwar leader Oda Makato reflected a common view of the Japanese peace movement. He viewed his country as "a kind of 'forced aggressor' in the war." Because of the Mutual Security Treaty, "Japan had to cooperate with the American policy of aggression. In this sense Japan was a victim of its alliance...but it was also an aggressor toward the small countries in Indochina."[80]

The war protected and enriched the growing Japanese economy. At the same time, it revived painful memories of the cruelties and losses of Japan's war on the Asian mainland. It revived sensitivities to the Japanese militarism that was responsible for that war and to the unpopular alliance with the United States that was reinforced by the war in Indochina. The air war against Vietnam, Laos, and Cambodia, launched in part from bases in Japan, was perhaps most disturbing to Japanese. It reminded many of their suffering from U.S. wartime attacks and firebombings. Once again, the United States was "attacking Oriental people with yellow skin," and Japan was complicit.[81]

Carl Oglesby and Richard Shaull were among the first outside the U.S. government to understand that the war in Indochina was, in part, being fought to keep Japan within the U.S. sphere. They cited an observation made by President Eisenhower a month after the French defeat at Dien Bien Phu: "In its economic aspects...[loss of Indochina] would take away that region that Japan must have as a trading area, or it would force Japan to turn toward China and Manchuria, or toward the Communist areas in order to live." Japan's only "remote chance...for a long term alternative to the developing market of China," Oglesby and Schaull concluded, lay "with the more slowly developing and less organizable markets of the South Pacific, South Asia, and Southeast Asia."[82]

As described previously, before Japan's wartime defeat U.S. policy-makers saw U.S. control over Japan as critical to the postwar global balance of power. Japan was a material and strategic prize of the greatest value and would be the keystone to the structure of U.S. power in Asia and the Pacific.[83] U.S. political and military leaders were prepared to use any means necessary to prevent Japan from falling into the the Sino-Soviet orbit, lest the balance of power in Asia, and possibly the world, be tilted away from the United States.

Securing Japan's periphery, while maintaining political and economic chasms between Japan and China, preoccupied strategic planners in Washington through much of the 1950s. Fear of a Korean "sword pointing at the heart of central Japan" was a critical factor in the U.S. decision to go to war in Korea.[84] The Joint Chiefs of Staff advised the Eisenhower administration that the "[o]rientation of Japan toward the West is the keystone of United States policy in the Far East.... the loss of Southeast Asia to Communism would, through economic and political pressures, drive Japan into an accommodation with the Communist Bloc."[85] This anticipated Eisenhower's theory of falling dominos and informed his decision to recommend the use of nuclear weapons to break the Vietnamese siege of Dien Bien Phu.

To consolidate U.S. control over Japan, and to integrate the distant nation into the U.S. global system, the U.S. military occupation created a Japanese state that ambiguously incorporated mutually exclusive principles: a pacifist constitution, "a military alliance with the United States through which Japanese military and...diplomatic functions were largely relegated to the United States," and surreptitious continuity of the imperial state through the retention of Emperor Hirohito, and the "reverse course" that marginalized democratic forces and reintegrated people associated with the previously purged wartime order.[86]

The Mutual Security Treaty, imposed on Japan in 1951 in exchange for an end to the occupation, legitimized the continued presence of U.S. bases in Japan, and allowed their use without consultation of Japanese authorities. The treaty permitted the United States to bring whatever weapons it chose into Japan, including nuclear weapons. Despite the constitutional ban against the establishment of a Japanese military, the treaty provided for the metamorphosis of Japanese police forces, created by General MacArthur to compensate for the dispatch of U.S. troops to Korea, into Japan's Self Defense Forces. The limits of Japanese sovereignty were codified in the United States' right to use its military to repress disturbances within Japan during, for example, labor unrest.

In 1960, the most glaring inequities of the treaty were modified under the broad and intense pressures of the AMPO (anti- Mutual Security Treaty) struggle, the most massive popular movement in Japanese history. In essence the United States agreed to withdraw the nuclear weapons it had secretly stored in Japan and to renounce its right to quell domestic disturbances, in exchange for continued U.S. control of Okinawa, where U.S. bases were concentrated, and transit rights for U.S. forces. Contrary to the public text, a secret agreement provided for the continued presence of U.S. nuclear weapons in Japan.[87]

Much and little had changed by 1965, when Lyndon Johnson met with Prime Minister Sato to discuss U.S.-Japanese cooperation in Indochina, and the president prepared to escalate the war in Vietnam. Japan's wartime defeat was twenty years in the past. The U.S. military occupation was thirteen-year-old history, and the paroxysms of the AMPO revolt were fading. Factionalism, ideological debates, and Soviet and Chinese efforts to influence the Japanese Left had divided and demoralized it. Prime Minister Ikeda's program of economic revitalization, which promised "income doubling" within a decade, had filled much of the political vacuum and focused public consciousness on material gain and consumerism. The United States was at the pinnacle of its popularity in Japan, with polls showing forty-nine percent of the Japanese people considered the United States their favorite foreign country.[88]

This popularity could not survive the transformation of Japan into a forward base for the war against Vietnam. The war shocked and disgusted millions of Japanese, and many acted to oppose the war and end their government's complicity. Despite these efforts, Japan served the United States as a critically important base throughout the war. Japanese industry was the primary overseas supplier of U.S arms and other war materiel, further boosting Japan's economy. At the more than one hundred U.S. military bases and installations across Japan, the greatest number being concentrated in Okinawa, bombing attacks were launched, ground troops were trained, communications and logistical support were provided, U.S. casualties were tended to, and GIs enjoyed "R&R" (rest and recreation) at the expense of the "host" nation, particularly of Japanese women.

Tokyo's support for the U.S. military operations in Southeast Asia preceded Lyndon Johnson's escalation. The groundwork was laid in 1961, in response to a challenge to the use of U.S. bases in Japan to support military operations in Laos. A Diet member asked if U.S. bases in Japan could be used for operations outside of the Far East, a region previously defined as north of the Philippines. The government's response was that the "United States could take military actions short of actual combat in areas surrounding the Far East…if the security of the Far East itself was threatened," and it implied that related U.S. operations in Japan "did not require prior consultations." The same question and answer were repeated in 1962 when U.S. troops were dispatched to Thailand.[89]

When U.S. bases were used to support the August 1964 bombing of North Vietnam in retaliation for the non-existent Tonkin Gulf incident, the government's line remained consistent in the Diet: "events just outside the Far East might threaten its peace and security, allowing American forces to use their bases in Japan for noncombatant purposes without consulting with Japan in advance." The foreign minister took Japanese policy a step further in support of U.S. actions, saying "we trust the American statement. America's actions were unavoidable" and "fall within the sphere of self-defense rights."[90] The Japanese Communist and Socialist parties, the principle labor federation, and 134 peace and other organizations did not concur. They organized a major rally on August 10 to protest the bombings. When the government signalled its continuing commitment to Washington's Asian agenda by approving outstanding U.S. requests for port calls by U.S. nuclear powered submarines at Sasebo and Yokosuka after the adoption of the Tonkin Gulf Resolution, the vessels were met with broad and popular protests.[91]

When Prime Minister Sato traveled to Washington to meet with Lyndon Johnson in January 1965, he was well aware of growing Japanese opposition to Washington's widening war. His government calculated that supporting the war could achieve two Japanese foreign policy goals. It might help to avoid possible trade conflicts with the United States as Japanese businesses slowly expanded their market in China, despite U.S. efforts to "contain" the communist state. Sato's government also hoped that support for the U.S. war in Indochina would speed the return of Okinawa, an increasingly volatile political issue on the occupied islands and within Japan itself.

Johnson and Sato struck a deal that supported Johnson's military needs and provided the Japanese government room to maneuver. Their communiqué "recognized Japan's desire to regain Okinawa" but reaffirmed that U.S. bases there were "essential to peace in the Far East." While kowtowing to Washington's fantasy that Taiwan was the legitimate government of China, they noted without comment Japan's trade with the mainland. Both nations "agreed that continued perseverance would be necessary for freedom and independence in South Vietnam." As Thomas Havens later wrote, "In exchange for American flexibility on Okinawa and China, Sato now seemed to be marching jowl to jowl with Johnson on the war."[92] Foreign Minister Etsusaburo Shiina put it differently: "the Security Treaty between Japan and the United States puts Japan under obligation to allow U.S. forces to use facilities and areas in Japan within the scope of the Treaty.... under the Security Treaty...Japan does not take a neutral position between the two states, North Vietnam and the United States."[93]

The later Nixon-Sato communiqué of November 1969 reaffirmed U.S. access to its bases in Japan and Okinawa for the duration of the war. On the eve of the mandated review of the Mutual Security Treaty, the two leaders reaffirmed the alliance and proclaimed a new order in which Japanese Self Defense Forces would play a larger role in keeping with the Nixon Doctrine. To pacify Japanese public opinion, the United States conceded reversion of Okinawa to Japan in 1972. Many on the Japanese Left saw the agreement as an alliance between "U.S. imperialism and Japanese militarism, the latter now being revised and strengthened as a subordinate ally, [the two being] common enemies of the Japanese and Asian peoples."[94]

The "Rolling Thunder" of U.S. bombers attacking North Vietnam a month after the Sato-Johnson agreement profoundly shocked the Japanese body politic. Many, including hibakusha, naturally identified with people being killed and tormented by U.S. aerial bombardment. Drawing on Japanese political traditions and learning from and coordinating with U.S. peace activists and with the Vietnamese, a powerful Japanese peace movement grew. Beheiren, which brought together activists from the New Left, Christian peace groups, and many community-based activists, was the mainstream of the movement, calling for peace in Vietnam, self-determination for the Vietnamese, and an end to Japan's complicity in the war. Coalitions led by the Japanese Communist Party, which had a proud tradition of having been the only political party of the 1930s and '40s to oppose Japanese militarism, and which had long played a leading role supporting the hibakusha and working for the abolition of nuclear weapons, worked more closely with the NLF and North Vietnam's government. They called for solidarity with the Vietnamese, a united front against imperialism, and the abolition of the Mutual Security Treaty to end Japan's complicity in the war.[95]

Near Hiroshima, hibakusha could hear U.S. bombers taking off from their base at Iwakuni and read about the consequences of the aerial attacks several days later in their newspapers. They could also read reports from the war in the south, like the following dispatch by Katsuichi Honda who observed, and then became the target of, U.S. helicopter gunfire: "they seemed to fire whimsically…even though they were not being shot at from the ground nor could they identify the people as NLF. They did it impulsively for fun, using the farmers for targets as if in a hunting mood. They are hunting Asians."[96]

The war brought many of the hibakusha's painful memories to the surface. As Mrs. Misao Nagoya's speech revealed, they knew in their bodies, as well as in their minds, that the United States could resort to the most brutal violence imaginable. Many feared that "the United States would use any means whatsoever to win the war" including nuclear weapons.[97]

When Chieko Watanabe, who had been permanently maimed in Nagasaki, addressed the August 1965 World Conference Against Atomic and Hydrogen Bombs, the Japanese press had reported deployment of nuclear weapons at the U.S. air base in Danang. She condemned the United States' use of toxic gas and napalm that were "incinerating…Vietnam and murdering its people." She warned that Japanese subordination to the United States could create more hibakusha in Vietnam. The following year Yoshio Inoue, a Hiroshima hibakusha, also publicly warned that the U.S. aggression against Vietnam included planning for nuclear war.[98]

The Madman's DUCK HOOK

Richard Nixon will be remembered as among the most complex, vulgar, and brutal of U.S. presidents. When he assumed power in 1969, he understood that the era of unchallenged U.S. dominance was drawing to a close. The Soviet Union had achieved rough parity with its nuclear arsenal, making mutual assured destruction a certainty in the event of nuclear war between the superpowers. This inspired Nixon to place multiple nuclear warheads on U.S. missiles and to accelerate the research and development of a new generation of first-strike missiles which were deployed by Ronald Reagan. The economic competition resulting from Japanese and Western European postwar regeneration also necessitated a "downsizing of U.S. imperial commitments" and refinements in their implementation.[99] This led to the Nixon Doctrine: U.S. allies and clients would fight to defend interests they shared with the United States on the peripheries of the U.S. empire. In Vietnam this meant "Vietnamization." Elsewhere it meant Indonesia, Israel, Iran, and other nations serving as regional, sub-imperial powers. The North Vietnamese described the Nixon Doctrine as simply "changing the color of the corpses."

John Foster Dulles's Machiavellian protégé could not avoid the stark choices posed by the Tet Offensive and the continuing challenges of the U.S. peace movement that had driven Lyndon Johnson from office. He responded with unique and unexpected answers: fight as the United States had done during the World War II by threatening and possibly using nuclear weapons, and attack the peace movement.

During the 1968 election campaign, like Lyndon Johnson in 1964, Richard Nixon presented himself as a peace candidate with "a secret plan to end the war in Vietnam." His well kept secret plan was built on lessons learned as Vice President, when Eisenhower forced North Korea to accept U.S. terms for ending the Korean war. As his chief of staff, H.R. Haldeman, later recalled,

> Nixon not only wanted to end the Vietnam war, he was absolutely convinced he would end it in his first year.... He saw a parallel in the action President Eisenhower had taken to end another War. When Eisenhower arrived in the White House, the Korean War was stalemated. He secretly got word to the Chinese that he would drop nuclear bombs.... In a few weeks, the Chinese called for a truce and the Korean War ended.[100]

In retrospect, Nixon's path to this belief and strategy came naturally to him. Fawn Brodie, the historian, wrote that Nixon was "a man shaped by the racism of his era, including the demonology of Asians and the 'Yellow Peril' concepts.... Nixon—as vice president—had anticipated an "eventual confrontation of white- vs. dark-skinned races."[101] Marginalized by Dwight Eisenhower, at least after Nixon's "Checkers" speech, the vice president had forged an alliance with John Foster Dulles. Nixon learned from a man he described as "one of the great diplomats of our time," and the secretary of state used Nixon as "another set of eyes and ears in Washington."[102] In 1954, when Dulles first enunciated the policy of massive retaliation, Nixon immediately supported it. "We have adopted a new principle. Rather than let the communists nibble us to death all over the world in little wars," the vice president said, "we will rely in the future on massive, mobile, retaliatory powers."[103] Nixon supported the use of nuclear weapons at Dien Bien Phu, even without consulting the French and British. After briefing Vice President Nixon about the destructive capabilities of nuclear weapons, Robert Oppenheimer reported that he had "just come from a meeting with the most dangerous man I have ever met."[104]

Following his election in 1968, Nixon chose Henry Kissinger to serve as his national security advisor. Nixon was from the West and the Republican Party's right-wing. Kissinger's presence, it was thought, would allow him to govern with the "blessings of the...Eastern Establishment."[105] There were additional reasons for Kissinger's appointment. The Harvard professor had served on Lyndon Johnson's team negotiating with the Vietnamese in Paris. Those negotiations continued through most of the 1968 election campaign, during which time Kissinger also secretly served the Nixon campaign as a source of information about the ostensibly secret negotiations.[106] That Kissinger had written a seminal work advocating U.S. use of tactical nuclear weapons, *Nuclear Weapons and Foreign Policy*, was not entirely incidental to Nixon's choice or his agenda.[107]

It is now widely recognized that in 1969 Nixon could probably have ended the war in exchange for an American withdrawal according to a publicly announced schedule. This would have required admitting what Lyndon Johnson had recognized: the war was a lost cause. Instead, Nixon resolved that he would "not be the first President of the United States to lose a war." He prepared for, and threatened North Vietnam with, savage assaults and the possibility of nuclear attacks. When those threats and his escalation of the war failed to break the Vietnamese, Nixon widened the war to Cambodia.[108]

Since the publication of H.R. Haldeman's memoirs, the broad outlines of Nixon's secret plan to end the war in Vietnam during the first year of his presidency have been a part of the public record. Nixon lacked the military credentials to make his nuclear threat credible. To compensate for this handicap he developed the Madman Theory. Nixon wanted "the North Vietnamese to believe I've reached the point where I might do *anything* to stop the war. We'll just slip the word to them that, 'for God's sake, you know Nixon is obsessed about Communism. We can't restrain him when he's angry—and he has his hand on the nuclear button'—and Ho Chi Minh himself will be in Paris in two days begging for peace."[109]

Nixon had earlier signalled this approach in what he thought was an off-the-record briefing of Southern delegates at the 1968 Republican National Convention. Asked how he would end the war, he had responded "I'll tell you how Korea was ended.... Eisenhower let the word go out—let the word go out diplomatically—to the Chinese and the North Koreans that we would not tolerate this continual ground war of attrition. And within a matter of months they negotiated." He had told his speech writer, Richard J. Whalen, that if elected president, "I would use nuclear weapons."[110]

Nixon underestimated the will of the Vietnamese and their leaders' ability to discern the correlation of political forces within the United States more accurately than Nixon could.

As they prepared to assume power, Henry Kissinger, Nixon's national security advisor-designate, arranged with the Rand Corporation to develop a set of options for the war in Vietnam. Daniel Ellsberg, who had recently completed research on the Pentagon's secret history of the war, was given the assignment. Ellsberg concluded that U.S. military victory in Vietnam was not an option. Under pressure from Kissinger's aides, Ellsberg agreed to add a threat option to his report, but he cautioned that he "did not see how threatening bombing is going to influence the enemy, because they have experienced four years of bombing." The only threat that Ellsberg thought the NLF and North Vietnamese might find credible was the threat to "stay there for a long time; not to win." Kissinger's response was revealing: "How can you conduct negotiations without a credible threat of escalation?"[111]

A second report prepared by Ellsberg for Kissinger posed questions separately to the Pentagon, the State Department, and the CIA about the progress of the war, ostensibly to identify differences in analysis and bureaucratic tensions that could affect the president's exercise of power. The study revealed deep pessimism within the government about the war. "Doubts were expressed about the efficacy of bombing and pacification, and about the South Vietnamese army's ability to stand up to the North Vietnamese and Vietcong without heavy American air support. The most optimistic estimates envisioned a period of 8.3 years before the U.S. could pacify NLF controlled areas. The more pessimistic projections were 13.4 years.[112]

Kissinger's power and status depended on pleasing his "Prince," a vocation that would not be advanced by honoring Ellsberg's conclusions. Kissinger thus ignored the studies he had commissioned and followed the guiding principle of the administration's policy: South Vietnam would "remain non-Communist forever." Hanoi would be shown that "the Nixon administration would stop at nothing—not even the physical destruction of North Vietnam's cities and waterworks—to end the war on terms it declared to be honorable." The Soviet Union would be challenged with the warning "that its relationships with the United States in all areas, especially foreign trade, would be linked to its continuing support for Hanoi." The U.S. anti-war movement would also be challenged to buy time to pursue military victory.[113]

Without the knowledge of Defense Secretary Melvin Laird, Pentagon officials were drawn into planning Operation DUCK HOOK, a scenario enabling the president to order the mining of Haiphong harbor, the bombing of Hanoi, the destruction of North Vietnam's dike system, a land invasion of North Vietnam, and the atomic bombing of railroad lines linking Vietnam with China and the Soviet Union. Applying Kissinger's nuclear warfighting concepts, the North Vietnamese would be exposed to a "carefully orchestrated series of threats, culminating in dropping a tactical nuclear weapon...if they ignored a final ultimatum set for November 1, 1969," later termed "the November Ultimatum."[114]

As Nixon and Kissinger became more deeply engaged in the day-to-day planning of the war, from picking targets for the secret Operation Menu B-52 bombings in Cambodia, to the details of Operation DUCK HOOK, they bought themselves political time by addressing the public in moderate tones. Having ruled out a total, unilateral withdrawal by the U.S., Nixon announced the withdrawal of 25,000 U.S. troops from Vietnam on May 14. Ten weeks later, just five days after receiving the initial plans for savage bombing of North Vietnam, Nixon presented the Nixon Doctrine as a way to assure the public that the United States would not again be "dragged into conflicts such as the one we have in Vietnam." In mid-August, Defense Secretary Laird announced that the U.S. objective in Vietnam was no longer the defeat of North Vietnam. Instead, in accordance with the Nixon Doctrine, U.S. forces would concentrate on assisting the South Vietnamese army to "strengthen its ability to repel a North Vietnamese attack." In September, with the peace movement's October Moratorium approaching, the president announced the withdrawal of an additional 35,000 U.S. troops from Vietnam, bringing the total number below 500,000, and rumors were leaked to the press of a possible breakthrough in negotiations with North Vietnam in Paris.[115]

While Nixon deceived the U.S. public, he signalled his threats to Hanoi. On July 15 he sent a bland letter to Ho Chi Minh, "renewing his offer to negotiate an end to the war but proposing no new peace terms." Jean Sainteny, a French diplomat who had served in Hanoi and who was close to Kissinger, was entrusted with the mission. "He was to tell Ho Chi Minh that 'unless some serious breakthrough had been achieved by November 1,'" the president would be "obliged to have recourse 'to measures of great consequences and force.'"[116] Nixon used a meeting with President Nicolae Ceasescu in Bucharest on August 2 to send a message to Hanoi. He told the Romanian tyrant, "We cannot indefinitely continue to have two hundred deaths a week in Vietnam and no progress in Paris. On November 1 this year...if there is no progress, we must re-evaluate our policy."[117] On August 4, Henry Kissinger personally, and secretly, delivered the threats to North Vietnam in Paris: "If by November 1 no major progress has been made toward a solution, we will be compelled—with great reluctance—to take measures of the greatest consequence."[118]

Later that month Kissinger assembled a working group to continue refinements of Operation DUCK HOOK. In addition to military personnel assigned to the National Security Council, several civilians, including Anthony Lake, Winston Lord, Roger Morris, and Helmut Sonnefeldt were instructed to

> map out what would be a savage blow.... you are not to exclude the possibility of a nuclear device being used for purposes of a blockade in the pass to China if that seems to be the only way to close the pass.... I refuse to believe that a little fourth-rate power like North Vietnam does not have a breaking point.[119]

Roger Morris, Kissinger's aide responsible for coordinating DUCK HOOK's targeting proposals, later testified that the operation provided for attacks by at least two low-yield nuclear weapons, one of them a mile and a half from the Chinese border.[120] Within the White House and the DUCK HOOK planning group, Morris recalled, "Savage was a word that was used again and again...a savage unremitting blow on North Vietnam to bring them around.... That was the whole point."[121]

In late September, with the peace movement's Moratorium and the November Ultimatum's deadline approaching, and no word from Hanoi, Nixon stepped up the pressure and the theatrics. During a White House meeting between Kissinger and Soviet Ambassador Dobrynin, the president phoned Kissinger as they had previously arranged. After completing his conversation with Nixon, Kissinger turned to Dobrynin and told him, "the president has told me in that call that as far as Vietnam is concerned, the train has just left the station and is now headed down the track."[122] At about the same time, "want[ing] to attract some attention in Hanoi," Nixon met with a group of Republican senators. As he recounted it in his memoirs, he deliberately leaked his planning for the mining of Haiphong and an invasion of North Vietnam. As anticipated, this threat was duly reported in the media.

On October 1, with still no response from the Vietnamese, Nixon took the unprecedented action of ordering U.S. military forces to DEFCON 1 alert status, maximum force readiness. For twenty-nine days Nixon used the highest form of controlled violence or force short of war in an effort to intimidate Hanoi through Soviet messengers. As Seymour Hersh described it:

> aircraft were pulled off their routine training and surveillance duties and placed in take-off position on runways across the United States, fully armed, fueled, ready to fly attack missions anywhere in the world. No public announcement was made of the special alert.... [it] amounted to a secret between the White House and the Soviet Union.... the United States had gone, without announcement and for no obvious reason, to the most advanced alert status possible.

The alert was finally ended in response to the pleas of Strategic Air Command commanders who feared the B-52 fleet would deteriorate if normal flight, training, and maintenance operations were not resumed.[123]

If the Vietnamese doubted Nixon's resolve, his staff did not. Charles Colson later recalled Haldeman telling him "We'll be out of Vietnam before the year is out. But the Old Man is going to have to drop the bomb. He'll drop the bomb before the year is out and that will be the end of the war."[124]

Some members of Kissinger's staff were less sanguine. Roger Morris, William Watts, and Anthony Lake reinforced one another's doubts and scruples within the National Security Council. On October 13, two days before the national Moratorium, Watts, who brought the authority of years at the Ford Foundation and as a member of Nelson Rockefeller's staff, addressed a top secret memorandum to Kissinger. He warned that the November Ultimatum could provoke widespread domestic violence. Blacks and others in the U.S. ghettos would believe that Nixon was committed to his foreign agenda, but not to solving domestic problems. "The resultant feeling of disappointment and rage could be hard to contain." Young people, including students, would join Black rioters. "Widespread mobilization of the National Guard could become inevitable, and use of U.S. army units...could also ensue. The administration would probably be faced with handling domestic dissension as brutally as it administered the November plan."[125]

On October 21, Lake and Morris sent Kissinger a memo arguing that Vietnamization could not work. The administration should cut its losses with the Thieu government in Saigon and negotiate a caretaker government acceptable to both Washington and Hanoi. If necessary, Thieu might have to be assassinated like Diem before him.[126]

It was the peace movement, which remained frustrated as the bombing, ground war and U.S.-South Vietnamese repression continued, and the North Vietnamese government's refusal to be intimidated, that ultimately prevented Nixon from carrying out his threats. Nixon later wrote: "I had to decide what to do about the ultimatum.... after all the protests and the Moratorium, American public opinion would be seriously divided by any military escalation of the war.... On October 14, I knew for sure that my ultimatum failed.... A quarter of a million people came to Washington."[127]

Earlier when Kissinger found the North Vietnamese absolutely intractable, Nixon had been "as bitter and disappointed" as Haldeman had ever seen him. "No threat, and no offer, could obscure one great fact known to the world at large," Haldeman wrote. "The American people had turned against the war.... The response to Eugene McCarthy's Democratic primary campaign in 1968 convinced the North Vietnamese that it was only a matter of time before the U.S. would *have* to pull out.... So why negotiate."[128]

In their secret meetings, Nguyen Co Thach, North Vietnam's foreign minister, reportedly told Kissinger that he had read Kissinger's books: "It is Kissinger's idea that it is a good thing to make a false threat the enemy believes is a true threat. It is a bad thing if we are threatening an enemy with a true threat and the enemy believes it is a false threat. I told Kissinger that 'False or true, we Vietnamese don't mind.' There must be a third category—for those who don't care whether the threat is true or false." Given the calculations that led the NLF and North Vietnamese to see the costly Tet Offensive as a victory, there is every reason to believe Thach's recollections.

Kissinger, Thach maintains, was unable to threaten them, because if he did so "we would turn our backs." Kissinger was unable to intimidate the Vietnamese because "we knew that they could not stay in Vietnam forever, but Vietnam must stay in Vietnam forever."[129]

In the president's mind, the peace movement "destroyed whatever small possibility there may have existed for ending the war in 1969."[130] He felt he was in a difficult position. If he did not follow through on his threats "the Communists would become contemptuous of us and even more difficult to deal with." Preparing for his previously scheduled speech on November 3, Nixon discarded the draft, announcing the escalation he had secretly threatened. Instead he warned that he would "not hesitate to take strong and effective action" to prevent a U.S. defeat that would "result in a collapse of confidence in American leadership." He successfully appealed to "the great silent majority of…Americans" to support him in preventing the massacres and repression that he claimed would inevitably follow a U.S. withdrawal from Vietnam. With his aides manipulating the press through orchestrated telegrams of support, Nixon won the support of seventy-seven percent of his audience and time to continue and to widen his war in pursuit of "peace with honor."[131]

Three years later, after Nixon reneged on the peace agreement that Kissinger initialed in Paris in October 1972, the president fell back to "Madman" musings and threats of escalation. Threats were leaked to the U.S. press before they were ostensibly conveyed to Hanoi via Pakistan and China. As Ngo Vinh Long concluded, these threats may have been less than met the eye. In November, with George McGovern soundly defeated, Nixon discovered that the October agreement was indeed acceptable. His Christmas bombings of Hanoi and other North Vietnamese cities were designed to disguise this reversal and the ultimatum delivered at his behest to President Thieu in Saigon. Thieu was forced to decide "whether you desire to continue our alliance or whether you want me to seek a settlement with the enemy which serves U.S. interests alone." Nixon's reputed 1972 nuclear threat was probably designed to make the brutal bombings of North Vietnamese cities appear somewhat restrained to an outraged U.S. Congress and populace.[132]

From Chieko Watanabe's 1965 speech warning of the danger of nuclear war in Vietnam, that possibility preoccupied the World Conference Against Atomic and Hydrogen Bombs until the end of the war. In the following years, its World Conferences protested U.S. efforts to "maintain their domination over Vietnam," warned that "the danger of nuclear war was increasing, " that "nuclear weapons continue…as the means of nuclear blackmail," and expressed "firm determination never to allow the tragedy of Hiroshima or Nagasaki to be repeated in Vietnam or any other part of the world."[133]

Through it all, in Nagasaki, Chieko Watanabe heard "the wails of the Vietnamese people." She identified with "Vietnamese being thrown into the Mekong River with their hands tied behind their backs," knowing that the Vietnamese had come "close to suffering the same fate as I did…and that it was the worldwide public opinion against nuclear weapons that prevented their use by America which wanted badly to use them."[134]

NOTES

1. *Give Me Water*, Tokyo: A Citizens' Group to Convey Testimonies of Hiroshima and Nagasaki, 1973, p. 55.
2. H.R. Haldeman, *The Ends of Power*, New York: Times Books, 1978, p. 83.
3. Seymour Hersh, *The Price of Power: Kissinger in the White House*, New York: Summit Books, 1983, p. 126.
4. World Conference against Atomic and Hydrogen Bombs, "No More Hiroshimas," Tokyo, Oct–Nov. 1970.
5. Hersh, op. cit., p. 124.
6. "The Pentagon Papers" is the name given to "The Defense Department History of United States Decisionmaking on Vietnam." They were secretly researched and assembled at the request of Secretary of Defense McNamara, and made public through the courageous efforts of Daniel Ellsberg in 1971. Excerpts were first published in June 1971 in *The Washington Post* and *The New York Times*. A collection of excerpts was edited by Neil Sheehan and published as *The Pentagon Papers* in New York by Bantam Books in 1971. The complete study was published as *The Senator Gravel Edition, The Pentagon Papers: The Defense Department History of United States Decisionmaking on Vietnam*, Boston: Beacon Press, 1971.
7. Len Ackland, ed., *Credibility Gap: A Digest of the Pentagon Papers*, Philadelphia: AFSC, 1972.
8. Sheehan, op. cit., p. 278.
9. Assistant Secretary of Defense John McNaughton, January 1966, cited in Ackland, op. cit., p. 111.
10. Hersh, op. cit., p. 119.
11. Ngo Vinh Long, "Vietnam: Conventional War and the Use of Nuclear Threats" in *The Deadly Connection: Nuclear War and U.S. Intervention*, edited by Joseph Gerson, Philadelphia: New Society Publishers, 1984, p. 214.
12. Daniel Ellsberg, *Papers on the War*, New York: Simon and Schuster, 1972, p. 9.
13. These statistics are taken from *Indochina Newsletter*, Boston: November–December 1982. They are drawn from studies by the Committee on Foreign Relations of the U.S. Senate, the Congressional Research Service, the *Boston Globe*, the Committee on the Judiciary of the U.S. Senate, The International Institute for Strategic Studies, the Indochina Resource Center, the American Friends Service Committee, Project Air War, the Center for International Studies of Cornell University, the Coalition to Stop Funding the War, the Department of Defense, and Amnesty International.
14. Ibid.
15. Ibid.
16. Long, op. cit., p. 211.

17. Sheehan, op. cit., p. 9.
18. Michio Kaku and Daniel Axelrod, *To Win a Nuclear War: The Pentagon's Secret War Plans*, Boston: South End Press, 1987, p. 88.
19. Fawn M. Brodie, *Richard Nixon: The Shaping of His Character*, Cambridge: Harvard University Press, 1983, p. 320.
20. David Halberstam, *The Best and The Brightest*, Greenwich, Conn.: Fawcett Publications, Inc., 1972, pp. 170–171.
21. Kaku, op. cit., p. 89; Brodie, op. cit., p. 322.
22. John Prados, *The Sky Would Fall*, p. 92, cited in Kaku, op. cit., p. 90.
23. Brodie, op. cit., p. 322.
24. Daniel Ellsberg, "A Call to Mutiny" in Gerson, op. cit., p. 55, and Kaku, op. cit., p. 92.
25. Kaku, op. cit., p. 91.
26. "Remembering Dien Bien Phu," *Boston Globe*, May 7, 1994.
27. Charles Fourniau, *Le Vietnam Face a la Guerre*, Paris: Editions Sociales, 1966, p. 45.
28. Dwight D. Eisenhower, Mandate for Change, cited in John Gerassi *North Vietnam: A Documentary*, Indianapolis: Bobbs-Merril Co., 1968, p. 23.
29. George McTurnan Kahin and John W. Lewis *The United States in Vietnam*, New York: Delta Books, 1967, p. 77.
30. From an interview with Noam Chomsky in *Indochina Newsletter*, Boston, November-December, 1982.
31. Hugh Higgins,*Vietnam*, London: Heinemann, 1982, p. 51.
32. Ibid., 51–55.
33. Ibid., pp.53–54.
34. Ibid., pp. 56–58.
35. Ibid., pp. 57–58.
36. Ibid., p.66.
37. Sheehan, op. cit., p. 233.
38. Higgins, op. cit., p. 68.
39. Sheehan, op. cit., pp. 279, 282.
40. Chomsky, op. cit.; Higgins, op. cit., p. 68.
41. Sheehan, op. cit., p. 256.
42. Higgins, op. cit., pp. 71–74.
43. Edward Herman, *Atrocities in Vietnam: Myths and Realities*, Philadelphia: Pilgrim Press, 1970, pp. 50–56 and 63.
44. Ellsberg, op. cit., p. 234.
45. Herman, op. cit., p. 51.
46. Kaku, op.cit., p. 155.
47. Ibid., p. 165.
48. Ackland, op. cit., p. 83.
49. Chomsky, *At War With Asia*, cited in Higgins, op cit., p. 78.
50. Frank Harvey, *Air War-Vietnam*, New York: Bantam Books, 1968, pp. 139–140.
51. Harrison Salisbury cited in Gerasi, op. cit., pp. 46–47.
52. Long, op. cit., p. 210.
54. Gerassi, op. cit., pp. 52–53.
54. Ibid., p. 53.
55. Ibid., p. 78.
56. Joseph Buttinger, *Vietnam: A Political History*, cited in Higgins, op. cit., p. 92.
57. Noam Chomsky and Howard Zinn in *Indochina Newsletter*, op. cit.
58. John Pardos and Ray W. Stubbe, *Valley of Decision: The Siege of Khe Sanh*, Boston: Houghton Mifflin, Co., 1991, p. 289.
59. Malcome Browne, "Battlefields of Khe Sanh: Still One Casualty a Day," *New York Times*, May 13, 1994.
60. Pardos, op. cit., p. 7.

61. Ibid., p. 289.
62. Ibid., p. 297.
63. Ibid., p. 412.
64. Ibid., p. 291
65. Tony Palomba, "First Strike: Shield for Intervention," Gerson, op. cit., p. 82.
66. Kaku, op. cit., p. 158.
67. Ibid., pp. 158–59.
68. Ibid., p. 156.
69. Prados and Stubbe, op. cit., p. 291.
70. Gen. William C. Westmoreland, *A Soldier Reports*, Garden City: Doubleday & Co., 1976, p. 338.
71. Prados and Stubbe, op. cit., p. 292.
72. Ibid., p. 292.
73. "Japan's Stand May Delay Reversion of Okinawa," *Asahi Evening News*, Tokyo, March 9, 1968.
74. Pardos and Stubbe, op. cit., p. 413.
75. Ibid., pp. 810.
76. *Washington Post, National Weekly Edition*, May 23–29, 1994.
77. The NLF estimated it lost 5,000 dead, 10,000 wounded, and 7,000 taken prisoner in the Tet Offensive's assault on Saigon alone. *Washington Post, Weekly Edition*, May 23–29, 1994.
78. Noam Chomsky in *Indochina Newsletter*, op. cit.
79. Higgins, op. cit., p. 81.
80. Thomas R. H. Havens, *Fire Across the Sea: The Vietnam War and Japan 1965–75*, Princeton: Princeton University Press, 1987, p. 27.
81. An example of this view is reflected in a letter from Junko Kayashige to the author.
82. Carl Oglesby and Richard Schaull, *Containment and Change*, New York: Macmillan Co., 1967, pp. 128–129.
83. Joseph Gerson, "Japan: Keystone of the Pacific," in *The Sun Never Sets…Confronting the Network of U.S. Foreign Military Bases*, Joseph Gerson and Bruce Birchard, eds. Boston: South End Press, 1991, pp. 167–196.
84. Ibid., pp. 173–174.
85. Joint Chiefs of Staff Memorandum of March 12, 1954, in *The Pentagon Papers*, cited in Ackland, op. cit., p. 109.
86. Gerson, op. cit., p. 176.
87. Ibid., pp. 177–178. See also *The New York Times*, April 7, 1987.
88. Havens, op. cit., pp. 3–4
89. Ibid., pp.12–13.
90. Ibid., pp. 21–22.
91. Ibid., pp. 22–23.
92. Ibid., p. 25.
93. *"Sixty-Five Years" History of the Japanese Communist Party*, Tokyo: Japanese Communist Party, 1988.
94. Gerson, op. cit. pp. 178–179; Japanese Communist Party, op. cit.
95. Havens, op. cit., p. 69; Japanese Communist Party, op. cit.
96. Cited in Higgins op. cit., pp. 85–86.
97. Junko Kayashige, op. cit.
98. Japanese Communist Party, op. cit.; "Speech given at World Conference Against Atomic and Hydrogen Bombs," Tokyo: Gensuikyo, 1967.
99. "Many Nixons," *The Nation*, May 16, 1994.
100. Haldeman, op. cit., p. 82.
101. Brodie, op. cit., p. 323.
102. Mosley, *Dulles: A Biography of Eleanor, Allen and John Foster*, p. 342, cited in Brodie, op. cit., p. 320.

103. *New York Times* cited in Brodie, op. cit., p. 321.

104. Ibid., p. 108.

105. Kaku, op. cit., p. 163.

106. Hersh, op. cit., p. 24.

107. Hersh, op. cit., pp. 16–20; Haldeman, op. cit., p. 84; Kaku, op. cit., p. 163.

108. Niel Sheehan, "The Graces of Indochina," *New York Times*, April 28, 1994.

109. Haldeman, op. cit., p. 83. Emphasis in the original.

110. Hersh, op. cit., p. 52.

111. Ibid., p. 48.

112. Ibid., pp. 49–50.

113. Ibid., p. 51.

114. Kaku, op. cit., p. 164.

115. Hersh, op. cit. p. 121.

116. Ibid., p. 120.

117 Ibid., pp. 123–124.

118. Richard Nixon, *R.N.: The Memoirs of Richard Nixon*, New York: Grosset & Dunlap, 1978, cited in Kaku, op. cit., p. 165.

119. Hersh, op. cit., p. 126.

120. Ellsberg, op. cit., p. 48.

121. Hersh, op. cit., p. 127.

122. Hersh, op. cit., p. 124.

123. Hersh, op. cit., pp. 124–125; Kaku, op. cit., p. 165.

124. Hersh, op. cit., p. 128.

125. Ibid., p. 127.

126. Ibid., p. 128.

127 Ibid., p. 129.

128. Haldeman, op. cit., p. 98. Emphasis in original.

129. Hersh, op. cit., p. 134.

130. Nixon, op. cit., p. 497–499.

131. Hersh, op. cit., pp. 129–131.

132. Hersh, op. cit., p. 626; Long, op. cit., pp. 210–211.

133. General Resolution, 15th World Conference Against Atomic and Hydrogen Bombs, Hiroshima, 1966, 1967, 1968, 1969.

134. Water, op. cit., pp. 55–56.

CHAPTER FIVE

The Middle East
Nuclear Extortion and "The Prize"

We considered using the Bomb in Suez, and we did use it diplomatically.

— Richard Nixon[1]

We are confronted with a serious situation. The United States has sent military forces which are comparable to those it used during the Vietnam War. If Iraq [does] not accept the terms, the result might be another general war. And there is a strong chance that it might develop into a nuclear war.

— Takeshi Ito, *Nihon Hidankyo*[2]

President Truman made the right decision when he used the bomb on Hiroshima.... Speculation goes that casualties may have exceeded a million people.

— Richard Cheney, Secretary of Defense[3]

ON THE NIGHT of January 17, 1991, a barrage of four hundred sea-launched cruise missiles struck the technological, military, and economic infrastructures of Baghdad, on the orders of President George Bush. Complemented by aerial bombardments, the United States and its French and British allies struck at Iraq's power plants, its communications grid, and critical centers of the Iraqi military hierarchy. To demonstrate that in the New World Order "What we say goes,"[4] President Bush had ordered the attacks to "decapitate" Iraq's political and military leadership from its army in Kuwait and southern Iraq. This opening assault was followed by an estimated 100,000 sorties by U.S. war planes, which hit Iraq with more bombs in two months than were used against Europe in the Second World War. Iraqi troop concentrations in the south were decimated by fuel-air explosives, whose concussive power approached that of nuclear weapons.

The combination of high-technology and saturation bombings created a situation in which, as Jurgen Habermas observed, "the victims remain shadow figures; we can only speculate whether there were a hundred thousand, two hundred thousand, or more."[5]

The transformation of human beings into "shadow figures" was not the only, or even the primary, analogy between the devastation of Iraq and the atomic bombings of Hiroshima and Nagasaki. The quick, awesome, and overwhelming defeat of Iraq, like the first atomic bombings, was designed to reconsolidate into the structures of the U.S. global empire strategically important resources for the anticipated competitions of a new era. As Hiroshima and Nagasaki heralded the Cold War era, the high-tech bombing of Iraq back into the "preindustrial age" warned the world of U.S. capability, and will, for a new postwar period.

Despite the war's high-tech weaponry and the innovative use of the United Nations to manipulate the U.S. Congress and public, the war itself demonstrated how little had really changed. Through the assembly of George Bush's Desert Shield and the unleashing of his Desert Storm, the president of the United States demonstrated, as had his predecessors of the previous forty-five years, that the United States would use any means necessary, including nuclear weapons, to maintain its dominance of Middle East oil, "the jugular vein of Western capitalism."[6]

There were novel approaches to the use of nuclear weapons during the Gulf War. President Bush used rising fears of Iraq's nuclear weapons program to manipulate public opinion and build support for his war. There was open discussion about whether Israel would retaliate with nuclear weapons if Saddam Hussein launched chemically armed missiles against it. And after the war, public attention was turned to the UN-authorized destruction of Iraq's nuclear weapons program. As in the past, it was the United States that repeatedly used its nuclear arsenal during the conflict to ensure escalation dominance. During the war, Iraq was encircled with an estimated one thousand nuclear warheads, and President Bush, Vice President Quayle, Defense Secretary Cheney, and British Prime Minister Major all diplomatically threatened to use them. As McGeorge Bundy later reflected, that the U.S. nuclear weapons targeted against Iraq had "not exploded does not of itself exhaust the more subtle question of whether they are used."[7]

The Middle East's Predicament

Throughout the twentieth century the peoples and nations of the Middle East have been dominated by outside powers. Contrary to the rhetoric that the First World War was a war to end war, it was fought primarily to determine whether Germany or the more entrenched colonial powers, Britain and France, would carve colonies from the oil-rich corpse of the Ottoman Empire. When oil began to replace coal as the most efficient source of energy, control of Middle East oil became, as Winston Churchill described it, "the prize" of global mastery. Centuries of Ottoman rule were followed by British, and to a lesser extent French, hegemony, sealed in the secretly negotiated terms of the 1916 Sykes-Picot Agreement.[8]

The next thirty years were an era of British dominance. European concepts of nation and nationalism were exported altruistically, and in the service of "divide and rule." New structures of power were created to facilitate European rule through old elites. Then, as now, "the key to the international politics of the Middle East [lay] in the relations between outside powers and local forces, whether governments, rulers, tribal chiefs or warlords."[9] National boundaries were drawn in the sand and mountains. And, on the margins, France ruled Syria, Lebanon, and much of North Africa, and the United States established a foothold in Saudi Arabia.

Britain remained master of "the prize" until it was succeeded by the United States at the end of the Second World War. As the war drew to a close, U.S. planners understood they were about to win "a stupendous source of strategic power, and one of the greatest material prizes in world history."[10] Although the United States replaced Britain as the preeminent imperial power in the Middle East, its influence was not unrivaled. During what Avi Shlaim terms the superpower period, the United States shared power and divided responsibilities with Britain and France, until their disastrous invasion of Egypt (in alliance with Israel) in 1956. Throughout the Cold War, Washington was constantly concerned with, and at times preoccupied by, Soviet ambitions in the region.

Until 1991, when the United States became the sole great power dominating the Middle East, U.S. policy for the region was defined by three goals that were usually mutually supportive but sometimes in tension: controlling the production and distribution of the region's oil, marginalizing Soviet influence, and ensuring Israeli survival and security. Within this framework, U.S. policy makers had their differences. Cold Warriors saw Russians, or their agents, behind every sand dune, and they tended to view Israel as "a bulwark against Soviet penetration and a bastion of regional order." Regionalists sought stability by addressing regional conflicts, like the Israeli-Palestinian-Arab conflict, on their own terms.[11] There were also those whose identity and commitments lay primarily with Israel.

The hibakusha's understanding of Middle East conflicts and tensions during the Cold War was not unlike that of most people in the United States. The conflicts seemed far away, and it was difficult to keep informed about which countries were fighting for what reason in what appeared to be ethnic or religious wars. Only with Henry Kissinger's very public DEFCON 3 alert at the end of the 1973 October war, did hibakusha and the Japanese peace movement seriously begin to address the possibility of nuclear war in the Middle East.[12]

A Chronology

1516–1918	Ottoman Empire controls most of the Middle East
1916	Sykes-Picot Agreement
1917	Balfour Declaration
1922	League of Nations formalizes British and French mandates
1939–45	World War II—Radical Decline of French and British power
1945	Franklin Roosevelt meet Saudi King Abdul Aziz following the Yalta Conference, marking the "special" U.S.-Saudi relationship.
1956	Suez War
1962	France defeated by Algerian National Liberation Front
1968	Britain announces its withdrawal from "East of Suez"
1980	Carter Doctrine
1989	Collapse of Berlin Wall, end of Cold War
1991	Desert Storm War

Axiom Number One

Writing in 1978 about U.S. efforts to maintain its control over Middle East oil, Noam Chomsky stated: "Axiom One of International Affairs [is] that the United States will take any possible steps to ensure that its allies do not gain independent access to these resources to any significant degree, and surely that the Soviet Union does not. All other issues will be subordinated to this concern."[13] Elsewhere he recalled that as early as 1949, when George Kennan advocated the reindustrialization of Japan, he reinforced his position by observing that the United States would be able to exercise a veto power over future Japanese policies. U.S. control of Middle East oil provided the United States "a stranglehold on Europe and Japan."[14]

As the allied victory in Europe became increasingly inevitable, U.S. strategists increasingly turned their attention to the use of the Middle East "prize" to the advantage of the United States. In 1943 Secretary of State Cordell Hull recommended that Britain be allowed to expand its Middle East oil facilities "only if such increase is clearly necessary from the military view-point and the need could not be met by providing for increased supplies of American Middle East oil." The following year the broad outlines of U.S. postwar strategy were outlined in a State Department memorandum: Where possible the import of Middle East oil should be substituted for U.S. produced oil in Europe, Asia, and South Asia. An agreement should be negotiated with Britain on the development and distribution of Middle Eastern oil, so that "the unilateral political intervention that has characterized Middle Eastern petroleum affairs heretofore" was eliminated. The United States should "forestall those factors" that might lead to the loss or "failure to exploit" U.S. oil concessions in the Middle East, and it should "guard against political complications that might develop." In 1945, the concern about British unilateral political intervention was explained more fully:

> We want a cessation of British political interventionism in the process of obtaining petroleum concession in areas directly or indirectly dependent upon British sovereignty. This political interventionism...has taken the form of interposing innumerable and ingenious obstructions...in the path of efforts by United States nationals to obtain concessions in areas within the British sphere of political influence.[15]

To a great extent, these strategies were implemented by the "Seven Sister" oil companies, with the assistance of State Department staff and CIA agents. As necessary, they were reinforced by presidential initiatives and doctrines, a network of U.S. military bases, covert operations and overt military interventions, and on multiple occasions with the threat of U.S. nuclear attack.

The proximity of the Middle East to the Soviet Union inevitably meant that regional developments would affect Soviet security. Yet, ever since Harry Truman had visions in 1945 of a "giant pincer movement against the oil-rich areas of the Near East and the warm-water ports of the Mediterranean,"[16] U.S. presidents, to varying degrees, followed in taking measures to block any expansion of Soviet influence in the Middle East.

Because the Soviets understood the centrality of Middle East oil to U.S. imperial power, their leaders were, with rare exceptions, cautious in actions that could be interpreted as challenging U.S. power in the region. At most Soviet aims did "not exceed the attainment of equality of influence or perhaps a kind of condominium with the United States." Soviet leaders were "improvisers, who wish[ed] to make their presence felt but otherwise lack[ed] long-term goals."[17]

As had been the case since the Spanish-American War and the interventions of the Wilson administration, the United States' commitment to freedom and democracy coincided neatly with its imperial ambitions. The Russian threat was repeatedly invoked "to scare the Hell out of the country," and to permit presidents to take whatever action they thought necessary to implement Axiom Number One. In the names of freedom and anti-communism, the Truman, Eisenhower, and Carter Doctrines were proclaimed. The United States would intervene under the Truman Doctrine "to support free people who are resisting attempted subjugation by armed minorities or by outside pressures." The Eisenhower Doctrine called for "the employment of the armed forces of the United States to secure and protect the territorial integrity and political independence of nations requesting such aid against...aggression from any nation controlled by international communism."[18] Later, the Carter Doctrine asserted that "any attempt by any outside force [i.e., the Soviet Union] to gain control of the Persian Gulf will be regarded as an assault on the vital interests of the United States of America, and such an assault will be repelled by any means necessary."

Thus, according to Senator Henry Jackson, when the Soviet Union was slow to withdraw from northern Iran after the Second World War, President Truman informed the Soviet ambassador "that Soviet troops should evacuate Iran within 48 hours—or the United States would use the new superbomb that it alone possessed."[19] In 1948, when the CIA informed President Truman that "a victory for the Greek guerrillas would endanger U.S. control over Middle East oil, 40% of the known world reserves," the president initiated a counterinsurgency effort on behalf of Greek royalists who had collaborated with the Nazis. "In the civil war that followed, 160,000 Greeks were killed, 800,000 were made refugees, tens of thousands became permanent exiles and tens of thousands more were sent to concentration camps."[20]

During the Eisenhower administration, fears of communism were used to justify the CIA-directed coup in Iran that returned the Shah to power, to attempt (unsuccessfully) to topple Gamal Abdel Nasser in Egypt, and to dispatch Marines to the beaches of Beirut. Expelling the "Soviet threat" also dominated the Nixon-Kissinger approach to the region, served as the rationale for creation of the Rapid Deployment Force, and was used to support the 1982 Israeli invasion of Lebanon.[21]

Just as the Balfour Declaration's commitment of British support for "the establishment in Palestine of a national Home for the Jewish People" was an act of British national interest, U.S. support for Israel has been less than fully altruistic. U.S. economic, political, and military aid and the maintenance of a regional military balance of power in Israel's favor have been rooted in a multitude of foreign policy and domestic political considerations.

Cold Warriors saw Israel "militarily, politically, and morally...as an asset, a bulwark against Soviet penetration."[22] Before the Nixon Doctrine formally transformed Israel and Iran into the hammer and anvil of U.S. regional power, the Johnson administration understood that Israeli military power could be used to contain and weaken the Arab nationalism that threatened oil-rich conservative monarchies allied with the United States.[23] Under the Carter Doctrine and Reagan's strategic cooperation framework, Israel also came to serve the United States as an unsinkable aircraft carrier for the Rapid Deployment Force, later the Central Command.

Israel's shared Western values and origins as a colonial settler state, the roles Israel plays in Christian theology and imagination, and the need to compensate for anti-Semitic guilt have all served as popular ideological underpinnings for the more strategic U.S.-Israeli relationship. They also reinforced "the power of the American Israel Public Affairs Committee (AIPAC), popularly known as the Jewish lobby."[24] Until its power was challenged in the campaign to consolidate U.S. control in the Middle East after the 1990–91 Gulf War, AIPAC's power rivaled or exceeded that of oil interests in framing and influencing U.S. foreign policy.

The goals of assuring U.S. control over Middle East oil, marginalizing Soviet influence in the region, and providing support to Israel regardless of its military conquests and occupations have usually reinforced one another. That most Arab nations saw Israel and the repression of the Palestinians, not the Soviet Union, as the greatest threat to their security was long the central contradiction within U.S. Middle East policy.

The historical record indicates that the United States has practiced nuclear extortion on at least eight occasions in the pursuit of its entwined Middle East policy objectives. Apart from Truman's reported 1946 threat to use the "superbomb," the threats fit roughly into four categories: threats to ensure or reinforce U.S. power and escalation dominance, in response to Soviet nuclear threats at the height of the Suez war in 1956, and in the wake of the 1958 antimonarchist revolution in Iraq; implicit threats, made with the dispatch of the nuclear-armed Sixth Fleet to the eastern Mediterranean, to ensure that the Soviet Union did not intervene in the 1967 Six Day War and to prevent Syrian and Soviet intervention during the 1970 Black September civil war in Jordan; Henry Kissinger's highly visible DEFCON 3 alert, designed to prevent Soviet intervention to save the encircled Egyptian Third Army in the closing days of the 1973 October war; and the Carter Doctrine and the Bush administration's post-Cold War model of preparing for, and repeatedly threatening, nuclear attack to maintain U.S. hegemony in the Middle East. Lessons taken from repeated U.S. threats to use nuclear weapons in the Middle East and the Soviet Union's 1956 Suez War-related nuclear threat have contributed to the development of the French and Israeli nuclear arsenals, and fuel the nuclear weapons programs of Iran and several Arab states.[25]

Suez

The 1956 Suez War and the 1958 Iraqi revolution and Lebanese civil war, were vastly different in scope, regional ramifications, and in the intensity of the nuclear threats they provoked. Their similarities lie in U.S. preparations for nuclear war and the threats made to prevent Soviet intervention in support of Arab nationalists, whom the United States was determined to weaken or contain. In both cases, the U.S. nuclear arsenal and threats were employed to ensure that no other power intervened in ways that weakened or challenged U.S. ambitions or goals.

The causes of the 1956 Suez War were as simple and as complex as colonialism. The United States, which had decided to weaken the Egyptian government, unintentionally precipitated Gamal Abdel Nasser's decision to nationalize the Suez Canal. It then supported Nasser when Britain, France, and Israel invaded Egypt to retake the canal and drive the Arab nationalist government from power. When the Soviet Union threatened London and Paris with missile attacks to force their withdrawal from Egypt, the United States moved to immobilize Moscow by threatening the Soviet Union with nuclear war. While the Suez crisis preoccupied the world's attention, Stalin's successors brutally crushed the Hungarian uprising.

The crisis began in a period when the Soviet Union and Eastern Europe were enjoying the increased freedom resulting from Khruschev's de-Stalinization program. Eisenhower's National Security Council anticipated that the U.S.S.R. would pursue "a less tense relationship with the Western powers," but feared the Soviets would simultaneously "increase efforts...to extend the area of Communist influence or control."[26] In the Middle East, this fear translated into a U.S. policy fixated on removing what little influence the Soviets had and preventing any possibility of its expansion.

President Eisenhower and his secretary of state, John Foster Dulles, were not initially predisposed against the Egyptian Free Officers Movement. Ousting Britain's client, King Farouk, had presented the United States with opportunities to expand its influence at Britain's expense. Nasser's government received U.S. economic assistance, and the CIA unsuccessfully attempted to buy the new leader's loyalty.[27] Nasser was initially more moderate than many understood. In 1955 and early 1956 he engaged Egypt in secret peace negotiations with Israel, sponsored by the United States. These peace efforts were sabotaged by what U.S. Ambassador Raymond Hare described as Israeli "military, quasi-military and political actions aimed at keeping frontiers in turmoil."[28]

The U.S. nuclear warfighting doctrine of the time was described in the Basic National Security Policy. It provided that "It is the policy of the

United States to integrate nuclear weapons with other weapons.... Nuclear weapons will be used in general war and in military operations short of general war as authorized by the President.... The United States will not preclude itself from using nuclear weapons even in a local situation."[29]

Eisenhower, who had criticized the atomic bombings of Hiroshima and Nagasaki, was not sanguine about the probable consequences of a U.S.-Soviet nuclear exchange. He had been sobered by a military study which he summarized in his diary: "The United States experienced practically total economic collapse.... Members of the federal government were wiped out and a new government had to be improvised.... something on the order of 65 percent of the population would require some kind of medical care.... It would literally be a business of digging ourselves out of ashes, starting again.... The damage inflicted by us against the Soviets was roughly three times greater."[30]

Britain and France were then dying empires, and were only beginning to acknowledge the disturbing changes that would inevitably follow the decline of their global power and status. Resistance and desperate efforts to retain as much of the old order as possible characterized their responses to the postcolonial order. Britain had nuclear weapons. France was working to develop them, collaborating with Israel since 1951 as it suited French needs.[31]

Despite the Egyptian revolution of 1952 and Britain's subsequent reluctant agreement to withdraw its troops from the Suez Canal Zone, the waterway continued to serve as the lifeline for what remained of the British empire, and it was essential to the economies of Europe. Two-thirds of Britain's oil passed through the canal, and two-thirds of the nearly fifteen thousand ships that annually transversed the canal in 1955 carried oil to Europe. Approximately 1.3 million of the two million barrels of oil that European nations imported daily from the Middle East came via the canal. Sixty thousand British troops moved between England and British military bases east of Aden via the canal each year. The canal's closure would, as British Foreign Minister Macmillan later reported, "finish Britain as a world power."[32]

While nearly all Arab nations were nominally independent, France was resisting a nationalist revolution in Algeria. The Algerian revolutionaries, the Front Nationale de Libération (FNL), were supported by Nasser's Egypt. In addition to its investment in, and economic dependence on, the Suez canal, the French government was increasingly preoccupied with Gamal Abdel Nasser's pan-Arabism and the support he provided to the FNL.

The situation became more complex in September 1955. Israeli border attacks against the Egyptian army sabotaged peace negotiations, humiliated Nasser, and led his government to turn to Britain, France, and the U.S. in search of weapons to achieve parity with Israel.[33] Nasser's requests were denied, ostensibly in keeping with the 1950 Tripartite Agreement that limited arms sales to the region. In desperation, Nasser solicited weapons from the Soviet Bloc. To the West's stunned amazement, an agreement was negotiated to supply Egypt with 200 Czech-built bombers, 230 tanks and 200 troop carriers.[34] Although Nasser was clear in stating that his goals were self-defense, independence, and nonalignment, Dulles and Eisenhower saw Nasser's action as a betrayal. From their perspective, Nasser had "opened the Middle East to penetration by the Soviet Union," and they moved to weaken, if not overthrow, his government.[35]

On July 13, 1956, President Eisenhower instructed Secretary of State Dulles to inform the Egyptians that the United States was withdrawing its earlier offer to finance the construction of the Aswan High Dam, the project on which many of Nasser's dreams of economic development depended. A plan was developed to surround and isolate Egypt with an informal network of pro-Western nations: Iraq, Jordan, Libya, Saudi Arabia and Syria. Dulles also moved to reorganize his Middle East team "to give it a stronger anti-Nasser cast." Among those displaced was the U.S. ambassador to Egypt, Hank Byroade. Byroade later remembered that when he informed Nasser that he was being recalled to Washington, Nasser's "face went black. He stared at me for a full two minutes.... He just stared. I am sure he feared we were going to assassinate him and I was being removed because we had been so close."[36]

When the United States publicly announced its decision to withdraw from the Aswan Dam project, Nasser described the action as "an attack on the regime and an invitation to the people of Egypt to bring it down."[37] He had reason to be concerned. Only three years earlier, the CIA had coordinated the overthrow of another independent minded nationalist, Mohammad Mossadeq in Iran.

Nasser responded decisively. He decided not to abandon the construction of the Aswan Dam, but to finance it by nationalizing the Suez Canal. The canal's revenues would subsidize the economic, social, and political transformation of Egypt.

Although Nasser's plan was drawn up in a matter of days, it was careful to avoid providing any legal justification for the violent reaction Nasser anticipated. The nationalization respected all applicable international law and was entirely legal. It provided that "share- and bondholders in the canal company would be compensated for the precise value of their holdings." Free rights of passage through the canal would continue to be respected. On the first day after the canal's nationalization, forty-nine ships passed through the canal, four more than average. Ships chartered by Israel had unhindered access to the canal.[38]

British Prime Minister Eden responded with panic and outrage, that Nasser had "his hand on our windpipe." Despite advice that Nasser's actions were entirely legal, Eden ordered the British Chiefs of Staff to devise a campaign to retake the canal. When the British cabinet gathered, the major question it faced was whether U.S. support for economic sanctions and military actions against Egypt could be expected.

The French response was, if anything, tougher than Eden's. Foreign Minister Pineau accused Nasser of plunder and publicly stated that France would not accept Nasser's unilateral action. Prime Minister Mollet announced that there would be "an energetic and severe counterstroke."[39] French and British leaders agreed to a joint invasion to retake the canal.

Structures of power and patterns of diplomacy for the coming decades were established during the secret and public diplomacy of the Suez crisis.

In June 1956, just weeks before Nasser's nationalization of the canal, Israeli Prime Minister David Ben Gurion and his protégé, Moshe Dayan, had agreed on the necessity of preemptive war against Egypt before the Soviet bloc weapons changed the regional balance of power. Israel's immediate goal would be to destroy the Egyptian army, and thus end its support and training of Palestinian *fedayeen*. A humiliating defeat of Egypt would, they thought, lead to Nasser's fall and weaken pan-Arabism, the force they considered to be the greatest threat to Israeli security.[40] "All that remained was for the right occasion to arise that would provide the justification for a full-scale attack without incurring the extreme wrath of the United States, Britain, and France."[41] The nationalization of the Suez Canal and Prime Minster Mollet's public vow to retaliate, provided Shimon Peres, another of Ben Gurion's protégés, the opening he had been instructed to find.

By August, despite U.S. efforts to channel British and French energies and resources into diplomacy and international conferences, and in spite of Dwight Eisenhower's counsel that his European allies avoid force until all peaceful means had been exhausted, an agreement was negotiated whereby Israel would attack Egypt in alliance with France and Britain. The plan called for Israel to invade the Sinai Peninsula. The French and British would demand that both Egypt and Israel withdraw ten miles from the Suez Canal. When Nasser predictably refused to withdraw from Egyptian territory, France and Britain would invade Egypt, reconquer the canal, and drive Nasser from power.

Two additional Israeli war aims were not raised until September and October. One, the purchase of a French heavy water research reactor and further assistance in developing Israeli nuclear weapons, was achieved as a result of the war.[42] The other, the conquest of the West Bank of the Jordan river and the partition of Jordan and Lebanon, was deferred.[43]

In September Eisenhower communicated to his European allies "that from this point onward our views on the situation diverge.... American public opinion flatly rejects the thought of using force," and he let the Israelis know that he would not pander to their ambitions, despite the approaching presidential election.[44] The United States apparently had little to lose. Eisenhower saw the British "invit[ing] on themselves all the Arab hostility to Israel" and wondered if British, French, and Israelis were really "going to *dare* us—dare *us*—" to defend the Tripartite Agreement, which not only limited arms sales but also provided that action be taken in support of Middle East victims of aggression.[45] The U.S. role as the predominant foreign power in the Middle East would thus be consolidated. As the invasion and U.S elections approached, Eisenhower again warned his allies,"The United States has pledged itself to assist the victim of any aggression in the Middle East. We shall honor our pledge."[46]

The Israeli invasion of the Sinai Peninsula began on October 29. Unable to defend his forces in the eastern Sinai, Nasser ordered their withdrawal to the canal zone. On October 31, as Egyptian forces were in retreat, Eisenhower honored his pledge. All U.S. military, developmental, and technical assistance to Israel was halted. Export licenses for the shipment of munitions, other military goods, and agricultural products were terminated. When Britain and France launched their attack, according to the prearranged scenario, the United States introduced a resolution in the UN General Assembly condemning the invasion and demanding their withdrawal. The United States attacked the British currency and threatened Britain with reductions in its supply of oil. In relatively short order, Eisenhower forced the new tripartite alliance to accept a cease-fire and military withdrawal.[47]

Even as the Soviet Union used the Anglo-French invasion as political cover for its own invasion of Hungary, Eisenhower ended the Suez war with Soviet assistance and an exchange of nuclear threats, to which I now turn.

In response to the Anglo-French invasion, Soviet Premier Bulganin wrote Eisenhower that "if this war is not stopped, it is fraught with danger and can grow to a third world war." Because the United States and the Soviet Union had "all modern types of arms, including atomic and hydrogen weapons," he proposed that the U.S. and the Soviet Union join to "crush the aggressors."[48]

As Britain, France, and Israel began to accede to U.S. pressures for a cease-fire, the Soviets moved offensively on the diplomatic front. In separate letters to Prime Ministers Eden and Mollet, Bulganin threatened to attack London and Paris with missiles if they did not immediately withdraw from Egypt. He inquired and threatened: "In what position would Britain [or France] have found herself had she been attacked by more powerful states possessing all types of modern weapons of destruction." Soviet aircraft were, reportedly, dispatched to Syria, and "the danger of a great-power confrontation suddenly was looming larger and was more significant and frightening than the crisis in the Middle East." The White House concluded that the Kremlin was bluffing, but there were fears that Soviet long range bombers could attack Israel, not Britain and France, with nuclear weapons.[49] At the very least, the Soviet threats distracted attention from the invasion of Hungary.

Eisenhower responded directly and publicly to Bulganin's proposal for joint action. He called it unthinkable and warned that the United States would oppose the Soviet Union if it moved forces to the region. Less publicly, Admiral Radford, the chairman of the Joint Chiefs of Staff, provided the president with recommendations for increased U.S. military readiness to be "implemented by degrees.... interceptor aircraft were placed on advanced alert, tanker squadrons were deployed, and two aircraft carriers, a cruiser and three divisions of destroyers were all ordered to set sail to...reinforce the Sixth Fleet." Eisenhower told his aides, "If those fellows start something, we may have to hit 'em—and, if necessary, with *everything* in the bucket."[50]   He made certain the Kremlin's leaders understood his intent. As Richard Nixon, for whom Eisenhower's actions later served as a model, recalled:

> In 1956 we considered using the Bomb in Suez, and we did use it diplomatically.... We were trying to use diplomatic leverage, but he wasn't about to join the Russians against our allies.... Eisenhower's response was very interesting. He got Al Gruenther, the NATO commander, to hold a press conference, and Gruenther said that if Khruschev carried out his threat to use rockets against the British Isles, Moscow would be destroyed "as surely as day follows night." From that time on, the U.S. has played the dominant role in the Mideast.[51]

The war illuminated the new structures of power in the Middle East. The United States, not Britain, was the dominant foreign power in the region. To ensure that the United States, and not the Soviet Union, filled the vacuum created by the French and British defeat, the Eisenhower Doctrine was proclaimed. The Soviets did, however, retain the power to influence regional political dynamics.

Nasser snatched political victory from military defeat. His prestige and the power of pan-Arabism were at their pinnacle, although his independence led to continuing U.S. efforts to isolate and contain his ambitions. Though forced to surrender the Sinai Peninsula, Israel also appeared to emerge from war as a victor. The Egyptian government had committed to keep the Gulf of Aqaba open to Israeli shipping, and UN forces were deployed to the Sinai Peninsula to serve as a buffer between the two countries. The French and Israeli governments also derived a dubious lesson from the war: they would be vulnerable in the future without nuclear weapons. This deepened their commitment and cooperation in pursuing nuclear capability. Within years, both joined the nuclear club: France overtly, and Israel covertly.

Lebanon and Iraq, 1958

The origins and tensions of the 1958 Iraqi revolution and Lebanese civil conflict were no less complex than those of the Suez crisis. Like the 1956 war, the immediate origins of the Lebanese and Iraqi uprisings in 1958 were legacies of European colonialism.

Midcentury Lebanon was in many ways a French creation. Beirut served as the Paris of the Middle East. It was an opening to the West, a banking center, and a resort for elite of the Arab world. Western districts of Syria had been fused with the predominantly Maronite Christian-dominated Mount Lebanon region. French control of Lebanon was buttressed by according disproportionate privilege to the Maronite minority. The National Covenant of 1943 modified and codified this confessional balance of power within Lebanon. The Muslim majority would not press to unify Lebanon with other (Moslem) Arab states, and Lebanese Christians would recognize the Arab (Moslem) "dimension of Lebanon and not ally themselves to any Western power."[52] The posts of president and prime minister, and percentages of seats in the parliament were contractually allocated to reinforce this agreement.

While the letter of the agreement was respected, its spirit was honored in the breach. In 1957 the United States clumsily intervened in the parliamentary elections that focused on the benefits of the Eisenhower Doctrine (or lack thereof) and the relative power of pro-U.S. and Arab nationalist forces in Lebanon. Throughout the election campaign, Wilbur Crane Eveland, the second-ranking CIA official in the region, commuted regularly between the U.S. embassy in Damascus and the presidential palace in Beirut, personally delivering hundreds of thousands of dollars to the pro-U.S., Maronite President, Camille Chamoun. "So obvious was the use of foreign funds by the president and the prime minister," Eveland later wrote, "that the two progovernment ministers appointed to observe the polling resigned halfway through the election period.... By the end of the third week the government's plurality was so great that consideration was being given to creating a senate to provide seats for defeated candidates of stature."[53]

This subversion of Lebanese sovereignty was not sufficient on its own to loose the first tremor of the Lebanese civil war. That required a revolution in Iraq.

The Iraqi monarchy, installed after the First World War by the British under the mandate of the League of Nations, fatally compromised itself by failing to break with Britain and Israel during the Suez War. On July 14, 1958, a coalition of nationalist forces within the Iraqi military overthrew the monarchy and replaced it with an Arab nationalist government that withdrew from the Baghdad Pact "shatter[ing] the Western-brokered chain of military alliances."[54]

In Washington the Iraqi revolution raised fears of expanding Soviet influence, and anxiety that, given the artificiality of the Iraqi-Kuwaiti border, the antimonarchist revolution might spread into the oil-rich sheikdom. In Jordan, the Iraqi revolution left King Hussein "wobbling on his throne." The Jordanian monarchy was stabilized only after Britain dispatched armed forces in response to the Hashemite king's appeal. In Lebanon, the Iraqi revolution unleashed resentments that had been festering for decades and that had intensified as a result of the recently rigged elections.[55] Although the Lebanese order was challenged by internal, not external, forces, President Chamoun invoked the Eisenhower Doctrine. Washington responded with signals to Moscow and Baghdad. Marines were dispatched to the beaches of Beirut where they reportedly were greeted by ice cream peddlers instead of the warring parties.

There has been some debate about whether tactical nuclear weapons accompanied the marines onto the shores of Lebanon. In the mid-1980s, one veteran of the landing bragged that he had carried ashore munitions that bore the markings of nuclear weapons. More authoritatively, the Brookings Institution has reported that "just before U.S. troops landed…a Pentagon official realized that their equipment included an Honest John rocket battery," and that "at the last minute it was arranged for the nuclear ordnance to be left aboard ship."[56]

Regardless of whether tactical nuclear weapons were physically prepositioned on ship or shore, President Eisenhower confirmed that he placed the Strategic Air Command on alert, and that he thought it desirable that the Soviets be aware of the nuclear alert. At least "1,100 aircraft were positioned for takeoff, and for several days the alert kept the show-of-force going." President Eisenhower later ignored General Twining's warning that the "forward deployment of tankers to refuel the bombers would be impossible to conceal and…that it might lead to misinterpretation of U.S. intentions." The president's response was to order Twining to "be prepared to employ, subject to my personal approval, whatever means might become necessary to prevent any unfriendly forces from moving into Kuwait." Eisenhower reflected in his memoirs, "These measures would probably bring us no closer to general war [nuclear war with the Soviet Union] than we were already."[58]

Both Moscow and Beijing received the signal. Nasser's confidant and advisor, Mohamed Heikal, wrote that Khruschev told the Egyptian leader "he thought the Americans had gone off their heads. 'Frankly,' [Khrushchev] said, 'we are not ready for a confrontation. We are not ready for World War III.'" Khruschev deflected Nasser's request for guarantees, telling him he "would have to lean with the storm, there was no other way because Dulles could blow the whole world into pieces."[59] The Chinese didn't get it quite right. The People's Liberation Army newspaper reported that "the United States openly threatened to carry out atomic warfare in Lebanon," and that "the socialist campis far ahead of the imperialistic nations in war potentialities."[60]

When the storm had passed, the Iraqi revolution had not been exported to Kuwait. The Lebanese National Covenant, the Jordanian monarchy, and U.S. power in the Middle East all remained intact.

The Six Day War and Black September

The 1967 Six Day War, during which Israel conquered the West Bank including East Jerusalem, the Gaza Strip, the Sinai Peninsula, and the Golan Heights, and the 1970 Jordanian Black September civil war have both been omitted from several histories of nuclear blackmail and atomic diplomacy. Lyndon Johnson and Robert McNamara remained discreet about their 1967 atomic diplomacy. While Richard Nixon was more forthright that the possibility of Syrian, Israeli, and Soviet intervention into the 1970 Jordanian civil war "was like a ghastly game of dominoes, with a nuclear war waiting at the end."[61]

Presidents Johnson and Nixon actively prepared for the possibility of nuclear war to ensure the continued dominance of the United States and its regional allies in the Middle East. Both men signaled their willingness to initiate nuclear war against the Soviet Union by deploying the nuclear-armed Sixth Fleet. William Arkin estimates that in each case the United States brought "more than one thousand nuclear weapons" to bear on the crisis: approximately one hundred atomic bombs carried aboard each aircraft carrier, an estimated fifty nuclear weapons carried aboard accompanying ships, and four hundred warheads on the missiles of Polaris submarines that were formally assigned to NATO. The Sixth Fleet also drew on the arsenal of atomic bombs, nuclear depth bombs, Honest John Rockets, and nuclear artillery shells stored at U.S. bases in Spain, Italy, Greece, and Turkey.[62]

In June 1967 Lyndon Johnson remained preoccupied with the Vietnam war. To compensate for the disproportionate commitment of military, economic, and political resources to Southeast Asia, he anticipated the Nixon Doctrine in the Middle East by forging an "unprecedented, covert military-security relationship" with Israel that would contain Arab nationalism. This policy was informed, in part, by William Brubeck's report to the president that "True Arab unity [would] not be achieved for many years, if then," and that federations of Arab political and military power "would not detract from Israel's military superiority over the Arabs." In exchange for an Israeli commitment to contain Arab nationalist challenges to the status quo, and thus to "the Prize," the United States became Israel's primary weapons supplier.[63]

The tensions and attacks which led to the 1967 war had been accumulating for years and intensified during the spring of that year. Palestinian *fedayeen*, some sponsored by neighboring Arab states, were attacking Israeli frontiers in their campaign to establish a Palestinian state. Knowing their own military capabilities, the Israelis had moved tanks into the Israeli-Syrian demilitarized zone with impunity since 1965, and attacked civilian irrigation projects to goad the Syrians.[64]

In May 1967, after Israeli retaliatory attacks against neighboring states, *fedayeen* raids, and after receiving probably erroneous reports that Israel was preparing to attack Syria, President Nasser called on the UN to withdraw its buffering forces from the Sinai Peninsula. Nasser followed the withdrawal of the UN peacekeepers with closure of the straits of Aqaba to Israeli shipping in violation of the terms agreed upon at the end of the 1956 Suez War. The Egyptian president may have believed that he had nothing to lose. Either the United States would intervene and arrange a last minute settlement, or his Soviet equipped forces would prevail. The Israelis saw the situation differently. General Mattitiyahu Peled, then a member of the Israeli Chiefs of Staff, has since described the eagerness of the Israeli military for war and his deep disappointment that following the Israeli victory the government did not resolve the Palestinian question by creating a Palestinian state on Israeli terms. The Israeli generals knew their military capabilities, and as President Nasser escalated the crisis, they urged their government not to succumb to U.S. diplomatic entreaties to negotiate an end to the confrontation. As the historian Albert Hourani later wrote, "the Israelis were not prepared to give Egypt a political victory which did not correspond to the balance of power between them."

As the war approached, the CIA advised President Johnson that no matter which side initiated the fighting, the Israelis would win within a week. Secretary of State Rusk counseled the president that he had two choices. He could either "unleash" the Israelis or mediate the crisis. The evidence, as summarized by Stephen Green, seems to indicate that Johnson covertly unleashed the Israelis while ostensibly seeking a negotiated settlement.[65]

In the course of the devastating six-day military rout, the Israeli government and the Johnson administration were confronted by the question of how much humiliation the Soviets could accept. This had been anticipated on the first day of the war when Israeli Prime Minister Eshkol requested U.S. assurances that Israel would be protected if the Soviet Union moved to defend its regional allies.

On June 7, two days into the war, Jordan accepted the UN proposed cease-fire. Egypt followed suit the next day. Although many guns had been silenced by June 8, Israeli forces continued to expand their hold on the West Bank and to prepare the conquest of the Golan Heights in Syria in violation of the calls for a cease fire. The offensive for the Golan was launched on June 9, and by the following day Syrian political leaders panicked. With no physical obstacles between Israeli forces and Damascus, forty miles away, they feared the Israelis would occupy their capital and oust the government, as they long had threatened. The Syrian government turned to Moscow, which immediately severed diplomatic relations with Israel and warned that the Soviets "jointly with other peace-loving states will undertake sanctions against Israel, with all the consequences flowing therefrom," unless the Israeli offensive was halted.[66]

Having achieved all their war aims, the Israeli government began to signal its willingness to comply with Moscow's demands, but the signals came too late to avoid a superpower confrontation. Before a cease-fire was implemented, Premier Kosygin used the hot line to the White House to underline the Kremlin's seriousness. He warned that the two nations faced a "very crucial moment," in which there was the risk of a "grave catastrophe." If Israel did not cease fire within hours, the Soviets would respond with "necessary actions, including military."[67]

President Johnson's formal response was that the United States was encouraging Israel to comply with the cease-fire, and that it expected Israel would do so. Unspoken was Johnson's decision that under no circumstances would the Soviets be allowed to intervene. At Robert McNamara's recommendation, Johnson signaled his resolve to use nuclear weapons if necessary to keep the Soviets restricted to the diplomatic margins. The nuclear-armed Sixth Fleet was ordered to the Eastern Mediterranean, within fifty miles of the Soviet squadron in the area. As Johnson wrote in his memoirs, "that message, which no translator would need to interpret to the Kremlin leadership, was that the United States was prepared to resist Soviet intrusion in the Middle East."[68]

As the Israeli implementation of the cease-fire progressed, the confrontation dissipated. Only a few members of the U.S. and Soviet elites knew at the time that there had been a nuclear threat. The war ended on the basis of UN Security Council Resolution 242, calling for Israeli withdrawal from territories occupied during the war, mutual recognition by the states of the region, and "just settlement" of the Palestinian "refugee problem."

Three years later, Richard Nixon's Black September nuclear threat resulted from his inability to distinguish indigenous threats to the Middle East status quo from fears of the Soviet Union. The administration believed that there were Soviets "behind every sand dune."[69]

The Hashemite Kingdom of Jordan had been carved from the Mandate of Palestine by the British in 1922, and was never a model of political stability. This was particularly true in 1970. Palestinian refugees, seeking safe haven during and after the 1967 Israeli conquest of the West Bank, had surged into the Hashemite kingdom, adding energy to the Palestinian state within a state that had been built in Jordan. King Hussein had been unable to prevent competing *fedayeen* organizations from using Jordan as a base for guerilla raids against Israel. The king was a loyal ally of the United States and since 1956 had received regular gratuities from the CIA to reward his participation in U.S.-sponsored regional alliances.[70] While his U.S. base of support was hardly insignificant, his power rested primarily on the intense loyalty of his army, comprised principally of non-Palestinian Bedouin.

On coming to power in 1969, Nixon and Kissinger framed their Middle East policies in Cold War terms. The next Middle East war would, they feared, lead to yet another nuclear confrontation, one in which the unthinkable, Mutual Assured Destruction, was the likely outcome. "If the Arabs were to lose again, the Soviets might feel obliged to intervene; if the Israelis were under severe military pressure, the Americans could not stand aside. The intervention by one superpower would almost automatically trigger a reaction from the other." To promote U.S. interests in the region, and to avoid the dangers of a regional war, they concluded that the "military balance...must be maintained in Israel's favor."[71] This does not mean that they were entirely committed to the status quo.

The Jordanian civil war was precipitated by the Popular Front for the Liberation of Palestine (PFLP). The United States had brokered an agreement ending the Israeli-Egyptian War of Attrition, an enduring artillery duel across the Suez Canal that had escalated with Israeli bombing raids. The PFLP sought to revive the Arab world's, and particularly Jordan's, confrontation with Israel by creating a crisis. In early September PFLP guerrillas hijacked four airliners and nearly five hundred hostages, most of them from the United States. Three of the planes and the majority of the captives were taken to a remote airfield in Jordan.

On September 12, having released most of the hostages, the PFLP destroyed the three remaining airliners in response to rumors that U.S. troops had been ordered to move against them. A brief lull followed, during which King Hussein consulted with President Nasser. On September 15 Hussein moved to bring the confrontation to an unexpected climax. As part of his preparations, he informed President Nixon of his intention to appoint a military government that would initiate a civil war to destroy the power of the Palestinian Liberation Organization (PLO) in Jordan.[72]

Nixon and Kissinger reaffirmed their support for the king, but they feared that the Soviets were pushing the Syrians, and that the Syrians, in turn, were pushing the Palestinians to overthrow the Jordanian monarch. It was this fear that led Nixon to envision a "ghastly game of dominoes with a nuclear war waiting at the end." If Hussein were overthrown, the Israelis would attack "a Syrian-dominated radical government in Jordan. The Egyptians were tied to Syria by military alliances; and Soviet prestige was on the line with both the Syrians and the Egyptians. Since the United States could not stand idly by and watch Israel being driven into the sea, the possibility of a direct U.S.-Soviet confrontation was uncomfortably high."[73]

Fighting began in Amman on September 17 and soon spread to northern Jordan. The divided Syrian government responded by moving tanks to the Jordanian border. It was at this point that Nixon, preoccupied with election campaigning, and Kissinger, whose energies were focused on Vietnam and planning for a coup in Chile, decided to send messages to Damascus and Moscow. Nixon told the press that if Syrian tanks invaded Jordan, only Israel and the United States could stop them, and that he preferred that the United States do it alone. The Nixon Doctrine was briefly set aside and replaced by the revived Madman theory as the president confided to journalists that it might be helpful if the Soviets thought he was "capable of irrational or unpredictable action."[74]

In Washington, uncoded orders were transmitted to ensure that the Soviets would observe the U.S. mobilization that followed. Paratroopers in Europe were placed on alert, as was the 82nd Airborne Division at Fort Bragg. The Sixth Fleet, with its nuclear arsenal and a Marine force of twelve hundred men, was dispatched to the eastern Mediterranean.[75] Unlike their response to Lyndon Johnson's 1967 nuclear threat, Soviet ships avoided any harassment and moved out of the way as the Sixth Fleet assembled off the Lebanese coast.[76]

The crisis continued for nearly a week. Syrian tanks, hastily painted with Palestinian colors, briefly crossed the border into northern Jordan. Israeli forces, at Henry Kissinger's instigation, were then assembled along the Jordanian border and the Golan Heights. On September 23, with the Soviets "telling all who would listen that they were pressuring Syria to withdraw," Syrian tanks rolled back toward Damascus.[77] The PLO was forced to accept its military defeat and banishment from Jordan. Nixon and Kissinger exulted in their victory, continuing to believe that the Soviets, not the Israeli-Palestinian-Arab conflict, were the primary source of Middle East turmoil.

October 1973: Kissinger's Nuclear Brinkmanship

Gamal Abdel Nasser died shortly after helping to mediate the Black September crisis and was succeeded by Anwar Sadat. Sadat quickly moved to radically alter Egypt's approach to the Israeli-Palestinian-Arab conflict. In early 1971 he responded positively to UN mediator Gunnar Jarring's inquiries, while "Israel stated flatly that it would not return to the lines of June 4, 1967," as provided by the intent, if not the letter, of UN Resolution 242.[78] Sadat also launched a diplomatic initiative of his own, offering an interim agreement in which Israel would withdraw only partially from the Sinai Peninsula and Egypt would reopen the Suez Canal.

The political and diplomatic ground for Sadat's initiatives was less than fertile. After the Six Day War, Egypt was referred to in Israel as "a dead body" that could be ignored for the next fifty years.[79] In Washington, Lyndon Johnson had adopted a policy which made greater demands on the Arab states than those described in the U.N. Security Council Resolution 242. Before the United States would press Israel to negotiate, it required that Egypt and other Arab countries recognize Israel's "right of national life, justice for the refugees (not self-determination for Palestinians), innocent maritime passage, limits on the arms race, and political independence and territorial integrity" for all states in the region.[80]

Nixon and Kissinger built on Johnson's precedent, with a commitment to expel Soviet influence from the Middle East. Given Israel's role within the Nixon Doctrine, Nixon and Kissinger were disinclined to pursue comprehensive settlement of the Israeli-Palestinian-Arab conflict or to challenge Israel's increasingly harsh military occupation. During Nixon's first term, the United States joined Israel in rejecting Sadat's initiatives. The joint U.S.-Israeli policy was "to let Sadat sweat it out…until he had little choice but to sue for peace on Israel's terms."[81]

The no peace, no war, deadlock was untenable for the Egyptians, economically, politically, and in terms of national self-respect. Rather than capitulate to these terms, dictated by the balance of power, Sadat opted to restructure the balance and break the diplomatic deadlock. In August 1972, when the Soviet Union continued to refuse to sell to Egypt weapons Sadat had requested, Sadat, believing that the United States held ninety-nine percent of the cards in the Middle East diplomatic game, expelled Soviet advisors from Egypt. This won Egypt little more than a back channel, of dubious value, for communicating with Henry Kissinger.[82]

In September 1973, after months of intense and secret planning, Sadat unexpectedly convened the Egyptian National Defense Council. There, at Sadat's request, General Ahmad Isma'il briefed the government leadership about the planned Egyptian-Syrian offensive: It would "pressure Israel into accepting the conditions for a peaceful solution." Because "reinforcements and supplies from the Soviet Union were limited," the Egyptians would not be able reconquer all of Sinai. "It would be a long war" and Egypt would suffer heavy losses, but Israel "would suffer even greater losses."[83]

On October 6, 1973, with little warning, heavy concentrations of Egyptian and Syrian aircraft simultaneously struck Israeli positions in the Sinai Peninsula and the Golan Heights. Soon thereafter, Egyptian troops crossed the Suez canal, a feat Israelis had thought would be impossible because of the Bar-Lev line's fortifications and the rigging of the canal with oil pipes that could "transform every inch of the canal confrontation line into a murderous mass of fire."[84] The "dead body" of Egypt had risen with a vengeance. In Israel and the United States, it was widely believed that "the Arabs" were once again attempting to destroy Israel and "drive the Jews into the sea." President Sadat, however, announced early in the war that Egyptian and Syrian war aims were limited to breaking the deadlock in diplomacy that had persisted since 1967. Sadat sought to shock the superpowers into taking responsibility for negotiating a comprehensive peace settlement between Israel and its Arab neighbors. "This indeed is what happened, but in a way which increased the power and participation of one of the super-powers, the USA."[85]

Once the war began, President Nixon was, at best, marginal to U.S. decision-making and diplomacy. He was in Florida when war began, agonizing over how to respond to legal demands that he surrender Watergate-related tape recordings. During the three-week war, Vice President Agnew was forced to resign, Gerald Ford was selected to replace Agnew, and the president escalated the constitutional confrontation by firing the attorney general and special prosecutor in what became known as the "Saturday night massacre." Although Henry Kissinger had to deal with rivals in the Pentagon who, unlike him, had closer ties to the oil industry than to Israel, he had a relatively free hand in framing U.S. policy during the war. This was kept secret from the public to protect Nixon's fading reputation, but as war-related diplomacy moved to end game and nuclear confrontation, the Kremlin addressed its proposals and ultimatums to the secretary of state, not the president.[86]

Kissinger approached the war preoccupied, as always, with the Soviet Union. On October 6 he promised Soviet Ambassador Dobrynin that the White House would continue to press for congressional support of most-favored-nation trade status for the Soviet Union, if they "showed restraint" during the war. Brezhnev's answer the following day was, "We feel we should act in cooperation with you." Kissinger assumed that Israel would quickly regain the offensive and worked to delay calls for a cease-fire until it had regained its prewar positions. If Israel "came out a little ahead but got bloodied in the process, and if the U.S. stayed clean" in terms of Arab perceptions of the United States, Kissinger believed that U.S. power and influence in the Middle East would be augmented and the Soviets would be further marginalized.[87]

On October 9 Prime Minister Golda Meir's government placed Israeli military forces on a nuclear alert that continued secretly until the 16th. This has since been described by a number of scholars, perhaps best by the journalist, Seymour Hersh.[88]

The previous night, with Israeli forces still on the defensive, Golda Meir convened her kitchen cabinet for an all-night meeting. With fears that Israel might succumb to the Egyptian and Syrian offensive, they made three critical decisions. Israeli forces would be rallied for a major counterattack. The Israeli nuclear arsenal (the "Temple weapons") would be armed and targeted against the possibility of continuing military defeats. The Israelis would notify Washington of their preparations for nuclear war and reiterate their demands for the urgent resupply of weapons and munitions for what was becoming an extended war. Israel's nuclear-capable Jericho missiles were armed, as were eight U.S.-supplied F-4 aircraft, and Egyptian and Syrian military headquarters near Cairo and Damascus were targeted.

It was assumed that Moscow would be informed of the nuclear alert and dangers by its agents within Israel and would press the Egyptians and Syrians not to advance beyond the prewar 1967 boundaries. Meir's advisers also assumed that "such a drastic step would force the United States to begin [the] immediate and massive resupply of the Israeli military" that had been requested, promised, and delayed. At the time, the CIA estimated the Israelis had at least twenty nuclear warheads.[89]

Although the Israeli nuclear threat had little apparent effect on Egyptian and Syrian decision-making, this was not the case in Washington. Israeli Ambassador Simcha Dinitz met with Kissinger in the early hours of

October 9 and exhorted the secretary of state to provide new weapons and resupply Israel's diminishing reserve of munitions. Given the disparity of Israeli and Arab manpower, Kissinger was told, Israel would have to "do something decisive." Kissinger also was informed that Golda Meir was willing to come secretly to Washington for a one-hour meeting with the president, an offer that Kissinger interpreted as "either hysteria or blackmail." Kissinger ended the meeting with assurances that the United States would replace all Israeli war materiel consumed during the war, assuming that this would provide Israel with the confidence to move to the offensive.[90]

The war materiel did not flow as quickly as Kissinger anticipated. He did not want it ferried by U.S. aircraft, lest it further alienate the United States from the Arab world. The Pentagon created obstacles by preventing Israeli transports from landing at U.S. supply bases, and charter airlines were hesitant to incur the risks of flying weapons into a war zone. At this point Golda Meir sent a message to Washington: "Israel had suffered very heavy casualties and its resources were running very low.... If the United States did not begin immediately to resupply it on a massive scale, it might soon be forced to use every means at its disposal to ensure its national survival."[91] At this time, in response to Henry Kissinger's frantic demands, the obstacles to the resupply of Israel evaporated. In spite of Kissinger's diplomatic concerns, Secretary of Defense Schlesinger ordered U.S. planes to airlift eighty tons of war material directly to Israel.

As William Quandt, director of Middle East Affairs in Jimmy Carter's National Security Council, later wrote, Kissinger was responding from fear that Israel might resort to the use of its nuclear weapons: "Without being told in so many words, we knew that a desperate Israel might activate its nuclear option. This situation by itself, created a kind of blackmail potential.... But no one had to say it."[92] Herman Eilts, the former U.S. ambassador to Egypt, also recalled a reference by Kissinger to the threat: "There was concern that the Israelis might go nuclear. There had been intimations that if they didn't get military equipment and quickly, they might go nuclear." During his postwar shuttle diplomacy, Kissinger described the incident to Anwar Sadat, who in turn told Mohamed Heikal that the U.S. airlift to Israel had been initiated to prevent escalation to nuclear war. Sadat quoted Kissinger as telling him that the Israelis had three nuclear warheads which it was prepared to use, and that "It was serious, more serious than you can imagine."[93]

Within a week of the U.S. airlift, Israeli forces crossed to the western shore of the Suez canal and threatened to surround and isolate the Egyptian Third Army, twenty-five thousand troops still east of the canal.

It was at this point that Kissinger traveled to Moscow, at Soviet urging, to negotiate a cease-fire.[94]

Without consulting the Israelis, whom he was, functionally, also representing, Kissinger and the Soviet leaders quickly reached agreement. A cease-fire in place would be adopted by the United Nations Security Council. Reference would be made to UN Resolution 242, although no specific demands would be made for Israeli withdrawal from Arab territory. At the urging of the two superpowers, negotiations "between the parties concerned" would be urged.

When Kissinger arrived in Israel to apprise its leaders of the agreement he had negotiated, he anticipated Golda Meir's rage. Israeli army commanders had been pleading with her to postpone a cease-fire until the Third Army was fully encircled. Their arguments fell on sympathetic ears, given the government's eagerness to gain some military or political advantage to bolster its postwar negotiating position. In the course of laboring to win Israeli support for the U.S.-Soviet agreement, Kissinger recalled aloud that "in Vietnam the cease-fire didn't go into effect at the exact time it was agreed on." Some slippage in the implementation of the cease-fire was possible.[95]

Predictably, there was slippage. As UN Security Council Resolution 338 was scheduled to go into effect, the Israeli offensive was renewed, completing the encirclement of the Third Army. Egyptian and Soviet leaders protested bitterly, believing that Kissinger had intentionally deceived them to buy time for the Israelis.[96] Kissinger answered their protests by joining in a renewed UN call for a cease-fire, this one requiring the warring parties to return to their positions of October 21. When Golda Meir threatened continued noncooperation, Kissinger pacified her by asking "How can anyone ever know where a line is or was in the desert?"[97]

On October 24, when the cease-fire was supposed to be in force, the Egyptians reported renewed Israeli attacks. The Soviets responded by warning the Israelis that they faced "the gravest consequences" if they did not halt their siege of the Third Army. U.S. intelligence detected Soviet airborne divisions being placed on alert—an indication that the Soviets might actually intervene. Sadat, with his military forces facing the possibility of annihilation by thirst and starvation, was desperate. Privately he urged the United States to send troops to protect his forces. Later he publicly called for U.S. and Soviet forces to enforce the cease-fire.

Kissinger and the Soviets had created a situation in which they had little room to maneuver. As Kissinger perceived it, "If the United States held still while the Egyptian army was being destroyed after an American-sponsored cease-fire and a secretary of state's visit to Israel, not even the most moderate Arab could cooperate with us any longer."[98] At the same time, he faced the political constraints posed by Golda Meir's charges of U.S. "collusion" with Egypt and the USSR, while Senators Jackson and Javits claimed Kissinger had sacrificed Israel's needs for the imperatives of détente. Soviet leaders were in a similarly difficult situation. "Their credibility was on the line: with the Egyptians—with whom it was already low...with the Syrians, who had not yet accepted the cease-fire; and indeed, with all the Arabs. The Soviets were not pursuing a forward diplomatic strategy, they were simply trying to hold on."[99]

The crisis climaxed on the night of October 24–25 with a nuclear alert resulting in large measure from Kissinger's diplomatic dishonesty. That evening, Ambassador Dobrynin informed Kissinger that the Soviet Union would endorse a UN resolution calling for the dispatch of U.S. and Soviet troops to enforce the cease-fire. When Kissinger responded that the U.S. would veto such a resolution, Dobrynin warned that minds in Moscow "had probably been made up." At 9:30 p.m. Dobrynin phoned with a message from Brezhnev: "If you find it impossible to act jointly with us in this matter, we would be faced with the necessity urgently to consider the question of taking appropriate steps unilaterally."[100]

Kissinger interpreted Brezhnev's response as an ultimatum. He later wrote, "We had not worked for years to reduce the Soviet military presence in Egypt only to cooperate in reintroducing it as the result of a UN resolution. Nor would we participate in a joint force with the Soviets which would legitimize their role in the area.... we were determined to resist by force if necessary the introduction of Soviet troops into the Middle East." He concluded that the only way to ensure that Soviet forces did not return to Egypt was to "shock the Soviets into abandoning the unilateral move they were threatening."[101]

With Alexander Haig advising Kissinger that President Nixon was too distraught to be consulted, Kissinger convened a rump session of the National Security Council. He was joined by Secretary of Defense Schlesinger, CIA Director Colby, and Joint Chiefs Chairman Thomas Moorer. They made three important decisions: A letter was sent to Sadat urging the withdrawal of his request for U.S. and Soviet forces and urging that he call, instead, for UN peacekeeping forces, which by definition would exclude the superpowers. A message was dispatched to Brezhnev, informing him that the United States "could in no event accept unilateral action.... such action would produce incalculable consequences which would be in the interest of neither of our countries and which would end all we have striven so hard to achieve."[102] They decided to demonstrate the meaning of "incalculable consequences" by placing U.S. nuclear forces and troops across the globe on nuclear alert, believing it would lead the Soviets to back down.[103]

The alert included the Strategic Air Command, the North American Air Defense Command, and field commands. The aircraft carrier *Franklin Delano Roosevelt* and its support squadron were redeployed from the Straits of Gibraltar to the eastern Mediterranean where they joined the *Independence* and other warships. The aircraft carrier *John F. Kennedy* and its escorts were also ordered to the Mediterranean. Sixty B-52s were moved overnight from Guam to the U.S. to join the SAC alert. The 82nd Airborne Division was placed on alert, as were other U.S.-based units.[104]

Kissinger's diplomatic appeals and nuclear extortion achieved their intended purposes. On the morning of October 25, Washington was informed that Sadat's government would withdraw its earlier request and call for the UN to send an international force instead. Brezhnev responded by supporting the revised Egyptian call, and communicated his hopes for continued U.S.-Soviet cooperation. UN Security Council Resolution 340 was adopted, no longer urging, but demanding, that Israelis and Egyptians return to the positions of October 22.[105] Although the confrontation in the Sinai continued for several more days, the U.S. alert ended the following day.

Kissinger continued to press the Israelis to break the siege, but to little avail. In the end it was Anwar Sadat who broke the impasse. He agreed to initiate direct Egyptian-Israeli talks at the military level, provided a convoy was first allowed through the Israeli siege to keep the Third Army alive. The Israelis agreed, and shortly thereafter General Abdel el-Gamasy and Major General Ahron Yhariv met to begin negotiating terms of disengagement.[106]

The October War, caused largely by U.S. diplomatic intransigence, brought the world to the brink of nuclear cataclysm twice within a two-week period. It ended with the dislocations of the Arab oil embargo that the war engendered still to be addressed. Henry Kissinger achieved his objectives at the risk of Mutual Assured Destruction, which would have dwarfed the unimaginable destruction of Hiroshima and Nagasaki. The Soviet Union was further marginalized in the Middle East, while Egypt was moved into the U.S. sphere and soon integrated into the structures of the Nixon Doctrine. Diplomatic and strategic frameworks for the resolution of the Israeli-Palestinian-Arab conflict, consistent with U.S. and Israeli objectives, had been created.

Years later, while flying between Boston and Philadelphia, I met a staff member of the Rand Corporation who had an intriguing story to tell. In 1973, his job was to prepare weekly estimates of the likelihood that a Middle East war would begin during the following ten days. In late September 1973, he had reported that an Egyptian-Syrian attack against Israel was probable on Yom Kippur. He had advised that the surprise of striking on a holiday would not be as beneficial to the Egyptians and Syrians as they might expect since Israel''s military reservists would be at home and more easily mobilized.

When the war ended, my seat-mate was called into his supervisor's office and told that their unnamed client had been most appreciative of his thoughtful and accurate reporting. He was given a $5,000 bonus. He took the check, but soon changed his field of concentration to specialize in non-profit management. Although he never explicitly say so, he led me to believe that Rand's unnamed client had been Henry Kissinger.

The Carter Doctrine

The Desert Storm war of 1990–91, with which George Bush consolidated the early structures of the post-Cold War order, was facilitated, if not entirely made possible, by actions flowing from the Carter Doctrine, proclaimed in January 1980. President Carter's achievements were checkered. He exceeded his predecessors in institutionalizing U.S. human rights commitments, and during his first year in office he opted not to build the B-1 bomber. His administration also negotiated the SALT II treaty. But under pressure from Republicans and the right-wing of his own party during his last years in office, he continued Richard Nixon's efforts to reconstruct a U.S. nuclear first-strike capability by deciding to base Pershing II and ground-launched cruise missiles in Europe. Aid was provided to *Contras* in Nicaragua and to the Salvadoran military. And, in response to the collapse of the Nixon Doctrine in the Persian Gulf, President Carter proclaimed his own doctrine, explicitly reaffirming the U.S. commitment to use "any means necessary" to maintain U.S. dominance in the region.

The U.S. military presence in and surrounding the Persian Gulf certainly preceded the Carter-Reagan augmentation of U.S. forces in the region. A U.S. military mission was dispatched to Saudi Arabia during the Second World War, and Franklin Roosevelt declared that its defense was essential to the United States.[107] At the end of the war, the United States had a network of military bases that stretched across North Africa and into the Middle East. When the British announced their military withdrawal from east of Suez, the United States moved to fill the military vacuum with the construction of air and naval bases on the Indian Ocean island of Diego Garcia. Indigenous opposition was silenced by deporting the entire population, twelve hundred people, to Mauritius and Seychelles.[108] With the Nixon Doctrine, the shah of Iran became the United States' regional enforcer. Toward that end, the United States sold more than ten billion dollars worth of the world's most sophisticated and deadly weapons to the Iranian dictator.

Even as the United States relied on the shah to defend U.S. interests throughout the Gulf region, "the prize" grew in economic and strategic importance. In this period the Gulf region was the source of sixty percent of the world's proven oil reserves. The region became a vital export market for the U.S., and billions of petrodollars were reinvested in U.S. banks and business. Many strategic analysts came to believe that the region was as important to U.S. global power as were Europe and East Asia. Some said the Middle East was more important, because without the U.S. hand on the Middle East oil taps, Western Europe and East Asia would become increasingly independent.[109]

The overthrow of the Shah in December 1978 and the subsequent hostage crisis shattered the Nixon Doctrine. Fear that the Soviet Union would intervene to fill the resulting military vacuum led the Carter administration to signal its military commitments with the dispatch of twenty-five warships, including three nuclear-armed aircraft carriers and eighteen hundred marines to the Persian Gulf. Plans were even developed to defend Iran against a Soviet invasion, despite Iranian hostility to the United States.

Anxiety in Washington became hysteria in late 1979 when the Soviet Union invaded Afghanistan. Although Afghanistan's mountainous geography precludes it from serving as an invasion route between Moscow and Teheran, Jimmy Carter's National Security Adviser Zbigniew Brzezinksi concluded that "the third front" of the confrontation with the Soviet Union had been joined. The president was thus moved to proclaim the Carter Doctrine in his 1980 State of the Union address: "Any attempt by an outside force to gain control of the Persian Gulf region will be regarded as an assault on the interests of the United States and will be repelled by the use of any means necessary."[110]

In addition to its futile effort to functionally annex the Persian Gulf, there were at least two fundamental faults with the Carter Doctrine. Even with the decision to deploy Pershing II and cruise missiles in Western Europe, there were serious doubts that the United States had, or could reconstruct, a credible first-strike nuclear capability to threaten the Soviet Union with "any means necessary." Additionally, as illustrated by the overthrow of the shah, the takeover the Grand Mosque in Mecca by religious extremists in November 1979, and the continuing turmoil caused by the Israeli-Palestinian-Arab conflict, the principal threats to U.S. power in the Middle East were indigenous and had little to do with the Soviet Union.

The Carter Doctrine was, of course, dual-capable. It provided the rationale for a military buildup that could be used against the nations and peoples of the Middle East as well as against the Soviet Union. As his doctrine replaced Nixon's, President Carter called for the creation of a Rapid Deployment Force (RDF) to speed the projection of U.S. military power into the Gulf region in times of crisis. To reinforce the RDF, basing agreements were negotiated with Oman, Somalia, and Kenya; to avoid the appearance of recolonization, the Carter and Reagan administrations "demanded firm political agreements with friendly regimes to allow the U.S. access to their own bases in times of crisis." The model for these agreements was Saudi Arabia. There, an infrastructure of Saudi bases had been built to U.S. specifications under the supervision of the U.S. Army Corps of Engineers and stocked with prepositioned U.S. weapons and munitions.[111]

The Reagan administration built on the Carter Doctrine. The Pentagon's mid-decade formulation of U.S. military priorities placed maintaining influence in the Middle East second only to its role in Western Europe and the defense of North America: "Our principle objectives are to assure continued access to Persian Gulf oil and to prevent the Soviets from acquiring political-military control of the oil directly or through proxies....we should be prepared to introduce American forces directly into the region should it appear that the security of access to Persian gulf oil is threatened."[112]

Cruise missiles were based in Comiso, Italy, whence they could strike targets in the Middle East and North Africa. One billion dollars was allocated to modernize military bases in a dozen countries in the Middle East, Southwest Asia, and North Africa. The RDF was renamed and transformed into the Central Command, and it was given responsibility for U.S. military operations from North Africa to Pakistan. This was the first regional command created since the end of the Second World War, and it accorded the Middle East equal status with Europe and East Asia within the Pentagon.[113]

One aspect of the Central Command was given little publicity. It was armed and routinely trained to fight with tactical nuclear weapons. As one embarrassed commander explained to me in the mid-1980s, "We taught our troops two things: to dig their trenches *real* deep, and to keep their units spread far apart, so that if the wind blows the wrong way we don't lose everyone."[114]

Desert Storm, Nukes, and the New World Order

Unlike previous Middle East wars which felt distant, many hibakusha and other Japanese felt the immediacy of the Gulf War. They were frightened and horrified by the nuclear threats emanating from Washington, and some were reminded that "every time the United States came close to nuclear war, it was against people of color." With television broadcasting only the "good news" of the "Nintendo war," some were reminded of Japanese wartime propaganda, and wondered what destruction was actually being wrought. Many also feared that, in response to U.S. pressures, Japanese soldiers would again be sent to fight abroad. For the first time in Japanese history, there were mass demonstrations calling for an end to war in the Middle East. Japanese political leaders and diplomats had some sympathy with the people in the street. They understood the United States was fighting a war for "narrow national interests."[115]

Like the atomic bombings of Hiroshima and Nagasaki, the 1990–91 Gulf War was fought to impose the contours of a postwar era. From the beginning, the Bush administration designed its responses to Saddam Hussein's conquest of Kuwait to reaffirm U.S. control over Middle East oil, a critical lever of power over its competitors and allies, particularly Japan and Western Europe. It also used the war to reinforce its global structure of alliances and its access to bases and military facilities. In a world of three economic superpowers and only one military superpower, the Bush administration demonstrated that U.S. military power would be the determining factor.[116]

On the morrow of the U.S. victory, which was fought with repeated U.S. threats to resort to nuclear arms, the new wisdom in Tokyo was that "Japan is Number Two." Across the Atlantic, Jacques Delors concluded that unless Europe developed an integrated and independent military by 1995, it would be unable to compete with the United States. Those in the United States who had feared the collapse of the Cold War would cost them their jobs in the national security establishment and military industries were temporarily reassured that while everything had changed, everything remained essentially the same.

So powerful was the return to history that some were reminded of colonialism. King Hussein, a former CIA asset, whose throne had been described as a domino whose fall could lead to nuclear war, warned, "The real purpose behind this destructive war…is to destroy Iraq and rearrange the area in a manner far more dangerous to our nations' present and future than the Sykes-Picot Agreement."[117]

Borders drawn in the sand by a British colonial official in 1922 served as the rationale for the Iraqi invasion of Kuwait. In fact, the Iraqi conquest of Kuwait resulted more directly from the eight-year Iraq-Iran war which preceded it. Saddam Hussein invaded Iran in 1980 to reestablish Iraqi control over the Shatt al-Arab waterway leading to the Persian Gulf, to assert Iraq's primacy in the region, and to end Iranian efforts to overthrow the government in Baghdad and replace it with an Islamic state modeled after Iran's.[118] When the war ended in July 1988, with the U.S. fighting Iran in tacit alliance with Iraq, the Reagan administration no longer perceived the government in Baghdad as a Soviet-oriented state. It was the United States' "junior partner in preserving the status quo in the Gulf." The Bush administration appears to have followed the Reagan administration's misreading of Iraq.[119]

The Iraq-Iran war left Baghdad deeply indebted to Kuwait and other Gulf states. It was in this context that the Iraqi government pressed the Kuwaiti sheikdom to forgive its debt, protested increased Kuwaiti oil production that added to the global glut of petroleum and reduced Iraqi oil revenues, claimed Kuwait was stealing Iraqi oil from the Rumalia oil fields - five percent of which extended into Kuwaiti territory, urged resolution of the long-standing border dispute, demanded greater access to the Gulf through the leasing of Warba and Bubiyan islands, and began to view Kuwaiti wealth as a shortcut to postwar economic development and paying the costs of maintaining the Iraqi dictatorship.[120]

It cannot yet be determined if the Bush administration was inexplicably blind to the warning signs of Iraqi aggression, or if it consciously lured Saddam into his invasion of Kuwait. The "usually compliant" al-Sabah family that ruled Kuwait was uncharacteristically rigid in its resistance to Iraqi demands, leading some to conclude that the United States had secretly promised to support Kuwait, "and that it might have been a Kuwaiti-U.S. conspiracy."[121] After overtly opting to use its postwar oil revenues to reconstruct the Iraqi military, including continued development of weapons of mass destruction, instead of concentrating on economic development, in January 1990 Saddam Hussein warned that the decline of the Soviet Union would lead to the United States becoming the unrivaled superpower in the Middle East. "If Arabs were not vigilant...everything, including oil prices would be ruled by the United States." On April 2, Saddam Hussein threatened to attack Israel with chemical weapons in the event of war, and ten days later he was assured by a U.S. delegation led by Senator Robert Dole that the Bush administration wanted to improve U.S.-Iraqi relations. In late April Hussein could only have been reassured when U.S. Assistant Secretary of State John Kelly opposed congressional efforts to impose economic sanctions on Iraq, because they would penalize U.S. exporters. In a meeting with U.S. Ambassador to Iraq April Glaspie on July 15, he was told that the United States had "no opinion on the Arab-Arab conflicts like your border disagreement with Kuwait." A week later, with Iraqi forces massed on the Kuwaiti border, Hussein must have been further reassured when Assistant Secretary of State Kelly informed Congress that the United States had no treaty obligations to defend Kuwait.[122]

The Bush administration's position regarding the "Arab-Arab conflict" in Kuwait changed dramatically following the August 2 Iraqi invasion. The administration's early commitment to use military force and not diplomacy, was, however, obscured from public scrutiny. Public attention was initially focused on refugees fleeing Kuwait and diplomatic efforts in the UN to win Iraqi withdrawal. The Bush administration had, however, already resolved that "no outcome would be tolerated other than [Iraqi] capitulation to force."[123]

Central Command forces were deployed to Saudi Arabia, ostensibly to protect Saudi oil fields. The Saudis, however, did not fear an Iraqi invasion. Like Saddam Hussein, they had little regard for what had been the Kuwaiti government, and they had recently concluded a nonaggression pact with Iraq. The Saudis had no evidence and little fear that Iraqi ambitions extended beyond Kuwait.[124] Only after Washington exhorted the Saudi monarchy to allow the dispatch of U.S. forces to Arabia (before the UN sanctions were imposed on Iraq) did the first wave of 500,000 U.S. troops arrive in Saudi Arabia. In late August, Thomas Friedman summarized the Bush administration's approach in the *New York Times*: diplomacy would be avoided to prevent rewarding Iraq with token gains.[125]

Jordan was isolated and punished for attempting to resolve the crisis diplomatically, as were the PLO and Yemen. Saddam Hussein's August 12 proposal to simultaneously resolve "all cases of occupation, and those cases that have been portrayed as occupation in the region," linking Israeli withdrawal from the West Bank, Gaza Strip, Golan Heights, and southern Lebanon to Iraq's retreat from Kuwait, was immediately rejected by the Bush administration, although it highlighted the double standards of U.S. policy. An Iraqi proposal, described as serious and negotiable by a State Department Middle East specialist, calling for withdrawal from Kuwait in exchange for minor border adjustments, was similarly dismissed by the Bush administration. As General Schwartzkopf finalized U.S. preparations for the rout of Iraqi forces, the Bush administration rejected renewed Iraqi proposals calling for linkage and French and Soviet efforts to mediate the crisis. As James Webb, Ronald Reagan's secretary of the Navy wrote, the Bush administration "relentlessly maneuvered our nation into a war."[126]

As the war approached, many of the hibakusha understood both the complexity and the seriousness of the situation. In its New Year's Message, Nihon Hidankyo denounced the "outrageous" Iraqi invasion of Kuwait and called attention to the fact that "President Saddam Hussein had threatened to use poison gas and top officials of the United States and the United Kingdom had suggested that nuclear weapons might be used in retaliation." They urged that "the United States, United Kingdom, France, the Soviet Union and all other governments involved not precipitate armed conflict or...contemplate the use of nuclear weapons under any circumstances." The hibakusha statement condemned Iraq and urged Saddam Hussein to renounce his threat to use poison gas. Finally, it called on the UN "to repeal the resolution endorsing the use of military force" against Iraq, and urged that the testimonies of hibakusha be used to convey the urgency of the moment.[127]

The 1991 Gulf War might have more aptly been termed "The War of Discriminate Deterrence." It was the immediate and direct descendent of the Reagan-Bush *Discriminate Deterrence* doctrine. George Bush may have been genuinely outraged by the implications of the Iraqi invasion of Kuwait, but greater strategic concerns were present from the beginning. The strategic rationale for the war was established in 1987, the year that Paul Kennedy's *The Rise and Fall of the Great Powers* stirred debates across the country and the Congressional Joint Economic Committee warned that the United States could not long remain both a great power and a debtor nation.[128] These challenges, and the need to contain the Pentagon's budget, led the Reagan administration to assemble its Commission on Integrated Long-Term Strategy, which included Henry Kissinger, Zbigniew Brzezinski, Samuel Huntington, former members of the Joint Chiefs of Staff, and other luminaries of the national security establishment. Their mandate was to recommend modifications in United States military strategy to ensure that the U.S. would remain the dominant global power in the first decades of what was becoming the Post-Cold War era.

The commission concluded that continued U.S. control of the Gulf, the Mediterranean, and the Pacific were essential to U.S. dominance for the long haul. It expressed deep concern that U.S. military power was decreasing relative to that of increasingly well-armed Third World nations, and that in the "next century, forty or more countries in Europe, Asia, the Middle East will have the means to build nuclear arsenals." In an era of austere military spending, the commission recommended that investment for air- and sea-lift capabilities and high-tech weaponry for "precisely controlled strikes against distant military targets" in Third World nations should be a priority. Thus the rationale and strategy of the 1991 Gulf War were cast when George Bush was still vice president.

Nuclear weapons were not initially an element of President Bush's mobilizing rhetoric, but in time he used the Iraqi nuclear program to his political advantage. Memories of the 1981 Israeli bombing of the Iraqi Osirak reactor, and Saddam Hussein's repeated public resolve to achieve military parity with Israel, became targets of opportunity for pollsters and then the U.S. president. A November 1990 *New York Times*/CBS poll indicated that "Americans saw the destruction of Saddam Hussein's nuclear, chemical and biological weapons capabilities as a compelling reason to go to war with Iraq."[129]

President Bush apparently carried an awareness of this poll with him to Saudi Arabia in November 1990 when he celebrated Thanksgiving with U.S. troops. In four carefully staged and widely reported rallies, he labored to build popular support in the United States for the coming war. Each of his speeches concluded with the argument that "Every day that passes brings Saddam Hussein one day closer to his goal of a nuclear weapons arsenal. And that is another reason… why more and more of our mission is marked by a real sense of urgency."[130] Although the postwar survey of Iraq's nuclear establishment brought some surprises, few analysts in the United States believed that Iraq was on the verge of achieving nuclear weapons capability.

By raising the specter of Iraqi nuclear weapons, the president not only built popular support for the war, he also prepared international opinion for targeting Iraq's nuclear weapons infrastructure during the war. He simultaneously laid the political and diplomatic groundwork for UN Security Council Resolution 687, which defined the terms Iraq would be required to accept in order to end the slaughter.[131] That resolution was the first occasion that international legitimacy was provided for the preemptive destruction of an incipient nuclear arsenal. The resolution and the precedent it established went beyond the expectations of *Discriminate Deterrence.*

In an early manifestation of what was later termed counterproliferation, the destruction of Iraq's nuclear weapons program was made an explicit administration war aim. When the U.S. attack was ordered, the destruction of Iraq's nuclear weapons infrastructure was given equal, possibly greater, importance than the liberation of Kuwait. The Sheikdom's liberation was the last war aim listed in Operations Order 91-001, with which President Bush initiated the war.[132]

As the war approached, and during the war, the U.S. and British governments used their nuclear arsenals diplomatically and on the battlefield. In a classic case of escalation dominance, nuclear attacks were threatened to ensure that Iraqi chemical and biological weapons were not used in desperation. The threats also provided a nuclear umbrella for vulnerable U.S. and allied advance units as they assembled in Saudi Arabia during the first chaotic weeks that the imperial force was assembled.

The U.S. naval flotilla encircling Iraq carried more than 700 tactical and strategic nuclear weapons, reinforced by another 300 land-based nuclear weapons in Turkey. There were also credible reports that land-based tactical nuclear weapons were shipped from Westover Air Force Base in Massachusetts to U.S. forces in Saudi Arabia. Britain also contributed five nuclear-capable ships, each carrying between eight and sixteen nuclear weapons.[133]

The first veiled threat of a U.S. nuclear attack came just six days after the Iraqi invasion of Kuwait. The Bush administration was ostensibly using diplomacy to win Iraqi withdrawal, but had already made the decision to go to war.[134] President Bush warned that the use of Iraqi chemical weapons "would be intolerable and would be dealt with very, very severely."[135] Two days later "Whitehall sources made it clear that the multinational forces would be ready to hit back with every means at their disposal...[including] using tactical nuclear weapons."[136]

As Desert Shield was assembled, including nuclear forces, the muffled drumbeat of nuclear threats continued. Under Secretary of State Paul Wolfowitz warned, "If we have to fight a war, we're going to fight it with all we have."[137] Secretary of Defense Cheney told the international press that the United States would use the "full spectrum" of its weaponry. "Were Saddam Hussein foolish enough to use weapons of mass destruction, the U.S. response would be absolutely overwhelming and devastating."[138] When asked if he would rule out the possibility of a nuclear strike in response to Iraqi use of weapons of mass destruction, Cheney opted not to reiterate the declared policy of successive U.S. presidents not to use nuclear weapons against nonnuclear nations.[139]

According to McGeorge Bundy, the president's "most clear-cut" nuclear warning was delivered by Secretary of State Baker when he handed the Iraqi foreign minister a letter from the president during their highly publicized meeting in Geneva on January 7. The letter warned that if Hussein resorted to the use of chemical weapons, "The American people would demand the strongest possible response," and "you and your country will pay a terrible price."[140]

In February, during the transition from air war to ground war, Secretary of Defense Cheney publicly threatened Iraq by referring to Hiroshima during a televised interview: "I basically think that President Truman made the right decision when he used the bomb on Hiroshima.... Speculation goes that [U.S.] casualties may have exceeded a million people." Soon thereafter he commented that he "would not at this point advocate use of nuclear weapons."[141] Vice President Quayle also warned that the United States would not rule out the use of nuclear weapons: "Our policy is very clear and that is we simply don't rule options in and out."[142]

Nuclear threats and planning were not limited to Washington. In Saudi Arabia, as General Schwarzkopf oversaw the development of the U.S. offensive, he urged that Washington "send a *demarche* to Baghdad...[that] if you use chemicals, we're going to use nuclear weapons on you." Perhaps more significant for the post-Cold War era was the recommendation of Air

Force Brigadier General Glossom, the officer responsible for planning U.S. bombing attacks. He proposed that nuclear weapons be used to destroy Iraq's biological weapons. Only the blast's intense heat, he advised, would ensure their complete destruction. Although this recommendation was vetoed by Colin Powell, it presaged one of the driving forces behind much U.S. postwar nuclear weapons development and planning.[143]

Finally, the destructive force of one derivative of the U.S. nuclear program was used during the ground war. "Depleted" uranium shells, extremely hard, six- to eight-pound projectiles capable of penetrating the armor of tanks, made from a byproduct of the enrichment process for constructing nuclear fuel rods and atomic bombs, were used for the first time in war. Ten thousand of these projectiles were fired by U.S. and allied tanks, artillery, and aircraft to destroy Iraqi tanks and their crews. A confidential report by the British Atomic Energy Authority estimated that "at least forty tons of depleted uranium was dispersed in Iraq and Kuwait during the war." The report described the continued presence of the shells in Iraq and Kuwait as a "significant problem" that could cause "tens of thousands of potential deaths." Others have reported that the extreme heat with which depleted uranium burns "creates an oxide dust that can be easily inhaled and ingested," that many U.S. troops were exposed to this toxic dust, and that the Pentagon used radioactive traces from these shells to identify friendly fire casualties of allied military vehicles. While these conclusions have been debated, they appear to be one of the "many causes" the Pentagon believes is responsible for Gulf War Syndrome.[144]

Months after the war's end tens or hundreds and possibly thousands of Iraqi civilians continued to suffer and die from the biological fall out (cholera and gastroenteritis) caused by the destruction of Iraq's technological infrastructure. Post-war casualties and deaths continued for years as economic sanctions drastically reduce essential supplies of medicine and food. The thirty-seventh World Conference Against Atomic and Hydrogen Bombs spoke for hibakusha, for much of the Japanese peace movement, and for considerable world opinion as it reflected on the Gulf War and outlined an agenda for the post-Cold War era:

> Iraq's aggression and annexation of Kuwait was a brutal action challenging world opinion…. The U.S. and its allied forces hastened into the use of military forces, closing the door on economic sanctions and other means of peaceful settlement. Although the outrage of Iraq at last failed, the Gulf War sacrificed uncountable human lives, children included, and caused environmental destruction on an unprecedented scale. Among others, we cannot forgive a statement openly made by some U.S. high officials that tried to justify the atomic bombing of Hiroshima and to threaten the possible use of nuclear weapons again…. A nuclear super-power-centered framework, such as the so-called "New World

Order," which aims to legitimize even their 'right to intervene against other countries in the name of the United Nations,' must not be permitted....At this crucial turning point in post-war history, we need to overcome the policy of strength, centering around the present nuclear powers, and open the way to establishing international justice and democracy by eliminating nuclear weapons, dismantling military blocs, respecting the sovereignty of the peoples and settling international conflicts by peaceful means.[145]

Notes

1. *Time* Magazine, July 29, 1985.
2. Nihon Hidankyo, "New Year's Message," Tokyo, January 1, 1991.
3. ABC News, February 3, 1991, cited in "Open Letter to the President of the United States of America," Tokyo: Nihon Hidankyo, July 31, 1991.
4. NBC News, February 2, 1991.
5. Jurgen Habermas, *The Past As Future*, Lincoln: University of Nebraska Press, 1994, p. 6; Dilip Hiro, *Desert Shield to Desert Storm: The Second Gulf War*, New York: Routledge, 1992, p. 250; See also the report of the *Harvard Study Team Report: Public Health in Iraq after the Gulf War*, Boston, May 1991.
6. Maxwell Taylor, *Christian Science Monitor*, June. 16, 1978.
7. McGeorge Bundy, "Nuclear Weapons and the Gulf," *Foreign Affairs*, Fall, 1991, p. 83.
8. See Albert Hourani, *A History of the Arab Peoples*, Cambridge: Harvard University Press, 1991, pp. 279–332; A.J.P. Taylor, *The Struggle for Mastery in Europe 1848–1918*, London: Oxford University Press, 1971, pp. 509–532; Daniel Yergin, *The Prize*, New York: Simon & Schuster, 1991, pp. 165–183.
9. Avi Shlaim, *War and Peace in the Middle East: A Critique of American Policy*, New York: Viking, 1994, p. 3.
10. Joe Stork, *Middle East Oil and the Energy Crisis*, New York: Monthly Review Press, 1975, p. 34.
11. Shlaim, op. cit., pp. 39–40, William B. Quandt, *Decade of Decisions: American Policy Toward the Arab-Israeli Conflict 1967–1976*, Washington, D.C.: The Brookings Institution, 1977, p. 9.
12. Interview of Mitsuo Kojima as recorded in letter of Rieko Asato, July 9, 1994. Interviews conducted by Junko Kayashige, summer 1994. World Conference Against Atomic and Hydrogen Bombs, Resolution, 1994.
13. Noam Chomsky, "The Drift Towards War and the Alternatives," in Peggy Duff, ed., *War or Peace in the Middle East?*, London: Spokesman Books, 1978, p. 27.
14. "The Gulf Crisis: How We Got Here," An Interview with Noam Chomsky and Eqbal Ahmad," in Greg Bates, ed., *Mobilizing Democracy*, Monroe: Common Courage Press, 1991, p. 7.
15. Stork, op. cit., pp. 35, 293.
16. Harry Truman, *Memoirs, Years of Decisions*, New York: Doubleday Inc., 1955, p. 523.
17. Seth P. Tillman, *The United States in the Middle East: Interests and Obstacles*, Bloomington: Indiana University Press, 1982, pp. 252–253.
18. Noam Chomsky, "Patterns of Intervention," in Joseph Gerson, *The Deadly Connection: Nuclear War and U.S. Intervention*, Philadelphia: New Society Publishers, 1986, p. 64.
19. Daniel Ellsberg, "Call to Mutiny," in Gerson, op. cit., p. 37.
20. Chomsky, op. cit., p. 64.
21. See Wilbur Crane Eveland, *Ropes of Sand: America's Failure in the Middle East*, New York: W.W. Norton & Co., 1980; Denis, F. Doyon, "Middle East Bases: Model for the Future," in Joseph Gerson and Bruce Birchard, eds., *The Sun Never Sets...Confronting the Network of Foreign U.S. Military Bases*, Boston: South End Press, 1991.; Seymour M. Hersh, *The Price of*

Power: Kissinger in the Nixon White House, New York: Sumit Books, 1983; Donald Neff, *Warriors at Suez: Eisenhower Takes America into the Middle East*, New York: Linden Press, 1981.

22. Shlaim, op. cit., p. 39.
23. Stephen Green, *Taking Sides: America's Secret Relations with a Militant Israel*, New York: William Morrow and Co., Inc., 1984, pp. 193–199, 204, 244.
24. Shlaim, op. cit., pp. 41–42.
25. McGeorge Bundy, *Danger and Survival: Choices About the Bomb in the First Fifty Years*, New York: Random House, 1988, pp. 475, 508; Seymour, M. Hersh; *The Samson Option: Israel's Nuclear Arsenal and American Foreign Policy*, New York: Random House, 1991, pp. 33–46.
26. Neff, op. cit., pp. 226–227.
27. Ibid., p. 87.
28. Green, op. cit., p. 116; Neff, op. cit. pp. 112–116.
29. Neff, op. cit., p. 227.
30. Ibid., p. 227.
31. Hersh, op. cit., pp. 33–46.
32. Neff, op. cit., pp. 281, 290.
33. Green, op. cit., p. 100.
34. Hersh, op. cit., p. 35.
35. Neff, op. cit., p. 253.
36. Ibid., p. 258.
37. Ibid., pp. 258, 262.
38. Green, op. cit. pp. 132–133.
39. Neff, op. cit., p. 280.
40. Hersh, op. cit., p. 40.
41. Green, op. cit., p. 130.
42. Hersh, op. cit., pp. 39, 43.
43. Neff, op. cit., pp. 34–43.
44. Hersh, op. cit., p.42.
45. Neff, op. cit., p. 360.
46. Ibid., p. 367.
47. Green, op. cit., p. 142; Shlaim, op. cit., p. 30.
48. Neff, op. cit., p. 403.
49. Ibid., pp. 404, 412–413.
50. Ibid., pp. 406, 412–413.
51. *Time* Magazine, July 29, 1985, cited in Michio Kaku and Daniel Axelrod, *To Win a Nuclear War: The Pentagon's Secret War Plans*, Boston: South End Press, 1987, p. 168.
52. David C. Gordon, *Lebanon: The Fragmented Nation*, Stanford: Hoover Institution Press, 1980, p. 42.
53. Eveland, op. cit., pp. 249–253.
54. Mohamed Abdel El-Gamasy, *The October War: Memoirs of Field Marshal El-Gamasy of Egypt*, Cairo: The American University in Cairo Press, 1993, pp. 15–16.
55. Shlaim, op. cit., pp. 32–33.
56. Richard K. Betts, *Nuclear Blackmail and Nuclear Balance*, Washington, D.C.: The Brookings Institution, 1987, p. 66.
57. Hopkins, *Development of the Strategic Air Command*, p. 71, cited in Betts, op. cit., p. 67.
58. Dwight D. Eisenhower, *Waging Peace 1956–1961*, Garden City: Doubleday & Co., 1965, pp. 276, 278.
59. Mohamed Heikal, *The Cairo Documents*, pp. 133–134, cited in Betts, op. cit., p. 67.
60. Betts, op. cit., p.67.
61. Richard Nixon, *RN: the Memoirs of Richard Nixon*, New York: Grosset & Dunlap, 1978, p. 483.

62. Interview with William Arkin, September 14, 1994; William M. Arkin and Richard W. Fieldhouse, *Nuclear Battlefields: Global Links in the Arms Race*, Cambridge: Ballinger, 1985, p. 102.
63. Green, op. cit., pp. 180, 193.
64. Ibid., p. 194.
65. Ibid., p. 199.
66. Donald Neff, *Warriors for Jerusalem: the Six Days That Changed the Middle East*, New York: Linden Press, 1984, pp. 276, 280.
67. Ibid., p. 280.
68. Ibid., p. 281.
69. Hersh, *The Price of Power*, op. cit., p. 234.
70. Neff, op. cit., p. 317.
71. Quandt, op. cit., p. 81.
72. Hersh, op. cit., p. 238.
73. Ibid., p. 238.
74. Walter Isaacson, *Kissinger: A Biography*, New York: Simon & Schuster, 1992, p. 294.
75. Kaku, op. cit., p. 169; Barry M. Blechman and Stephen S. Kaplan, *Force Without War: U.S. Armed Forces as a Political Instrument*, Washington, D.C.: The Brookings Institution, 1978, pp. 47–49.
76. Hersh, op. cit., p. 241.
77. Isaacson, op. cit., pp. 298–302, 304.
78. Shlaim, op. cit., p. 47.
79. El-Gamasy, op. cit., p. 198. When I first traveled in Egypt, in 1975, I was struck by the number of times members of the Egyptian elite, newspaper editors, politicians, etc. expressed their humiliation and anger about Israeli references to Egypt as a dead body.
80. Shlaim, op. cit., p. 43, parentheses added.
81. Shlaim, op. cit. pp. 46–47.
82. El-Gamasy, op. cit., p. 144.
83. Ibid., pp. 185–186.
84. El-Gamasy, op. cit., p. 204.
85. Hourani, op. cit., p. 419.
86. Isaacson, op. cit., pp. 514, 528.
87. Ibid., pp. 514, 516.
88. Hersh, *The Samson Option*, op. cit.; Raymond L. Garthoff, *Detente and Confrontation: American-Soviet Relations from Nixon to Reagan*, Washington, D.C.; The Brookings Institution, 1985; Isaacson, op. cit.; Henry Kissinger, *Years of Upheaval*, Boston: Little, Brown and Co,, 1982; Quandt, op. cit.; Nadav Safran, *Israel: the Embattled Ally*, Cambridge: Harvard University Press, 1978.
89. Hersh, op. cit., pp. 225–227.
90. Ibid., p. 229.
91. Safran, op. cit., pp. 482–483.
92. William B. Quandt, "How Far Will Israel Go?" *Washington Post Book World*, Nov. 24, 1991.
93. Hersh, op. cit., pp. 230–231.
94. Isaacson, op. cit., pp. 52–53.
95. Ibid., p. 528.
96. El-Gamasy, op. cit., p. 297.
97. Isaacson, op. cit., p. 528.
98. Kissinger, op. cit., p. 571.
99. Garthoff, op. cit., p. 374.
100. Isaacson, op. cit., p. 530.
101. Kissinger, op. cit., pp. 579–584.
102. Ibid., p. 591.
103. Isaacson, op. cit., p. 532.

104. Garthoff, op. cit., p. 379.
105. Ibid., p. 380.
106. Isaacson, op. cit., pp. 536–537.
107. Doyon, op. cit., p. 279.
108. Ibid., pp. 280–281.
109. Robert Tucker, "The Purposes of American Power," *Foreign Affairs*, Winter 1980/81.
110. Gerson, op. cit., pp. 177–178.
111. Doyon, op. cit., p. 286.
112. Shlaim, op. cit., p. 78
113. Ibid.,p. 116.
114. From a conversation between the author and a recently released U.S. Army Lieutenant during a conference organized by Physicians for Social responsibility at the Harvard School of Public Health.
115. Based on an informal survey conducted by Junko Kayashige and an interview with Junichi Ihara, Deputy Director, First American Division, Foreign Ministry of Japan, July 1991.
116. Joseph Gerson, "Legacies of the Storm: Desert Shield, Desert Storm and the Diplomacy of the Israeli-Palestinian-Arab Conflict, *Scandinavian Journal of Development Alternatives*, June-September, 1993; "The Gulf War and the New Order," in Robert Elias, and Jennifer Turpin, eds., *Rethinking Peace*, Boulder: Lynne Rienner Publishers, 1994.
117. Shlaim, op. cit., p. 130.
118. Ibid., p. 71.
119. Ibid., pp. 86–90.
120. Ibid., p. 92; Bob Woodward, *The Commanders*, New York: Simon & Schuster, 1991, p. 252; Gerson, "Legacies of the Storm," op. cit.
121. Shlaim, op. cit., p. 92.
122. Ibid., pp. 93–94.
123. Noam Chomsky, "What We Say Goes: The Middle East in the New World Order," in Cynthia Peters, ed., *Collateral Damage: The 'New World Order' At Home & Abroad*, Boston: South End Press, 1992, p. 65.
124. Woodward, op. cit., pp. 258–259.
125. Chomsky, op. cit., p. 64.
126. Ibid., pp. 65–66; Gerson, op. cit.
127. Nihon Hidankyo, "New Year's Message," Tokyo, January, 1, 1991.
128. Joint Economic Committee of the U.S. Congress, cited in *Japan Times*, August 11, 1987.
129. Cited in Michele A. Flournoy, "Implications for U.S. Military Strategy," in Robert D. Blackwill and Albert Carnesale, eds., *New Nuclear Nations: Consequences for U.S. Policy*, New York: Council on Foreign Relations, 1993, p. 137.
130. Hiro, op. cit., p. 250.
131. See note 5.
132. The order reads: "Attack Iraqi political-military leadership and command-and-control; gain and maintain air superiority; sever Iraqi supply lines; destroy chemical, biological and nuclear capability; destroy Republican Guard forces in the Kuwaiti Theater; liberate Kuwait."
133. See BASIC Report 90.6, "Environmental Dangers of the Gulf," Washington, D.C.: British American Security Information Council,   The American Friends Service Committee received credible reports of shipments of nuclear weapons through Westover Air Force Base in Chicopee, Massachusetts in November 1990.
134. Woodward, op. cit. p. 260.
135. *International Herald Tribune*, August, 9, 1990, cited in Milan Rai and Declan McHugh, "Nuclear targeting of the Third World," London: Campaign for Nuclear Disarmament, 1992.
136.*The Daily Star*, London, August 10, 1990, cited in. Rai, op. cit.

137. *Bulletin of the Atomic Scientists*, November, 1990.

138. *The Guardian*, December 24, 1990.

139. *The Boston Sunday Globe*, January 20, 1991.

140. McGeorge Bundy, "Nuclear Weapons and the Gulf," op. cit.

141. World Conference Against Atomic and Hydrogen Bombs, Tokyo, 1991; *The Financial Times*, February 4, 1991; cited in Rai, op. cit.

142. *Boston Globe*, February 2, 1991.

143. Rick Atkinson, *Crusade: The Untold Story of the Persian Gulf War*, Boston: Houghton Mifflin Co., 1993, pp. 86, 89.

144. Eric Hoskins, "Making the Desert Glow," *New York Times*, January 21, 1993; Laura Flanders, "Mal de guerre," *The Nation*, March 7, 1994; David Grown, "An Invisible Enemy: the cause of 'Gulf War syndrome' is as elusive as its treatment." *Washington Post Weekly Edition*, August 15–21, 1994; David Brown, "Gulf War Syndrome Study Pinpoints No Single Causes," *Washington Post*, December 14, 1944.

145. World Conference Against Atomic and Hydrogen Bombs, 1991, op. cit.

CHAPTER SIX

Approaching the Twenty-First Century

The Continuing Imperative of Nuclear Weapons Abolition

> The hibakusha feel that [we] must not die until the abolition of nuclear weapons is realized.
>
> — Masanori Ichioka[1]

> We will continue to maintain nuclear forces of sufficient size and capability to hold at risk a broad range of assets valued by…political and military leaders.
>
> — Bill Clinton[2]

> As long as this nuclear cult exists, as long as the belief is sustained that nuclear weapons bestow status, strength and security, the pressure to join the club will be irresistible…. In the long term, there are only two alternatives: allow the possession of nuclear weapons to all states that desire them, or deny them to all states by eliminating nuclear weapons.
>
> — Joseph Rotblat[3]

ECCLESIASTES AND HERACLITUS tell us that to every thing there is a season, and that one can not step twice in the same river. Change is constant. After five decades, the Cold War ideological underpinnings used to legitimize nuclear arsenals and atomic diplomacy abruptly vanished.

The legacies of the nuclear disarmament movements in the 1980s and the loss of ideological rationales have placed advocates of nuclear weapons and nuclear warfighting strategies on the political defensive. They do retain more than considerable power, but confronting the realpolitik and the moral logic of nuclear disarmament and abolition has, nonetheless, become unavoidable.

In 1986, in the pursuit of Soviet imperial interests and in response to existential imperatives, Mikhail Gorbachev took a major step toward the hibakusha's vision of a world free of nuclear weapons with a comprehensive proposal for nuclear weapons abolition by the year 2000.[4] Gorbachev's efforts, together with a worldwide movement for nuclear disarmament, opened the way for a succession of arms control agreements and unilateral reductions in nuclear arsenals. Since then, many of the nonaligned nations, seeking equality among states, have pressed for the implementation of Article VI of the 1968 Nuclear Nonproliferation Treaty (NPT). That article committed the declared nuclear powers to end the nuclear arms race "at an early date" and to move toward "general and complete disarmament." The inconsistencies of the two-tier, discriminatory, nonproliferation regime, in which some states are, functionally, more sovereign than others and the global accessibility of fifty-year-old nuclear technology have created a situation in which the world faces two nuclear options: "allow the possession of nuclear weapons to all states that desire them, or deny them to all states by eliminating nuclear weapons."[5]

Yet the nearer we approach the destination of nuclear disarmament, the more we slide away. In recent years, prevailing public opinion in the United States and much of the world has been that, except for a few rogue states, the dangers of nuclear weapons have vanished as if moved by the invisible hand of a natural force. Disarmament advocates and activists in North America and Europe have not been immune to this misperception. Their vision, commitment, and numbers have waned as a result, but the politically engaged hibakusha and their allies have not been similarly confused. On the eve of the fiftieth anniversaries of the atomic bombings of Hiroshima and Nagasaki, they again challenged the continued preparations for nuclear war, focusing on U.S. efforts to win an indefinite extension of the Nuclear Nonproliferation Treaty and on the arsenals of all the nuclear powers:

> What they call 'nonproliferation',…means that they aim to maintain indefinitely the world's most powerful nuclear forces, including more than 10,000 nuclear warheads. Russia has openly abandoned the policy of no-first use of nuclear arms, and other nuclear weapons states maintain their nuclear arsenals…. The U.S. military strategy…even includes possible use of nuclear arms as one of its options. The 'sanctions' against North Korea demanded by the U.S…is a specific expression of this dangerous military strategy. In order to maintain this discriminatory framework for nuclear monopoly, the United States and other pro-nuclear forces are aiming at indefinite extension of the Nuclear Non-Proliferation Treaty.[6]

Before reviewing the post-Cold War hierarchy of nuclear power and the widening calls for total nuclear disarmament, recent nuclear arms reduction treaties should be acknowledged, despite their limitations. They were hard won and valuable achievements.

First, in 1987 the Intermediate Nuclear Forces (INF) Treaty eased the hairtrigger confrontation in Europe. The United States agreed to withdraw its short range, first-strike Pershing II and ground-launched cruise missiles in exchange for the removal of Soviet SS-20 missiles that could destroy Western Europe.

This was followed by the 1991 Bush-Gorbachev Strategic Arms Reduction Treaty (START) I. The United States pledged to cut its long-range strategic nuclear weapons from 11,602 to 8,592, in exchange for Soviet reductions from 10,877 to 6,940. The superpowers thus agreed to destroy nearly one-third of their strategic nuclear arsenals.[7] The danger of a cataclysmic nuclear exchange remained, but the chances of accidental nuclear war and the danger of thermonuclear exchange diminished significantly.

Seeking to further remove the dangers of miscalculation and to gain what advantage was possible during the chaotic collapse of the Soviet Union, President Bush challenged Mikhail Gorbachev to make still deeper cuts. In October 1991 the U.S. president unilaterally announced that U.S. tactical nuclear weapons, except bombs dropped from planes, would be demobilized. The development of several nuclear missiles was also cancelled. More dramatically, President Bush signaled the end of the Cold War by ending the decades-old low-level alert of nuclear-armed U.S. strategic bombers.[8] Mikhail Gorbachev responded, as anticipated, with a broad unilateral initiative of his own: the Soviets would reduce their strategic nuclear arsenal to five thousand warheads, instead of six thousand as provided by START I. Their tactical nuclear weapons would also be retired. The development of several missile systems was halted, and Soviet missiles and nuclear-armed aircraft were also taken off alert.[9] Gorbachev upped the ante by announcing a moratorium on nuclear weapons testing and by demobilizing 700,000 troops.

As the Soviet Union disintegrated, the two superpowers (the United States and Russia) moved to protect START I by winning Ukrainian, Kazakh, and Belarusian commitment to respect the treaty. These new nuclear states agreed to destroy or to send to Russia the strategic nuclear weapons they had inherited. They also agreed to abide by the terms of the Nuclear Nonproliferation Treaty.

One month later, in February 1992, President Bush and Gorbachev's successor, Boris Yeltsin, announced the successful conclusion of negotiations for a second START treaty, START II. If START II if fully implemented, the United States and Russia will reduce their strategic nuclear arsenal to no more than thirty-five hundred warheads each by the year 2003. The treaty would become effective when all parties to START I, including Ukraine, Belarus, and Kazakhstan, formally ratified that treaty. START II favors the United States. As *The New York Times* reported, "The accord would effectively wipe out the centerpiece of the Russian arsenal, its land-based missile force, while preserving much of the sea-based force that the United States military strategists consider this nation's greatest strengthThe Russian concessions.appeared to be driven by [the] urgent need to secure economic aid to help prop up the faltering Russian economy."[10]

These treaties, agreements, and unilateral actions greatly reduced the dangers of accidental, or otherwise unanticipated, nuclear war. Boris Yeltsin's October 1994 speech to the United Nations, calling for full nuclear disarmament,[11] left open the possibility that his vision, like Mikhail Gorbachev's, is of a nuclear free world. This was certainly not the case for George Bush, and probably not for Boris Yeltsin. Daniel Ellsberg cogently described Bush's vision as having

> an end point where the United States and the Soviet Union retain thousands of nuclear warheads, at least some five to eight thousand, including reserve weapons...no Comprehensive Test Ban, a first use threat policy, and no [International Atomic Energy Agency] inspections of U.S. nuclear facilities...a continued stockpile of tactical nuclear weapons—indefinitely...It was Bush's ambition, as it is Clinton's ambition, to get an indefinite extension of the Nonproliferation Treaty...maintaining all of these privileges for the nuclear states, especially for the United States.[12]

A Hierarchy of Power

The "post-Cold War world is decidedly not post-nuclear." With these words Bill Clinton's first secretary of defense, Les Aspin, began his October 1993 announcement of the Pentagon's "fundamental reexamination of our nuclear posture."[13] The unprecedented destruction of Iraq's military infrastructure by conventional U.S. weapons during the Gulf War reinforced the Discriminate Deterrence mandate to emphasize the research, development, and warfighting capabilities of high-tech weaponry. Yet in the post-Cold War era, as in the Eisenhower years, the view that U.S. nuclear weapons remained essential "to sustain our commitments overseas" was shared by both Democrats and Republicans.[14] They continued, theoretically, to guarantee U.S. escalation dominance, to reinforce nuclear extortion and atomic diplomacy, and to provide the means for first-strike nuclear attacks in extreme situations.

Nuclear weapons in the post-Cold War era were not, of course, limited to the arsenals of the United States and Russia. China refused to join the other declared nuclear powers in a moratorium on nuclear weapons testing. CIA Director R. James Woolsey warned Congress that "more than twenty-five countries, many of them hostile to the United States and our allies, may have or may be developing nuclear, biological and chemical weapons—so called weapons of mass destruction—and the means to deliver them." The "enormous discrepancy between what Iraq initially declared and what has subsequently been discovered during the inspection process" disturbed the CIA, U.S. policy-makers, and others as they contemplated Iraq's future nuclear potential, Pakistan's and India's nuclear arsenals, the nuclear weapons programs of North Korea, Iran, Algeria, and Libya, and the possible leakage of nuclear materials, technology, and expertise from the former Soviet Union.[15]

Again, Daniel Ellsberg reminded those who listened that *Hiroshima* had resumed its former meaning. After representing the possibility of an all-out nuclear war threatening the destruction of the northern hemisphere and possibly global nuclear winter, *Hiroshima* again symbolized the possibility of limited, regional nuclear holocausts. Worse, in the post-Cold War era, the possibility of another Hiroshima had increased.[16]

Alexi Arbatov, confirmed Ellsberg's observation: "In both Russia and the United States, nuclear specialists have created the same scenario to justify the need for nuclear weapons...in both countries nuclear strategists are discussing the idea of hitting rogue Third World nations that might try to develop their own nuclear weapons. The...lists...are almost identical: North Korea is followed by such countries as Iran, Iraq, India and Pakistan."[17]

The Clinton administration's 1993–94 Nuclear Posture Review, "blessing the status quo,"[18] culminated several years of debate among U.S. policy-makers about the post-Cold War role of nuclear weapons. It also framed the challenge for people committed to further nuclear disarmament and to nuclear abolition.

There were conflicting lessons from the 1991 Gulf War. Some, like Army Chief of Staff Carl Vuono, concluded that "it was America's conventional forces, not its nuclear arsenal that...ultimately decided its outcome." Others argued that General Glossom's recommendation to use nuclear weapons against Iraqi weapons of mass destruction would have to be considered more sympathetically in the future. "It's not a mistake," General Lee Butler of the Strategic Command told the *New York Times*, "that Saddam Hussein never used chemical or biological weapons in the Persian Gulf." Accordingly, General Butler's command revised computer programs to enable U.S. presidents "to aim nuclear weapons at third world nations that threaten the interests of the United States or its allies."[19] Other U.S. planners concentrated on a lesson learned in several Third World nations that nations should "never fight the U.S. without nuclear weapons."[20] Thomas F. Ramos wrote that "No reasonable argument suggests that conventional weapons can be a credible deterrent against a nuclear armed adversary who has the will to use his nuclear weapons."[21]

The first Pentagon-related comprehensive analysis of U.S. post-Cold War nuclear warfare policy was undertaken by Thomas Reed, a former secretary of the Air Force. His report urged maintaining "a sizeable nuclear arsenal" to target "every reasonable adversary", including the former Soviet Union, China, and some non-nuclear Third World nations. Reed's report warned "more nuclear-weapons states are likely to emerge, especially in the...Third World.... With such weapons they can seek to deter the United States and others from interfering with their regional aggressions." These insurgent powers, Reed continued, should not "be allowed to believe that they can embark on major aggression against the United States, its deployed forces, or its allies and friends while enjoying ...sanctuary from American weapons, including nuclear weapons."[22]

Another 1991 review, headed by General Lee Butler, was initiated by the Bush administration, but it included men who later served in the Clinton administration: R. James Woolsey, John Deutch, Ashton Carter, Edward Warner, and Walter Slocombe. They concluded that it was premature to assume that the former Soviet Union would not threaten the United States in the future, or that Russian imperialism was a spent force. They also proposed the creation of a "nuclear expeditionary force" for possible use against "China or Third World targets."[23] Finally, Thomas W. Dowler and Joseph S. Howard II, of the Los Alamos laboratory, called for the development of mini- and micronukes, "true battlefield weapons," that could be used in the Third World to "prevent Dunkirk-like traged[ies.]"[24]

Although Bill Clinton was elected president by focusing public attention on domestic economic needs, he came to power with foreign and military policy agendas. Among Clinton's priorities was nuclear nonproliferation. Warren Christopher testified in his confirmation hearings, "We must work assiduously with other nations to discourage proliferation through improved intelligence, export controls, incentives, sanctions, and even force when necessary."[25] Clinton's National Security Adviser Anthony Lake, advocated that the administration isolate "backlash states" that are "likely to sponsor terrorism and traffic in weapons of mass destruction and ballistic missile technology." When U.S. interests were threatened, Lake warned "we clearly must be prepared to strike decisively and unilaterally."[26]

The Clinton administration quickly manifested its aggressive approach to nonproliferation. In May 1992 Martin Indyk, of the National Security Council, enunciated the new administration's policy framework for the Middle East which included "an abiding interest in the free-flow of Middle Eastern oil at reasonable prices," a commitment to "stemming the flow of weapons of mass destruction to this volatile region," confronting Iranian and Iraqi efforts "to rebuild their arsenals, particularly in the nuclear and ballistic missile fields," and containing "the threats posed by Iraq and Iran" through isolation and "dual containment."[27]

Clinton struck decisively and unilaterally the following month. On June 27, one day after warning the Iraqi government that its continuing refusal to allow United Nations inspectors to monitor missile test sites could have "quite serious consequences," U.S. cruise missiles again assaulted Baghdad.[28] Clinton, no novice to the manufacture of consent, hid his deadly warning to Saddam Hussein in a diversionary media campaign that described the attacks as punishment for an alleged assassination plot against George Bush.

The Clinton administration also forced the Chinese cargo ship *Yin He*, bound for Iran, to submit to an inspection for chemical weapons components.[29] While no such components were found, the coercive search was a highly visible message to all would-be suppliers of weapons and technology to Iran. In July Clinton travelled to Korea, where he pressed his counterproliferation campaign, threatening to annihilate North Korea if it developed and used nuclear weapons. Not surprisingly, Les Aspin's "Bottom Up Review" of the missions and structures of the U.S. military for the post-Cold War era concluded that the United States must contain "rogue leaders...pursuing nuclear, biological and chemical weapons capabilities." The review, whose report was adopted by the administration, recommended that the United States be prepared to fight and win two nearly simultaneous conflicts in "regions important to our interests...to defeat hostile regional powers, such as North Korea and Iraq."[30]

During the Clinton administration's second year, its commitment to contain nuclear proliferation was institutionalized in a policy called Counterproliferation. The secretary of defense's *Annual Report* described counterproliferation as "a broad national strategy...analogous to the strategy of containment in the Cold War era" that "focuses on weapons of mass destruction and their delivery."[31] The policy initiative, which its advocates claimed was supported by four billion dollars of the Pentagon's budget,[32] grew from fears that "proliferators may have acquired such weapons for the express purpose of blackmail or terrorism and thus have a fundamentally different calculus not amenable to deterrence."[33] (Or, I would add, the threat of escalation dominance.)

Counterproliferation was advertised as having two goals: preventing the proliferation of weapons of mass destruction (WMD), and protecting U.S. military forces who might be threatened by such weapons in time of war. *Prevention* included dissuasion, denial of access to technology, arms control efforts, international pressure, and agreements to inspect, monitor, convert, or even destroy such capabilities. *Protection* was the ability to "bring to bear military, political, economic, and commercial tools by the United States, its allies, and friends in an effort to persuade even the most ardent proliferator that the risks of the threat or use of WMD are not acceptable."[34]

Counterproliferation's offensive dimension provided new rationales for weapons research, development, acquisition, and deployment, and for military intervention. "In future conflicts," Secretary Perry wrote, U.S. "commanders will have to assume that U.S. forces are potentially threatened." They must, therefore, be "prepared to seize, disable, or destroy WMD in time of conflict if necessary."[35] Calls for "another Cold War-type effort," to confront efforts by as many as twenty nations to build and launch weapons of mass destruction, provided a new ideological framework for the practice of atomic diplomacy and nuclear war itself.

Counterproliferation was not promoted with the same visibility initially accorded to the administration's Nuclear Posture Review, publicly announced in October 1993. Noting that the "world has fundamentally changed," Secretary of Defense Aspin pointed to "the new nuclear danger" stemming "from the possibility of a handful of nuclear weapons in less reliable hands." It was time, he said, to review U.S. nuclear weapons and war doctrine, its related operations, safety, and security guidelines, and arms control "all in one look."[36]

One year later, after Aspin's replacement by William Perry, and after secret and largely bureaucratic debates, the Pentagon opted for the status quo. As one Congressional aide observed at the time, "the administration is so embarrassed that they have nothing new to say, they are keeping it low key."[37] As the results of the Review were leaked to the press and publicly announced, those with vested interests in the old order were relieved. The *Washington Post* editorialized that "the Clinton review embraces the Bush policy." Others, like Jack Mendelsohn of the Arms Control Association, were outraged that "this review was just a justification for existing programs."[38]

The Nuclear Posture Review, like the simultaneous Nuclear Nonproliferation Treaty review and Comprehensive Test Ban Treaty negotiations, demonstrated that "Newspeak" had survived the end of the

Cold War. The posture review conceded that the United States' nuclear arsenal could no longer be justified by the need for Mutual Assured Destruction. Instead, the arsenal was said to provide Mutual Assured Safety. The Soviet threat was replaced by a Russian threat. As Secretary of Defense Perry explained, the U.S. faced the "real danger that reform in Russia might fail and a new government arise hostile to the United States, still armed with twenty-five thousand nuclear weapons." This required the United States "to retain a nuclear hedge." And, as in the past, the review called for U.S. nuclear forces to be structured "to deal with hostile governments not only in Russia, but in other countries."[39]

The report, which President Clinton accepted and used to explain his decision not to press for further disarmament negotiations, argued that the U.S. nuclear arsenal should not be reduced below the levels mandated in START I. Trident submarines would continue to be armed with multi-warhead D-5 strategic nuclear missiles including the upgrading of older submarines from C-4 missiles to D-5s. B-52 and B-2 bombers would be retained for nuclear and conventional attacks. Four hundred and fifty to five hundred single-warhead Minuteman III missiles would remain in active service. In Europe, the United States would continue to deploy tactical nuclear weapons and the dual-capable aircraft they required. The option of launching tactical nuclear weapons from surface ships was to be eliminated, but the deployment of nuclear-armed Tomahawk cruise missiles aboard submarines was not.[40]

Advocates of the U.S. first use nuclear attack policy option also prevailed, as did the defenders of the nuclear weapons laboratories at Los Alamos and Livermore. The latter were to be retained "to design and fabricate a new warhead if needed." As one unidentified senior official said, "'We looked at whether we were content with the dramatic pace of arms reductions set in motion by the Bush administration and decided that 'the answer was, largely, yes.'"[41] As the Washington Post had editorialized, Clinton had indeed embraced George Bush's vision of maintaining U.S. nuclear hegemony.

The Nuclear Posture Review did not, however, take place in a vacuum. Its recommendations could not avoid the basic truths named by hibakusha, by other advocates of nuclear weapons abolition, and by members of the national security elite anxious to contain nuclear proliferation. The idea of Mutual Assured Safety with nuclear weapons is an Orwellian and dangerous illusion. Even *The New York Times* warned that the posture review failed to propose reductions in nuclear weapons necessary for "securing unlimited extension of the 1968 Nuclear Nonproliferation Treaty…and advancing multilateral efforts to curb trade in bomb-making material and technology." The sixth article of the Nuclear

Nonproliferation Treaty (NPT) requires a "good faith" effort by the nuclear powers to end the nuclear arms race and negotiate "general and complete disarmament." *The New York Times* warned that "the non-nuclear states, led by Mexico, are trying to get the nuclear powers to keep their end of the bargain.... they may have the votes to block extension."[42]

As I write, the Clinton administration is attempting to win indefinite extension of the NPT, which is scheduled to expire in April 1995. The dangers of nuclear weapons proliferation are, indeed, quite real. Yet, as hibakusha and others seeking to revise the treaty have observed, a treaty that attempts to prolong a discriminatory and unequal world order will not long endure. Hitoshi Motoshima, the mayor of Nagasaki has been one among many to question the purpose of indefinite extension of the NPT. "This approach," he told Japanese reporters, "will not rid humankind of nuclear warheads, so I can't be enthusiastic about indefinite extension of the NPT."[43]

Whatever its outcome, the NPT review will be a turning point, establishing the framework for nuclear arms races and struggles for nuclear disarmament in the closing years of this century and in the first decades of the next. As governments, diplomats, and popular movements politick over indefinite or limited extension of the NPT and demands to make the treaty less discriminatory, the review will bring the fundamental choice facing humankind more clearly into view: widespread nuclear proliferation or nuclear abolition.

There is a widely-held belief that despite resentment caused by the refusal of the nuclear powers to abide by their Article VI obligations, the Nuclear Nonproliferation Treaty will be renewed during the 1995 Review Conference. That extension may be indefinite, or it may be for a limited period of time, encouraging continued pressure for the negotiation of a Comprehensive Nuclear Test Ban Treaty and other arms control agreements. The treaty could also be modified to meet the demands of the nondeclared nuclear powers including Israel, India and Pakistan, for a less discriminatory NPT regime.[44]

Regardless of the outcome, the U.S. government remains committed to a "New World Order" in which "what we say goes." The Clinton administration is attempting to limit nuclear weapons proliferation while maintaining U.S. nuclear dominance. Linked to its support for "the indefinite and unconditional extension" of the NPT are U.S. efforts to negotiate arms control treaties that reinforce the current hierarchy of power.[45]

While it is anticipated that a Comprehenisve Test Ban Treaty will be signed in 1996, the negotiations have proceeded in the "War is Peace" tradition. In the spring of 1993, President Clinton, who distinguished himself from George Bush in part through his calls for a comprehensive test ban, proposed the resumption of U.S. nuclear weapons testing, an initiative which was reversed as a result of popular and Congressional protest. Later, with the tolerance of his administration, France and China delayed Comprehensive Test Ban negotiations to gain time for more nuclear weapons tests.[46]

More Machiavellian has been the question of what constitutes a nuclear weapons test. China, Iran, and Algeria have proposed that "peaceful nuclear explosions" be sanctioned by the treaty. Britain and France have claimed the need for "exceptional" tests every five to ten years to ensure the safety and reliability of their nuclear arsenals. The United States and Russia have pressed for hydronuclear experiments, underground explosions using less than four (U.S.) and up to one hundred (Russia) pounds of nuclear explosives, to be sanctioned by the test ban. Such experiments would facilitate, but may not be essential to, the design and development of new nuclear weapons.[47] And, to insure "the integrity of the nation's nuclear arsenal without having to resort to explosive testing," the Clinton administration supported the construction of a two billion dollar laser machine at Livermore Laboratory.[48]

A World Free of Nuclear Weapons

The vast majority of the world's people have been born since the atomic bombings of Hiroshima and Nagasaki, the Cuban missile crisis, and the proliferation of nuclear arsenals. For most people, nuclear weapons are part of the natural order, like volcanoes and meteors, that can be dangerous to, and even threaten, human existence. Only in times of crisis are most of us forced to face the man-made threat that has been woven so deeply into the fabric of modern civilization, the threats of holocausts or cataclysmic thermonuclear war.

The mayors of Hiroshima and Nagasaki have warned that "it is becoming increasingly difficult to pass the experiences of their cities on to new generations because of the deaths of atomic-bomb survivors, the disappearance of buildings and other sites testifying to the effects of the bombs, and the fading memories and emotions of survivors still living."[49] Junko Kayashige, who explained that "the only way for hibakusha to live is to fight nuclear weapons and get rid of them," and Senji Yamaguchi, who has lived "to completely ban nuclear weapons and to create an international treaty which would outlaw all nuclear weapons," will not live forever.[50]

In 1995, the fiftieth anniversaries of the bombings will briefly introduce the horrors of Hiroshima and Nagasaki and resensitize those who are attentive to the dangers of nuclear weapons. Yet, the reasons for the bombings will be concealed, and as a result of the Smithsonian Institution's capitulation to the demands of veterans groups and right-wing politicians, the old lie that "conceivably as many as one million" U.S. casualties were prevented by the atomic bombings will be repeated as authoritative truth.[51] But what will happen as we approach the fifty-first, the fifty-second, and the sixty-fourth anniversaries of the bombings? What will be remembered? What will be taught? How will the lessons of the bombings be reflected in governmental policies and national identities?

Power, it is said, surrenders nothing without a struggle. There is little power more awesome than that of the nuclear powers, but even the greatest mountains are eventually worn away.

When I began working for nuclear disarmament in the mid-1970s, like most people I assumed that the complete elimination of nuclear weapons was a utopian dream. I had been socialized to believe that abolition was either beyond the power of popular movements or technically impossible. Engaging with the hibakusha, activists in the Japanese peace movement, and the analysts and scientists they have assembled has deepened my understanding of the moral imperative of nuclear abolition. Perhaps more importantly, their spirit and commitment have helped me to see that it is possible for people to create the will and steadfastness necessary to force governments to disarm and to return the nuclear genie to its bottle.

The vision of a nuclear-free world is not new, and it has origins other than the hibakusha. Two months before Hiroshima and Nagasaki were savaged, Manhattan Project scientists in Chicago wrote the Franck Report, warning of the dangers of a nuclear arms race, raising the possibility of halting the production of fissile material, and calling for the creation of a supranational organization that could protect the postwar world from the danger of nuclear weapons. The first resolution of the United Nations General Assembly established the International Atomic Energy Commission and urged it to:

> proceed with the utmost dispatch and enquire into all phases of the problem, and...make specific proposals...for the elimination from national armaments of atomic weapons and of all other major weapons adaptable to mass destruction.[52]

Article VI of the 1968 Nuclear Nonproliferation Treaty called for general and complete disarmament, as did the United Nations General Assembly in 1969. The First United Nations Special Session on Disarmament, in 1978, concluded that: "removing the threat of a...nuclear war is the most acute and urgent task of the present day. Mankind is confronted with a choice: we must halt the arms race and proceed to disarmament or face annihilation."[53]

More recently, during his 1986 Reykjavik summit meeting with Mikhail Gorbachev, Ronald Reagan created panic among his advisors when he briefly agreed to a three-part fifteen-year proposal ending with the elimination of all nuclear weapons.[54] More recently, during Clinton's Nuclear Posture Review, General Charles A Horner, the chief of the U.S. Space Command, argued "the nuclear weapon is obsolete." Concerned that the U.S. nuclear arsenal encourages nuclear weapons proliferation, he was clear that he wanted "to get rid of them all."[55]

Joseph Rotblat, a Manhattan Project scientist and recent president of the Pugwash Conferences, has been among the most articulate advocates of nuclear weapons abolition, focusing on the pragmatic political and technological arguments. He remains morally clear that security based on the "threat of wholesale destruction, possibly genocide, is bound...to erode the ethical basis of civilization." He is also uncompromising in his conclusion that the Nuclear Nonproliferation Treaty "is an interim arrangement...and one cannot imagine an international law that permanently discriminates between nations. If some states are allowed to keep nuclear weapons, because they claim they are needed for their security, one cannot deny the acquisition of these weapons to other states."[56]

We do not lack political and technical proposals necessary to eliminate nuclear weapons. Missing are the moral and political will to envision a nuclear weapons-free world order and to transform that vision into a binding treaty.

Fifty years into the era of nuclear weapons we face numerous obstacles, many created by the history of U.S. atomic diplomacy and nuclear extortion. Other nations confront situations similar to those that led U.S. and Soviet leaders to prepare for and threaten nuclear war.

A first policy step toward the abolition of nuclear weapons would be a clear reaffirmation, by the United States and the other declared nuclear powers, of their commitments to implement Article VI of the Nuclear Nonproliferation Treaty. Second would be renunciation of first-strike nuclear warfighting doctrines: No More Hiroshimas!

What would be more secure than Mutual Assured Safety? The answer was outlined fifty years ago in the charter of the United Nations and, more recently, in the Palme Commission's Common Security recommendations. Essential principles are that: all nations have the right to security, military force is not a legitimate instrument for resolving conflicts, policies that seek the advantage of one nation over others are the cause of insecurity, and security cannot be attained through military superiority. The alternatives to Common Security are never-ending arms races, resulting economic and physical impoverishment, and the possibility of nuclear cataclysms.[57]

Empires are not conducive to a nuclear free world. Throughout the past half century, nuclear weapons have been used to secure and maintain imperial power. Thus we face a conundrum and an opportunity. Policy-makers in the United States will actively and powerfully resist the abolition of nuclear weapons as long as they have an empire to defend. People in the United States committed to nuclear disarmament, therefore, have a responsibility to envision and describe the structures and advantages of becoming a non-imperial nation, and to labor to create such a nation. This is a morally clear, but not politically simple, task.

History and politics do not, however, always proceed along straight or conventionally logical lines. The threat of physical coercion is not the only source of political power. There are also moral, intellectual, religious, social, and economic wellsprings of power. International and domestic political movements can create political environments in which politicians and policy-makers gain or retain power and advantage by actively advocating the elimination of nuclear weapons. Change is unavoidable. What is required is a political imagination, not unlike that of the disarmament movement of the 1980s, but with a clearer vision of purpose and the will, including the willingness to risk and to sacrifice, to achieve it. Many in Japan would call this "surrounding and isolating the nuclear powers."

Many of the technical steps necessary for the abolition of nuclear weapons have been identified, implemented, and calibrated in the nuclear, chemical, and biological arms control agreements of the Cold War and immediate post-Cold War era. A nuclear weapons abolition treaty would require intense negotiation of the specifics, but the essential elements are common knowledge:

Dismantling nuclear weapons and nuclear weapons installations. As they are being destroyed, placing them under international control, and thus beyond the reach of national governments, to increase confidence.

Ending production of weapons-grade fissile material, and verifying and containing existing stockpiles.

Verification, including societal verification in which the duties of, and protections for, citizens to notify international authorities of any violations of the nuclear weapons abolition treaty are clearly stated.

Intrusive inspection systems in which no installations or buildings are off limits at any time, including those of the declared nuclear weapons nations.

Investing a supranational authority, possibly the United Nations Security Council, with the authority to isolate, contain, or remove threats to the nuclear-weapons-free order, including governments which refuse to participate in, or attempt to break out of, the nuclear weapons-free regime.[58]

A number of steps are essential to creating the international political environment in which a treaty eliminating nuclear weapons would become possible. On the political agenda for the last years of this century are: continued education and debate about the meanings and consequences of nuclear war, negotiation of a *true* comprehensive test ban, a ban on production of weapons-grade fissile material, adoption of no-first-use policies, increased powers and responsibilities for the International Atomic Energy Agency, and accelerated reductions of the arsenals of the nuclear powers.

To what end these abstract, idealistic political efforts and demands? So that, as my parents would say, "Never Again to Anyone," and so that we do not participate in the crimes of silence. More immediate is the answer given by an anonymous hibakusha:

> I was twenty years old, nine hundred meters from the center of the explosion, when the A-bomb fell. I miraculously survived those flames of hell. I was married and three months pregnant then. The fetus was a victim of the A-Bomb before she was born. When I was told she was a victim of the A-bomb, I...was driven to despair. The only relief was that she was a gentle, cheerful girl. My husband died in 1983, anxious about his daughter.
>
> We have...an association of prenatal hibakusha.... It was said in those days that they would not live to be older than ten years, but they have now lived for more than forty years, living without the opportunity to have an ordinary human life. It seems to me that they tell us, even without words, of the horror of nuclear weapons and of the importance of living a life worthy of human beings.[59]

Notes

1. Transcript. World Conference Against Atomic and Hydrogen Bombs, Tokyo, 1988.
2. Cited in "Nuclear Posture Review," Washington, D.C.: Department of Defense, September 20, 1994.
3. Transcript. World Conference Against Atomic and Hydrogen Bombs, Tokyo, 1993.
4. Joseph Rotblat, Jack Steinberger, and Bhalchandra Udagaonkar, eds., *A Nuclear-Weapon-Free World: Desirable? Feasible?*, Boulder: Westview Press, 1993, p. 29; Strobe Talbott, *The Master of the Game: Paul Nitze and the Nuclear Peace*, New York: Alfred A. Knopf, 1988, pp. 314–329.
5. World Conference, 1993, op. cit.
6. "Hiroshima Declaration," World Conference Against Atomic and Hydrogen Bombs, Hiroshima, 1994.
7. *New York Times*, June 17, 1991; McGeorge Bundy, William J. Crowe Jr., and Sidney D.Dress, *Reducing Nuclear Danger: the Road Away From the Brink*, New York: Council on Foreign Relations Press, 1993, p. 25.
8. *New York Times*, October 1, 1991.
9. *New York Times*, October 6, 1991.

10. *New York Times*, February 17, 1992.
11. *Manchester Guardian Weekly Edition*, London, October 2, 1994.
12. *New Contexts, New Dangers: Preventing Nuclear War in the Post-Cold War Era*, Cambridge: American Friends Service Committee, 1993.
13. Department of Defense, Washington, D.C., October 29, 1993.
14. William J. Perry, Department of Defense, Washington D.C., September 22, 1994; Ambassador Linton Brooks, "The New Nuclear Threat," *Proceedings*, May 1994.
15. James R. Woolsey, Testimony before Senate Committee on Governmental Affairs, "Proliferation Threats of the 1990s, February 24, 1993; *Boston Globe*, June 12, 1994.
16. *New Contexts, New Dangers*, op. cit.
17. Alexei Arbatov, "START II, RED INK, AND BORIS YELTSIN," *Bulletin of the Atomic Scientists*, April 1993.
18. Interview of a senior staffperson of the House Armed Services Committee by the author, August 31, 1994.
19. *New York Times*, February 25, 1993.
20. Lewis A. Dunn, "New Nuclear Threats to U.S. Security," in Robert D. Blackwill, and Albert Carnesale, eds., *New Nuclear Nations: Consequences for U.S. Policy*, New York: Council on Foreign Relations Press, 1993, p. 41.
21. Thomas F. Ramos, "The Future of Theater Nuclear Weapons," *Strategic Review*, Fall 1991, pp. 41–47.
22. Thomas C. Reed and Michael O. Wheeler, *The Role of Nuclear Weapons in the New World Order*, December 1991, pp. iii, iv, 19, 26.
23. *Boston Globe*, July 12, 1993.
24. *New York Times*, March 24, 1994; William M. Arkin and Robert S. Norris, "Tiny Nukes for Mini Minds," *Bulletin of the Atomic Scientists*, April 1992.
25. Statement before the Senate Foreign Relations Committee, Washington, D.C., January 13, 1993, Washington, D.C.: Department of State, January 25, 1993, p. 47.
26. Anthony Lake, "Confronting Backlash States," *Foreign Affairs*, March/April 1994, pp. 45–55.
27. Martin Indyk, Address to the Soref Symposium, The Washington Institute, May 18, 1993, provided by the White House.
28. *New York Times*, June 26, 1993.
29. *New York Times*, September 6, 1993.
30. Les Aspin,*Bottom-Up Review, Force Structure Excerpts*, Washington, D.C.: Department of Defense, September 1, 1993.
31. William J. Perry, *Annual Report to the President and the Congress*, Washington: Department of Defense, 1994; "Path to Counterproliferation Acquisition Strategy," Washington, D.C.: Department of Defense, May 1, 1994.
32. *Los Alamos Monitor*, May 6, 1994.
33. Perry, op. cit.
34. Ibid.
35. Ibid.
36. Les Aspin, Transcript of Press Conference, October 29, 1993, Washington, D.C.: Department of Defense.
37. Walker, Op. Cit.
38. *Washington Post National Weekly Edition*, October 3–9, 1994; *New York Times*, September 23, 1994.
39. William J. Perry, "Remarks Prepared for Delivery by the Secretary of Defense William J. Perry to the Henry L. Stimson Center," Washington, D.C.: Department of Defense, September 20, 1994; "Press Conference with Secretary of Defense William J. Perry" News Release, Department of Defense, September 22, 1994.
40. "DOD REVIEW RECOMMENDS REDUCTION IN NUCLEAR FORCE," News Release, Department of Defense, September 22, 1994.

41. *New York Times*, September 22, 1994; *Janes Defense Weekly*, July 30, 1994.
42. *New York Times*, September 26, 1994.
43. *Mainichi Shimbun*, August 3, 1994, published in *Japan Views* September 1994.
44. *New Contexts, New Dangers*, op. cit.; from a confidential briefing paper prepared by a senior staffperson of the House Armed Services Committee, August 1994.
45. Hazel R. O'Leary, "Remarks to the Thirty-Eighth Regular Session of the General Conference of the International Atomic Energy Agency, Vienna, Austria, September 19–23, 1994." Provided by U.S. Department of Energy, Washington, D.C.
46. From a confidential briefing paper prepared by a senior staffperson of the House Armed Services Committee, August 1994.
47. Ibid.; Tom Zamora Collina and Ray E. Kidder, "Shopping Spree Softens Test-Ban Sorrows," *Bulletin of the Atomic Scientists*, July/August, 1994.
48. William J. Broad, "U.S. Will Build Laser to Create Nuclear Fusion," *New York Times*, October 21, 1994.
49. *Japan Times*, May 2–8, 1994.
50. Junko Kayashige, Letter to the author, August 1994; *New Contexts, New Dangers*, op. cit.
51. Kai Bird, "The Curators Cave In," *New York Times*, October 8, 1994.
52. Rotblat, op. cit., p. 20.
53. Ibid., p. 28.
54. Ibid., p. 30; Talbott, op. cit., pp. 314–326.
55. Associated Press, *Concord Monitor*, Concord, New Hampshire, June 16, 1994.
56. Transcript, World Conference Against Atomic and Hydrogen Bombs, Tokyo, 1993.
57. Independent Commission on Disarmament and Security Issues, *Common Security: A Blueprint for Survival*, New York: Simon and Schuster, 1982. pp. 8–10.
58. Transcript, World Conference Against Atomic and Hydrogen Bombs, op. cit.; Rotblat, op. cit., pp. 6–15, 48–51.
59. Transcript, World Conference Against Atomic and Hydrogen Bombs, op. cit.

About the Author

FOR TWENTY-FIVE YEARS, Joseph Gerson has been studying, organizing against and writing about U.S. military intervention and nuclear weapons. He is the regional program coordinator for the American Friends Service Committee in Cambridge, Massachusetts, a lecturer at Regis College, and the editor of two previous books, *The Deadly Connection: Nuclear War and U.S. Intervention* and *The Sun Never Sets… Confronting the Network of Foreign U.S. Military Bases.*

Selected Bibliography

Abel, Elie. *The Cuban Missile Crisis*. Philadelphia: J.B. Lippincott Co., 1966.

Alperovitz, Gar. *Atomic Diplomacy: Hiroshima and Potsdam*. New York: Vintage Books, 1985.

Arkin, William M. and Richard W. Fieldhouse. *Nuclear Battlefields: Global Links in the Arms Race*. Cambridge: Ballinger Publishing Co., 1985.

Atkinson, Rick. *Crusade: The Untold Story of the Persian Gulf War*. Boston: Houghton Mifflin, 1993.

Barnet, Richard J. *Intervention and Revolution: America's Confrontation with Insurgent Movements Around the World*. New York: World Publishing Co., 1968.

Betts, Richard K. *Nuclear Blackmail and Nuclear Balance*. Washington, D.C.: The Brookings Institution, 1987.

Blechman, Barry M. and Stephen S. Kaplan. *Force Without War: U.S. Armed Forces as Political Instrument*. Washington, D.C.: The Brookings Institution 1978.

Blight, James G., Bruce J. Allyn, and David A. Welch. *Cuba On the Brink*. New York: Pantheon Books, 1993.

Brodie, Fawn M. *Richard Nixon: The Shaping of His Character*. Cambridge: Harvard University Press, 1983.

Bundy, McGeorge. *Danger and Survival: Choices About the Bomb in the First Fifty Years*. New York: Random House, 1988

Burchett, Wilfred. *Shadows of Hiroshima*. London: Verso, 1983.

Buruma, Ian. *The Wages of Guilt: Memories of War in Germany and Japan*. New York: Farrar Straus Giroux, 1994.

Chomsky, Noam. *The Chomsky Reader*. Edited by James Peck. New York: Pantheon, 1987.

Cook, Haruko Taya & Theodore F. Cook. *Japan at War: An Oral History*. New York: The New Press, 1992.

Department of Defense. *The Pentagon Papers: The Defense Department History of United States Decision Making on Vietnam*. The Senator Gravel Edition, Vols. 1–4. Boston: Beacon Press, 1971.

Dower, John W. *Japan in War & Peace: Selected Essays*. New York: The New Press, 1993.

Ellsberg, Daniel. *Papers on the War*. New York: Simon and Schuster, 1972.

Field, Norma. *In the Realm of a Dying Emperor: Japan at Century's End*. New York: Vintage, 1993.

Foucault, Michel. *Power/Knowledge: Selected Interviews & Other Writings 1972–1977*. Edited by Colin Gordon. New York: Pantheon Books, 1980.

Freedman, Lawrence, and Efraim Karsh. *The Gulf Conflict 1990-1991: Diplomacy and War in the New World Order*. Princeton: Princeton University Press, 1993.

Garthoff, Raymond L. *Détente and Confrontation: American-Soviet Relations from Nixon to Reagan*. Washington: Brookings Institution, 1985.

Gerson, Joseph, ed. *The Deadly Connection: Nuclear War and U.S. Intervention*. Philadelphia: New Society Publishers, 1986.

Gerson, Joseph and Bruce Birchard, eds. *The Sun Never Sets: Confronting the Network of Foreign U.S. Military Bases*. Boston: South End Press, 1991.

Gerson, Joseph and Andrew Junker, eds. "New Contexts, New Dangers: Preventing Nuclear War in the Post Cold War Age." Cambridge: American Friends Service Committee, 1994.

Green, Stephen. *Taking Sides: America's Secret Relations with a Militant Israel*. New York: William Morrow and Co., 1984.

Gribkov, Gen. Anatoli I., and Gen. William Y. Smith. *Operation ANADYR: U.S. and Soviet Generals Recount the Cuban Missile Crisis*. Chicago: edition q, 1994.

Hersey, John. *Hiroshima*. New York: Bantam Books, 1959.

Hersh, Seymour M. *The Price of Power: Kissinger in the Nixon White House*. New York: Summit Books, 1983.

————.*The Samson Option: Israel's Nuclear Arsenal and American Foreign Policy*. New York: Random House, 1991.

Hesse, Hermann. *If the War Goes On...* New York: Farrar, Straus and Giroux, 1971.

Higgins, Hugh. *Vietnam*, Second Edition. London: Heinemann Educational Books, 1982.

Hiro, Dilip. *Desert Shield to Desert Storm: The Second Gulf War*. New York: Routledge, 1992.

Ienaga, Saburo. *The Pacific War 1931–1945*. New York: Pantheon Books, 1978.

Isaacson, Walter. *Kissinger: A Biography*. New York: Simon and Schuster, 1992.

Kahin, George McTurnan and John W. Lewis. *The United States in Vietnam*. New York: Delta Books, 1967.

Kaku, Michio, and Daniel Axelrod. *To Win a Nuclear War: The Pentagon's Secret War Plans*. Boston: South End Press, 1987.

Kennedy, Robert F. *Thirteen Days: A Memoir of the Cuban Missile Crisis*. New York: W.W. Norton & Co., 1971

Lifton, Robert Jay. *Death in Life: Survivors of Hiroshima*. New York: Random House, 1967.

Mead, Walter Russell. *Mortal Splendor: The American Empire in Transition*. Boston: Houghton Mifflin Co., 1987.

Nagai, Takashi. *The Bells of Nagasaki*. Tokyo: Kodansha, 1949.

Neff, Donald. *Warriors at Suez: Eisenhower Takes America into the Middle East*, New York: The Linden Press, 1981.

———. *Warriors for Jerusalem: The Six Days that Changed the Middle East*. New York: The Linden Press, 1984.

Nihon Hidankyo, eds. *The Witness of Those Two Days: Hiroshima & Nagasaki*, Volumes I & II. Tokyo: Nihon Hidankyo, 1989.

Quandt, William B. *Decade of Decisions: American Policy Toward the Arab-Israeli Conflict 1967–1976*. Berkeley: University of California Press, 1977.

Rotblat, Joseph, Jack Steinberger, and Bhalchandra Udgaonkar, eds. *A Nuclear-Weapons-Free World: Desirable? Feasible?*, Boulder: Westview Press, 1993.

Sherwin, Martin J. *A World Destroyed: the Atomic Bomb and the Grand Alliance*. New York: Viking Books, 1975.

Shlaim, Avi. *War and Peace in the Middle East: A Critique of American Policy*. New York: Viking, 1994.

Shohno, Naomi. *The Legacy of Hiroshima: Its Past, Our Future*. Tokyo: Kosei Publishing Co., 1986.

Stork, Joe. *Middle East Oil and the Energy Crisis*. New York: Monthly Review Press, 1975.

Thompson, E.P., and Dan Smith. *Protest and Survive*. New York: Monthly Review Press, 1981.

Tochiki, Fujiko, ed. *Give Me Water*, 2nd edition. Tokyo: A Citizens Group to Convey Testimonies of Hiroshima and Nagasaki, 1972.

Williams, William Appleman. *Empire As a Way of Life: An Essay on the Causes and Character of America's Present Predicament Along with a Few Thoughts About an Alternative*. New York: Oxford University Press, 1980.

———. *The Tragedy of American Diplomacy*. New York: Dell Publishing Co., Inc., 1962.

Index

New Society Publishers

NEW SOCIETY PUBLISHERS is a not-for-profit, worker-controlled publishing house. We are proud to be the only publishing house in the United States committed to fundamental social change through nonviolent action.

We are connected to a growing worldwide network of peace, feminist, religious, environmental, and human rights activists, of which we are an active part. We are proud to offer powerful nonviolent alternatives to the harsh and violent industrial and social systems in which we all participate. And we deeply appreciate that so many of you continue to look to us for resources in these challenging and promising times.

New Society Publishers is a project of the New Society Educational Foundation and the Catalyst Education Society. We are not the subsidiary of any transnational corporation; we are not beholden to any other organization; and we have neither stockholders nor owners in any traditional business sense. We hold this publishing house in trust for you, our readers and supporters, and we appreciate your contributions and feedback.

New Society Publishers
4527 Springfield Avenue
Philadelphia, Pennsylvania
19143

New Society Publishers
P.O. Box 189
Gabriola Island, British Columbia
V0R 1X0